The Waite Group's™

FRACTAL CREATIONS

Explore The Magic Of Fractals On Your PC

Timothy Wegner
Mark Peterson

**WAITE
GROUP
PRESS**

Waite Group Press, A Division of The Waite Group, Inc.
100 Shoreline Highway, Suite A-285, Mill Valley, CA 94941

Development Editor: *Mitchell Waite*
Editorial Director: *Scott Calamar*
Managing Editor: *Joel Fugazzotto*
Technical Review: *Harry Henderson, Robert Lafore, Monte Davis*
Book Design: *Barbara Gelfand*
Production Coordination: *Merrill Peterson*
Production: *Karyn Kraft, Nancy Terzian*
Poster and Glasses Design: *Juan Vargas*
Poster and Glasses Production: *Ray Zone*
Fractal Contributors: *Eli J. Bogajian, Pieter Branderhorst, Norman L. Hills, Alex Matulich, Douglas Muir, Mark Peterson, Bill Potter, Marc Reinig, Gary L. Skinner, Lee Skinner, Scott Taylor*
Photos on page 7, 8, and 9 are courtesy of the National Aeronautics and Space Administration (NASA)

ISBN: 1-878739-05-0

Printed in the United States of America

91 92 93 94 • 10 9 8 7 6 5 4 3 2 1

CONTENTS

CHAPTER 2

CHAPTER 3

PREFACE

FRACTAL CREATIONS — A GUIDEBOOK FOR FRACTAL EXPLORERS

This book is about creating fractals—dazzling and colorful images of infinite detail—on your PC. This is a hands-on book that comes bundled with Fractint, the preeminent PC fractal-generating program. All the images on the fold-out poster attached to the book were created with this powerful program, which is the result of a collaborative effort by an international team of volunteer fractal enthusiasts. With this software and a PC, you can quickly and easily begin creating your own fractals from any of the built-in fractal types. As you become more proficient, you will discover an inexhaustible number of options for coloring and transforming your images to suit your imagination. A beginner can create images of striking complexity and beauty. But even an expert will find more than enough controls and tools to challenge his or her adventurous creativity.

Fractal Creations includes the Fractint program, and the book contains a software installation and quick start guide, three chapters, and four appendices.

INSTALLATION AND QUICK START

This section of the book will tell you how to get the Fractint program up and running on your PC. If you are an experienced computer user eager to begin creating fractals, you may find that the quick start in this section is all you need to begin using the program. A more detailed guided tour is provided in Chapter 2.

Chapter 1: A Fractal Primer

The first chapter describes fractals, the different varieties of fractals, how they are generated, and their significance. The background provided here will enhance your enjoyment of creating fractals by providing insight into how fractals are generated and what they are.

Chapter 2: Using Fractint

This chapter has two parts. The first is an extensive tour of the main features of Fractint. You will go on a step-by-step tour through Fractint's basic functions right up to some of the more advanced functions. By the end of the tour you will know how to make many of those spectacular poster images that accompany the book. The second part of the chapter is a reference to the commands that allow you to control the operation of Fractint. You will also find more examples of the use of the various options and features that are described.

Chapter 3: Fractal Types

Fractint can generate the most extensive variety of fractals of any fractal program. At last count, the main fractal type screen, which lists the different kinds of fractals generated by Fractint, had more than 70 entries. As you will discover in Chapter 3, the actual number of possible kinds of fractals you can create with Fractint is much larger than that. This chapter tells you about all of those different kinds of fractals and is filled with dozens of examples that you can try.

Appendices

The appendices contain additional technical information about Fractint. They assume more mathematical and computer background than the rest of the book.

Appendix A discusses Fractint 's support for a variety of video modes and describes how you can tailor Fractint for your video graphics adapter.

Appendix B discusses CompuServe's Graphics Interchange Format (GIF). The GIF specifications are used by Fractint to save fractal images. These images can be viewed with other software on virtually any graphics-capable computer.

Appendix C covers the tricks and algorithms that make Fractint so fast. Here is where you will find a discussion of fixed-point arithmetic.

Most of Fractint's types involve complex numbers. Appendix D gives more background on manipulating complex numbers and transcendental functions.

Conventions Used In This Book

Throughout this book a special "keycap" font illustrates the keys you need to press such as (S) or the number (2), and special keys such as (ENTER) or the function key (F1).

Commands that need to be entered by the user are shown in a lowercase monofont typeface such as

`a:finstall` (ENTER)

In order to make file names stand out from the surrounding text, we have represented them in all uppercase letters such as:

FINSTALL.EXE

One caution. Please be careful because the beautiful fractal patterns created with Fractint have been known to induce hypnotic states. Use with care!

ACKNOWLEDGMENTS

The authors would like to acknowledge the many people who directly or indirectly helped with this book. First and foremost, heartfelt thanks go to our families, who provided cheerful support during the intense writing effort. Pieter Branderhorst and Bert Tyler spent long hours honing and refining the software that is bundled with the book. If there are two more pleasant and capable programmers anywhere, we haven't heard of them. Many people have contributed ideas and code to Fractint; their names are listed in the scrolling credits screen. One of the ironies of being a Fractint author is that we spent so much time developing the software that there is little time to use the program to make fractals. This book would not have been possible without contributions of beautiful images by talented fractal artists. Thanks to Lee Skinner, Norman Hills, Scott Taylor, Phil Wilson, Marc Reinig, and Douglas Muir. Thanks to Monte Davis, who spent much time on the Fractint documentation, which provided a critical reference for this book. The authors made extensive use of the excellent software written by fellow Stone Soup members Doug Nelson (Fdesign) and Lee Crocker (Piclab) in the course of generating images for the book. Larry Wood, Sysop of the CompuServe Graphics Forums, provided the communication medium that made this group project possible The specialty Software Development company provided an ITT math coprocessor which aided in the generation of many of the fractals in this book.

Finally, we wish to acknowledge our publisher, editor, and enthusiastic Fractint user Mitchell Waite. Mitch was directly involved every step of the way guiding two programmers-turned-authors in writing this book.

We hope you derive as much pleasure using Fractint as we had designing, building, and writing about it!

Tim Wegner and **Mark Peterson**
March 1991

Dear Reader:

From the time I was a child I have been fascinated by patterns. I can remember spending hours deciphering the symmetry of the crude linoleum squares that surrounded my playpen, getting lost in the design of the quilt that covered my bed, absorbing myself in the multidimensionality of the 14 knots of the rope holding me to the garage door (I was notorious for brazen escapes). Throughout childhood I remained a pattern junkie. Everything seemed connected: I saw clouds in the foam of a wave, branches in the trails of ant colonies, mountain ranges in the slime of a jelly fish on the beach.

This predisposition to patterns explains why I was instantly drawn to (no—hooked on) Fractint, the program that comes with this book. When a friend first sent me copy of Fractint, I expected a typically slow fractal pattern generator. (Fractals are notorious for eating up CPU cycles and usually take powerful computers running overnight to generate.) Imagine my surprise when Fractint created a 256-color Mandelbrot on my 386 PC in under two seconds—and with no math coprocessor! How could this be possible!

After further digging I discovered that Fractint uses a custom integer math routine, something brewed up by a group of programmers called the "Stone Soup Group." Even more amazing is the opening screen of Fractint, which shows over 30 contributors to the program. The most awesome thing about Fractint is the sheer beauty of the fractals it generates (some of which are shown on the back cover and poster of this book). Fractint's fractal selection menu reveals over 65 built-in fractal formulas, meaning that you can spend hours and hours exploring. The program even offers a formula "interpreter" that generates fractals from any math formula you type in, providing an infinite range of design possibilities. Even more exciting is Fractint's movable zoom box, which lets you magnify and display any part of a fractal you want to investigate. If you find a particularly attractive fractal, you can convert it to a three-dimensional image by using Fractint's 3-D imaging options—and you can see the result though red/blue glasses. And after you generate your fractal you can color-cycle it so that it continually shifts through 262,000 colors on a VGA monitor. The color cycling is dangerous in one respect: after ten hours went by I knew what Fractint's true nature was—a productivity destroyer!

If you are curious about fractals—what they mean, how to use them, or what they look like—there is no better way to find out about them then by playing with Fractint. Unlike other fractal books, this one requires absolutely NO programming. Fractint is more of a fractal processor and paint program; instead of writing programs to see fractals, you push keys. (Of course, if you want to learn about programming, Fractint's source code is available; the Appendices detail its speed secrets.) Or, if you are looking for the most beautiful and stimulating multicolored patterns you have ever seen, patterns that rival the most powerful light shows, then by all means try this book out. Fractint has been in development for over two years. It works on any PC and graphic display adapter, and its huge support group on CompuServe offers free source code to study and learn from.

If you have any technical questions about Fractint, you can contact the authors (see their biographies at the end of the book). If you have ideas for books you would like to see us publish, or if you are interested in writing a book for us, please write to our offices.

Sincerely,

Mitchell Waite

Mitchell Waite

THE
WAITE
GROUP

100 Shoreline Highway   Suite A-285   Mill Valley   California   94941   415-331-0575   Fax 415-331-1075

INSTALLATION

INSTALLATION AND QUICK START

This section describes how to install the Fractint software that is bundled with the book. It also includes quick-start instructions for those who wish to immediately begin generating fractals. A more complete guided tour is in Chapter 2.

HARDWARE REQUIREMENTS

Fractint for DOS is distributed in a compressed format on a 360K 5.25-inch PC disk, so you will need a 5.25-inch disk drive to install it. Fractint will run on any IBM-compatible PC with at least 512K memory. A hard disk is recommended for optimum performance, but not required. The uncompressed program will fit on a 1.2M 5.25-inch floppy disk, or either a 720K or 1.44M 3.5-inch diskette, but it will not fit on a 360K floppy disk. To view the fractals generated by Fractint, some kind of graphics video support is required. Fractint supports the IBM CGA, EGA, VGA, MCGA, and 8514A standards. It also works with most super-VGA, Targa, and Hercules-compatible monochrome graphics boards.

UNPACKING THE FRACTINT FILES

Before installing the software on your computer, make a backup copy of the disk and store the original away safely. Assuming your A: drive is a 5.25-inch drive, insert the backup disk in the A: drive and type:

A : (ENTER)

then look for the file called README.COM. You can view this file's contents by typing:

readme (ENTER)

at the DOS prompt. A simple file view utility will allow you to easily read the README file which contains any last-minute changes or instructions that did not make the book deadline. You might want to print out this document.

The software on the diskette supplied with this book is contained in the file FINSTALL.EXE. This compressed file is "self-extracting," that is, when it is executed it extracts the Fractint program and all of its support files.

Hard Disk Installation

To install Fractint onto a hard disk, first create a directory for the Fractint files. Assuming you wish to place the software in the directory "fractint" on drive C:, enter the following at the C:/> prompt:

```
md fractint (ENTER)
```

and then switch to the newly created directory:

```
cd fractint (ENTER)
```

With the diskette in A: you can uncompress the file by typing:

```
a:finstall (ENTER)
```

After a slight delay you will see the following message:

```
PKSFX (R) FAST!! Mini Self Extract Utility   Version 1.1
03-15-90
Copr. 1989-1990 PKWARE Inc. All Rights Reserved.
PKSFX Reg. U.S. Pat. and Tm. Off.
Searching EXE: C:\FRACTINT\FINSTALL.EXE
              **************************************************
              *     The Waite Group's Fractal Creations     *
              *           Fractint Version 15.11            *
              **************************************************
Do you want to extract these files now (y/n)?
```

Type:

```
y
```

You will see a series of messages that tell you the files are being exploded and extracted. Don't worry about the word "exploded," it's just a way of uncompressing files.

Now all the Fractint files are in your hard disk directory. If you wish to copy the README.COM file to your hard disk type the following:

```
copy a:readme.com
```

INSTALLING TO A FLOPPY DISK

You may also install Fractint onto a formatted 720K, 1.2M or 1.44M floppy disk. To do this you must have two floppy drives. Assuming that your 5.25-inch drive is A: and your target 720K, 1.2M, or 1.44M drive is B:, place the book disk in A:, a formatted empty disk in B:, and make B: the default drive by typing:

B: (ENTER)

Then decompress the files from A: to B: by typing:

a:finstall (ENTER)

and type

y

at the prompt.

If your diskette drives are set up differently, replace "A:" in these instructions with the drive letter of your 5.25-inch disk drive, and "B:" with the drive letter of your target disk drive.

EDITING YOUR PATH

If you'd like to be able to access Fractint directly from your root directory or from any directory, you may edit your AUTOEXEC.BAT file to add the new directory to the "PATH=" statement. The new AUTOEXEC.BAT line should look something like this:

PATH=c:\dos;c:\fractint...

FRACTINT QUICK START

Here are instructions for quickly getting Fractint running. For a more detailed guided tour, see Chapter 2.

To start Fractint, simply enter its name from the DOS command line:

fractint (ENTER)

(If you did not modify your AUTOEXEC.BAT file earlier, you will have to switch to the fractint directory first by typing: cd fractint.)

Once the program starts, the screen will look like Figure I-1.

You can press the (F1) key at any time to obtain the help screens. After you press (ENTER) at the credits screen, you will get the main menu. The highlight will be on the "Select Video Mode selection" menu item. Press (ENTER). You will get the Select Video Modes screen. Move the highlight up and down the list to select the appropriate mode for your computer. If you have a standard adapter

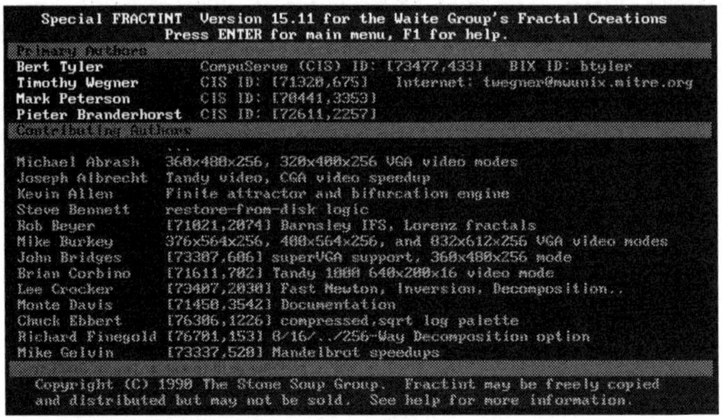

Figure I-1. The opening screen of Fractint.

(CGA, EGA, MCGA, VGA, or Hercules), Fractint should have detected your video equipment and highlighted a reasonable starting choice. These are as follows:

Key	Description	Colors
F2	*for EGA*	*16 colors*
F3	*or VGA, MCGA*	*256 colors*
F4	*for VGA*	*16 colors*
F5	*for CGA*	*4 colors*
SHIFT-F5	*for SVGA*	*256 colors*
F6	*for monochrome CGA, EGA, VGA*	*2 colors*
ALT-G	*for Hercules Monochrome Graphics*	*2 colors*

Press ENTER. (You can also select video modes directly by pressing the indicated function keys, such as F2 for 16-color EGA mode.)

The default image for the Mandelbrot set will now be drawn using the resolution of the mode just selected. This usually takes two or three passes. The first pass uses large, blocky bits of color. The second and third passes add more detail by breaking up the large blocks into smaller blocks. For the Mandelbrot set, this process is quite fast (usually about 3-6 seconds) for both passes on a PC AT. The actual speed depends upon many factors, not the least of which is your processor speed.

Press the PGUP key several times. A "zoom box" will appear on the screen and grow progressively smaller for each key press until it reaches a minimum size. Use the arrow keys or the mouse to move the zoom box. Move the zoom box to an interesting-looking detail in the Mandelbrot image such as an area on the edge of a blue lake. Press ENTER or double click on the left mouse button. The area within the zoom box will expand to fill the entire screen.

If you have an EGA or VGA, press the ⊕ key to start the colors cycling. You will be astounded! Exit from the color cycling mode by pressing (ESC).

To try some other fractal types, press (T) and select a type from the list using the cursor keys. Press (ENTER) to accept the default parameters, and the image for that fractal type will be displayed on the screen. You can save fractal images with the (S) command. Pressing (ESC) a few times will back you out to the main menu, and finally to a prompt asking if you want to quit. Answering "y" will bring you back to DOS.

Now that you've gotten an overview of running Fractint, you can turn to Chapter 1 to learn what fractals are, and to Chapter 2 to learn how to manipulate the beautiful fractals you've seen as well as to create others.

I coined the word *fractal* from the Latin adjective *fractus*. The corresponding Latin verb *frangere* means "to break:" to create singular fragments. It is therefore sensible—and how appropriate for our needs!—that in addition to "fragmented" (as in *fraction* or *refraction*) *fractus* should also mean "irregular," both meanings being preserved in *fragment*.

Fractal Geometry of Nature, p.4.
By Benoit B. Mandelbrot, W.H.Freeman and Co.,
New York, N.Y. 1982.

FRACTALS: A PRIMER

1

This chapter will teach you what a fractal is, where they came from, what can be done with them, and how they are created on a computer. Having read this chapter you'll be in an excellent position to appreciate the power of the Fractint program that comes with this book and is described in the next chapter.

WHAT IS A FRACTAL?

Fractals are beautiful, fascinating designs of infinite structure and complexity—the sort of intricate patterns that capture attention and evoke a sense of childlike wonder. A fractal is a mathematical object that has detailed structure no matter how closely you look at it, no matter how great the magnification. Look at Figure 1-1, which is a famous fractal called a Julia set. This fractal was generated on a computer with the software enclosed with this book and then printed out. If you hold the page at arm's length, you see spirals within spirals in repeating patterns, sequences of ever-shrinking structures vanishing into nothing. If you hold the page up close, your eyes will discover more detail right down to the limit of what the printer could record. What you see here is an infinite pattern somehow compressed into a finite space.

So what are fractals? As you make your way through this book, we will present ample evidence of the diversity of the universe of fractals and the multiplicity of ways of answering that simple question.

THE TRUTH ABOUT FRACTALS

We could go on and on about beauty and complexity, but let's begin this discussion with a healthy dose of reality. Far from being esoteric abstractions, fractals are much closer to home than you realize. In fact, it is the *nonfractal* objects that are unreal, abstract, and removed from our experience. Let's see why that is true.

From the beginnings of our education, formal and informal, we have been given simplified categories for organizing the world. The world is a sphere. Throw a baseball in the air, and its trajectory is a parabola. Nations are divided into the first world, the second world, and the third world. All of these statements have a strong element of truth, but none of them turns out to be accurate when you look closely. We have known since the Apollo days that the earth is really pear-shaped. After allowing for air resistance, the pear-shape of the earth, and even the gravitational field of the moon, the path of a baseball is *not exactly* a parabola. As is increasingly evident today, the elements of the first, second, and third worlds are intertwined in a complex way in the economies and societies of every country.

Figure 1-1 A Computer-Generated Fractal

This may sound like splitting hairs, but our everyday lives are full of clothes that don't exactly fit, lawns that are not all grass, and new cars with dents in their fenders. Yet we cannot do without our approximations and generalizations; we wouldn't make it through the day without simplifying assumptions. We say, "I'll meet you around 3:00," "enough to feed thirteen," or "about five people per car," instead of "meet me at 3:12:26," "enough food to feed five adults, two children, and six elderlies," or "exactly 4.67359 people per car." There is too much detail in the world to fully grasp. Indeed, there is too much detail in a single leaf for the mind to absorb.

It is irritating in the extreme to have one's simplified picture of the world shown to be inaccurate, but it happens to us all the time. It was Columbus who showed that the world was not flat, and Einstein (as an employee of the Trademark office) who showed that matter and energy are the same thing. The history of the investigation of fractals contains many stories of discoveries made by outsiders who collected up the forgotten crumbs of different disciplines and prepared a feast of chaotic structures and theories. Many scientists are finding that "curious counterexamples" turn out to be the basis of a whole new field of inquiry, and worse yet, a field developed by others! But we are getting ahead of ourselves.

Fractals are about looking closely and seeing more. Fractals have to do with bumps that have bumps, cracks that have crookednesses within crookednesses, and atoms that turn out to be universes. Fractals have to do with the rich structure of our universe that spans all scales from the uncountable galaxies at unthinkable distances to the mysterious inner electric flashes and vibrations of the subatomic realm. Let's see how looking closer results in fractals.

HOW LONG IS THE COASTLINE OF BRITAIN?

Benoit Mandelbrot, of IBM's Thomas J. Watson Research Center, did groundbreaking work in the theory of fractals and coined the word "fractal." He poses a simple question to introduce the notion of a fractal in his book *The Fractal Geometry of Nature*: How long is the coastline of Britain? This deceptively simple question turns out to expose a deep problem and give us insight into the question "What is a fractal?"

Consider how to approximate the length of the "coastline" of a circle of radius 1. Of course you know the answer in advance from high school geometry, using the formula for the circumference of a circle; it is $2 \times \pi$ where π = 3.14159..., or approximately 6.28. As a way of arriving at a similar result, you could inscribe a square inside the circle, and estimate that the circumference of the circle is the sum of the sides of the square, as shown in Figure 1-2. Notice that if the results are not accurate enough, all you have to do is make a polygon with more

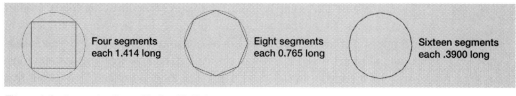

Figure 1-2 Approximating a Circle with Polygons

sides. Table 1-1 shows how the circumference of an inscribed polygon gets closer and closer to a limiting value, which is the "real" circumference.

This procedure is both mathematically correct and intuitively clear, and it works in much more general settings than this example. Estimating distances of curves by approximating them with a series of straight segments is a tried and true procedure that surveyors use when mapping terrain. Think of the side of the polygon (or the length of a sighting with a surveyor's scope) as a giant measuring stick. If the curve being measured is "well behaved"—which is to say, continuous and smooth—the answer can be made as accurate as desired by making the approximating measuring sticks smaller and smaller. Presumably this same logic can be used to find the length of the coastline of Britain. *Or can it?*

Let's try the same trick on a map of Britain, using measuring sticks 200 and 25 miles long. Figure 1-3 shows the measuring stick approximations overlaid on a map of Britain, and Table 1-2 shows the numerical results.

What is strange is that as the measuring stick gets smaller, the coastline estimation seems to grow larger—much larger than we would expect from the way the circumference approximation went! What is happening?

The difficulty is not too hard to see. The coastline of Britain is very, very irregular, full of large and small bays, inlets, tiny rivers, and complex, rocky shores. A long measuring stick does not bend with these many twists and turns, but cuts directly over them. A shorter measuring stick fits snugly inside these nooks and bays, thereby increasing the length estimate. Imagine doing this

Sides	Length of One Side	Circumference
3	1.732	5.20
4	1.414	5.66
8	0.765	6.12
16	0.390	6.24
32	0.196	6.27
64	0.098	6.28

Table 1-1 The Circumference of Polygons Inscribed in a Unit Circle

Length of Measuring Stick	Coastline
200 miles	*1600 miles*
25 miles	*2550 miles*

Table 1-2 Estimations of the Length of the Coastline of Britain

exercise crawling on your hands and knees, measuring the coastline of Britain with a measuring stick an inch long. Every small rock that you traversed around would increase your coastline estimate. Your answer for estimating the coastline would be astronomical!

There is a fundamental difference between a curve like a circle and a curve like the coastline of Britain. This difference separates the shapes of classical ge-

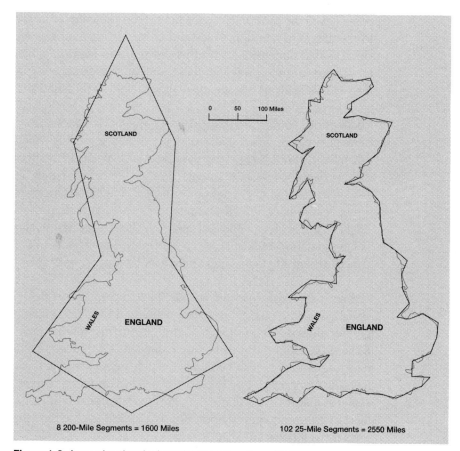

Figure 1-3 Approximating the Length of the Coastline of Britian

ometry from the shapes of fractal geometry. So here's your first definition: the coastline of Britain is a fractal, and our difficulty in measuring its length suggests a definition of fractal. For present purposes, we will use informal intuitive definitions, since the formal definitions are beyond the scope of this book.

> **DEFINITION:** If the estimated length of a curve becomes arbitrarily large as the measuring stick becomes smaller and smaller, then the curve is called a *fractal* curve.

While you might not be impressed by this observation of increasing distances measured as we go from circles to coastlines, what is magic is that the idea behind the fractal definition can be generalized to cover many other kinds of shapes besides curves. In all cases the basic idea is the same—the difficulty of measuring is due to the irregularity of the object being measured, and it is an irregularity that continues to the most microscopic level. This difficulty of measuring is related to the idea of dimension. Lines and curves are one-dimensional, planes and surfaces two-dimensional. It turns out that the idea of "dimension" can be broadened in such a way that these unusual curves have a dimension greater than 1. This leads us directly to an alternative way to define a fractal.

> **DEFINITION:** The *fractal dimension* of an object is a measure of its degree of irregularity considered at all scales, and it can be a fractional amount greater than the classical geometrical dimension of the object. The fractal dimension is related to how fast the estimated measurement of the object increases as the measurement device becomes smaller. A higher fractal dimension means the fractal is more irregular, and the estimated measurement increases more rapidly. For objects of classical geometry (lines, curves), the dimension of the object and its fractal dimension are the same. A *fractal* is an object that has a fractal dimension that is greater than its classical dimension.

Since the British coastline is, after all, a curved line, which is a one-dimensional geometric object, the fractal dimension of the coastline must be a little greater than 1. According to Mandelbrot, the mathematician Lewis Fry Richardson estimated it to be approximately 1.2. Indeed, mathematical "one-dimensional" curves can be defined which are so irregular that their fractal dimension approaches 2.0. These are called "space-filling" curves. In the discussion that follows, we will use the term "fractal geometry" to refer loosely to the theory of these bumpy shapes, just as classical geometry is the theory about regular "well-behaved" shapes.

EXAMPLES OF FRACTALS OCCURRING IN NATURE

Now that we know that the coastline of Britain is a fractal, where else are these fractals lurking? If you have begun to catch the gist of where this discussion is heading, you have probably already guessed the answer: nearly everywhere!

Mountains as Fractals

Have you ever noticed how difficult it is to estimate the distance to a far-off mountain? Nearby foothills and distant mountains have a very similar appearance. A mountain is thus a fractal; its roughness is the same at different scales. Indeed, the fractal characteristic of hills and mountains quickly becomes a practical matter for a hiker; a mild two-hour dash to the top can turn out to be a full day of traversing up and down through ravines and canyons that were invisible from a distance. The fun of scrambling up rocky hillsides is in part due to the fact that the fractal dimension of a mountain applies at all scales, including the scale of a human being. Figure 1-4 shows a range of snow-capped mountains as seen from the Space Shuttle. The snow-line traces the fractured boundaries of ravines, forming a fractal dimension and a pattern amazingly similar to some computer-generated fractals we will be discussing a bit later in the book.

Figure 1-4 Snow-capped Mountains from Space are Fractals

A good example of a fractal is found in the famous picture of a footprint on the moon (see Figure 1-5). Near the footprint is the gravelly crust of the moon's surface. Consider now the "earthrise" view of the earth and moon (see Figure 1-6). This picture is most famous for the beautiful view of the earth, but look at the lunar landscape and compare it with the lunar surface in the footprint picture. Take the footprint out of the picture, and the surface of the moon seen from two feet away looks somewhat like the moonscape viewed from two hundred miles away. When a tiny piece of a fractal is similar to the whole, we say that the fractal is *self-similar*. Understand that a self-similar object is generally a fractal, but not all fractals are self-similar. A fractal is defined by the irregularity that must exist at all scales, but this irregularity need not look the same. Both views of the moon's surface show fractal irregularities, but the fractal dimension appears to be higher in the footprint picture than in the more distant moon surface.

Clouds

Clouds are wonderful examples of fractals. Sophisticated travelers are supposed to prefer aisle seats on airplanes, but real fractal lovers choose window seats so they can watch clouds. You may wonder how something as soft and fluffy as a cloud can be a fractal, which we have defined in terms of jagged but measur-

Figure 1-5 Footprint on the Moon

Figure 1-6 Earthrise

able bumps and rough irregularities. Clouds are indeed roughly irregular and jagged; it's just that the colors reflected by the cloud blend smoothly into one another, giving the impression of smoothness. A little later in the book we will try to convince you that clouds and mountains from a fractal perspective are virtually the same thing.

Waves as Fractals

Not too long ago, before the study of turbulence (the complex movements of air or fluids) had advanced, it was believed that ripples on the surface of a lake were uniformly distributed. You can verify for yourself that this is not true, and that the pattern of ripples is very nonuniform, by simply taking a closer look at a body of water on a windy day. Every lake surface has smooth patches. On a windy day they might be small, and on a calmer day larger, but they are always there. But if you look closely at the rough areas of the surface—the areas full of wavelets—you will see that the "rough" areas are not completely rough, but themselves contain little glassy smooth areas. The surface of a lake is complex in the extreme, consisting of a nested pattern of smooth and rough areas that continues as you look closer and closer. This kind of nested mixture of the smooth and rough is a trademark of fractals. We can say that the lake's surface has a fractal dimension.

The Human Circulatory System

Blood flows from the heart in arteries and back to the heart in veins, but what happens in between? The arteries and veins are connected by a network of smaller and smaller vessels successively branching and rebranching until they finally meet in microscopic capillaries. A wonderful article in the February 1990 *Scientific American* entitled "Chaos and Fractals in Human Physiology" describes and vividly pictures this phenomenon. Branching patterns are a characteristic quality of certain classes of fractals.

Figure 1-7 A Fractal Fern

Fractal Ferns

A more common example of fractal branching can be found in the plant kingdom. Trees, shrubs, and flowers all develop with a branching growth pattern that has a fractal character. Figure 1-7 shows a computer-generated fractal fern based on a deceptively simple scheme of symmetry and self-similarity. (The fern was made using Fractint.) Each frond of the fern is a miniature of the whole. A real fern is not self-similar to the same degree, yet it is amazing how realistic this idealized fern looks.

Weather: Chaotic Fractals

Some of the most powerful supercomputers run complex mathematical models in an attempt to improve weather forecasts, yet the success of this effort has been moderate. A large investment in computational power purchases the ability to predict only a short time further ahead. The reason for this is not that the computers don't work or that the mathematical modelers are inept, but rather that the dynamics underlying the weather are chaotic. Weather is like the flow of water over Niagara Falls. If you launch a small leaf above the falls, where will it be a few minutes later after going over the falls? While a personal computer can easily project the orbit of the Voyager spacecraft far beyond the solar system, the largest supercomputer cannot with any accuracy predict the path of our ill-fated leaf. This is the difference between well-behaved and chaotic dynamic systems.

> **DEFINITION:** A *dynamic system* is a collection of parts that interact with each other and change each other over time. A dynamic system is *chaotic* if small changes in the initial conditions of the system make large changes in the system at later times.

The weather is a great example of a dynamic system. There are periods of relative calm and predictability, like the calm patches on a disturbed lake. But as anyone knows who has watched the weather report on TV, there are always fronts on the way, low pressure areas with huge spiral arms slowing moving to the east, and hurricanes brewing in the Gulf.

Satellite pictures of weather patterns have become a part of our cultural memory. They have a certain beauty to them, and, from our present perspective, a definite fractal character. If the weather forecaster could zoom the satellite picture, the audience would be treated to a succession of equally detailed pictures as the nation-sized low pressure areas would give way to a picture of the wind eddies around their city. These satellite pictures can be thought of as a graphical representation of the chaotic weather dynamics. So now we have another route to fractals—pictures of chaos.

QUALITIES OF A FRACTAL

The different qualities of fractals that have come up in the discussion of these examples are summarized below. Note that not all of these qualities apply to every fractal.

Qualities of Fractals

Fractional Dimension (fractal dimension)
Complex Structure at All Scales
Infinite Branching
Self-Similarity
Chaotic Dynamics

OF WHAT PRACTICAL USE ARE FRACTALS?

The second most common question about fractals after the question "What are they?" is some variation of "What earthly use do they have?". This is really a very reasonable question, but somehow we fractal fanatics are irritated by it. Imagine going to Paris to see the Mona Lisa in the Louvre and having someone ask you, "Fine, but what is it good for?" Let's see.

MATHEMATICS EDUCATION

Fractals are educational because they visually illustrate many basic mathematical concepts and make an ideal vehicle for challenging visually oriented people with those concepts. While appreciation for graphic images is not a substitute for learning the abstract foundations of mathematics, intrigue with dazzling fractal images can motivate a student to dig through math texts looking for abstract concepts that made possible the visual feast.

UNDERSTANDING CHAOTIC DYNAMIC SYSTEMS WITH FRACTALS

While we rarely think this way, the life of a person in our complex society is utterly dependent on both artificial and natural dynamic systems. As stated earlier, a dynamic system is a collection of parts that interact with each other and change each other over time. A few examples are power systems, the weather system, computer systems, or even the planetary ecosystem. We say that dynamic systems can exhibit behavior that is stable or chaotic. You may feel the word "chaotic" has negative connotations, but it is not necessarily a bad thing. When you are roasting marshmallows in front of a campfire, eyes transfixed on the swirls of smoke twisting up to the sky, you are observing a chaotic dynamic system made up of the air, the fire, and the wood. That kind of chaos is a pleasure, not a problem. But when chaotic interactions in power systems cause blackouts, that is usually a bad thing (although certain criminals would disagree). Useful computer algorithms (equations) are sometimes stable for some numeric inputs but exhibit chaotic behavior for others. This is an important concept to understand—certain formulas "blow up" and act unpredictably at certain times. If such an algorithm is used to calculate the position of a spacecraft just before reentry, the experience of the chaotic region of the algorithm could have serious consequences.

As we have already seen in connection with our example of the weather system, fractals are intimately connected with chaos. In fact, many computer-generated fractals are created precisely by operating otherwise well-behaved algorithms in regions where they exhibit chaotic behavior. The study of fractals cannot help but increase our knowledge of the chaotic behavior of dynamic systems. Indeed, fractal theory may not only help us predict the weather, but it can also help us understand the limits of our ability to predict it.

IMAGE COMPRESSION

Now let's move from chaos and weather to discuss an application of fractals for computers.

Most MS-DOS personal computer users have encountered compression utility programs like ARC and PKZIP that allow computer files to be stored in a very compact form. These compression programs take advantage of the redundancy in the pattern of bits that make up your file. Because graphic images consume so much disk space, the need for this kind of file compression becomes even more critical. For example, one of the typical new "super" VGA graphics adapters can display an image 640 pixels wide and 480 pixels high (*pixels* are the small dots that make up a computer screen image). Since each of these pixels can be any of 256 colors, it takes 8 bits (or 1 byte) of storage to store the color of each pixel. Multiply that out, and you discover that storing one graphics image from your screen at that resolution on your disk takes 307,200 bytes. That is as large as any major application you can buy for DOS. After compressing—with PKZIP, for example—the same image can be stored in less than half the space.

Fractals are complex images, but what is amazing is that in many cases they can be represented by simple equations that consume little space. In some cases it is possible to identify patterns of self-similarity in a graphics image and compress the image storage by describing the self-similarity rather than drawing the image. Taking this concept one step further, consider attempting to identify fractal patterns in any graphics image, and compress storage by representing the images with the rules generating the fractals. Imagine how powerful a technique this could be, as it might allow huge amounts of information to be reduced to a simple formula made of five or six characters! Michael Barnsley, one of the originators of the Iterated Function Systems approach to generating fractals which we will discuss shortly, has started a company that is building a commercial venture on this idea of graphics image compression. If Mr. Barnsley could find a way of dermining the fractal formula for an arbitrary text file, a disk that holds 20 megabytes might hold 2000 megabytes!

COMPUTER-GENERATED SIMULATION

Last but not the least of practical fractal applications, we come to computer-generated simulations. Movie special effects is a whole industry that uses many different technologies, ranging from animated artwork to miniature models. We have discussed how many natural objects from mountains to plants have a fractal nature. With the advent of high-resolution graphics workstations, it is possible with fractal formulas to generate realistic-looking computer images of mountains, trees, forests, and flowers. In the movie *Star Trek: The Wrath of*

Figure 1-8 View of a Fractal Planet from a Fractal Landscape

Khan the entire Genesis planet was a computer-generated fractal landscape. In the popular mind, computer-generated images have a mechanistic quality, perhaps due to the fact that popular computer drawing and paint tools come equipped with a repertoire of regular shapes such as lines, circles, and squares. But if the computer artist can supplement those with tools that create fractal shapes, with roughness, texture, branching, and cloudiness, then the mechanistic feel will be replaced by the earthiness of the natural world. Figure 1-8 shows a scene of a fractal planet as viewed from a fractal landscape. This example was generated with Fractint.

AN EMERGING VIEW OF NATURE

If you have begun to feel that more is at stake with fractals than beautiful pictures, education, or image compression, you are on the right track. The universe of fractals is part of a larger issue of understanding of the relationship between humanity and the natural world.

Ever since the Greek philosophers, our Western civilization has operated out of the idea that lines, circles, squares, and the other objects of classical geometry were somehow "more real" than nature itself, which contains few pure examples of these shapes. Plato postulated a world of ideal forms, where these perfect shapes resided unblemished. The world of human experience to Plato was but an imperfect and dim image of this ideal world. So, unable to live in this perfect world, people remake the natural world into a vision of imaginary perfection. Buildings must be square, shelves straight, and wheels round. Could it be that this deeply held world view is behind our impulse to bulldoze forests and build cities of rectangular skyscrapers laced with a gridwork of roads? Whatever the case, the irony is that classical geometry is used to model nature, and when the model doesn't fit, we blame nature rather than the model. What's worse, we then try to change nature to fit our preconceptions!

While this doesn't necessarily mean we should make buildings shaped like fractals, it does mean fractal geometry can often provide a much better "fit" for nature, and it can describe with great accuracy the structure of clouds, mountains, rivers, ferns, waterfalls, sunflower fields, and even weather. It may also tell us more about how the weather works, secrets of biochemistry, or insights about how people think. What is of critical importance is not the success of the theory but the reorientation of fundamental thinking. This emerging view of nature is more humble, less arrogant. The deepest wonder is for nature itself, not our attempts to model it and understand it.

THE COMPUTER AS A WINDOW TO CHAOS

Examples of chaotic phenomena occur in many disciplines, often as anomalous special cases. In many fields you will find the term "ill-behaved" used to describe chaotic phenomena. This is a very curious term indeed, reminiscent of the attitude that children are meant to be seen and not heard, and when they are heard, they are bad! But can the notion of "badness" be extended to a mathematical algorithm? That question will remain unanswered here, and this observation will have to suffice: where fractals are concerned, what is "bad" often turns out to be "good"!

For years, algorithms that exhibited chaotic behavior were ignored. Chaotic behavior represented as numbers is very hard to understand. But make this chaotic behavior visual and it can be directly grasped. With the advent of low-cost video adaptors, a personal computer can now be used as a tool to visualize such chaotic dynamics—a kind of window to chaos.

We've spent a good deal of time drawing parallels between nature and fractals and revealing ways in which fractals play a role in science. Now we are going to go into more depth and explain how a simple fractal is generated on a computer. You don't need to understand this to run the Fractint program that comes with this book, but knowing how the fractal is made can enhance your appreciation of its physical beauty. This section explores a whole category of fractals created by what are known as *escape-time* algorithms. The term *escape time* comes from the fact that the algorithm works by determining when an orbit "escapes" a circle, as will be explained shortly. The most famous fractal of them all, the Mandelbrot set, is an example of this kind of fractal. Let's have a look at how pictures of this fractal are created.

How the Escape-Time Mandelbrot Set Is Generated

To appreciate the Mandelbrot fractal, a few mathematical preliminaries are needed. We will be using these rules later, so it is important to understand them. A *set* is simply a collection of objects of some kind. In the case of the Mandelbrot set, those objects are the coordinates of locations on a mathematical map called a complex plane. These particular locations are unique because they are made up not of regular numbers we are used to but what are called complex numbers. You might think of this plane as being like the map of a city with rectangular streets and avenues. The horizontal x-axis might be considered a collection of avenues numbered from some large negative number to some large positive number. The vertical y-axis would be unusual in that it corresponded to complex numbers (from negative large to positive large) with names such as $2i$, $6.529i$, and so on.

Complex Numbers and the Complex Plane

What's so special about complex numbers? First, they are unusual in that they are composed of two parts, one a regular number, the other an imaginary number. The imaginary part is most interesting. With ordinary real numbers, you are not allowed to take the square root of a negative number, and this operation is not defined. With complex numbers this is allowed, and the result is a special number designated "i." Looking at this another way, the number i is defined to be the complex number such that $i^2 = -1$, which is another way of saying that $i = \sqrt{-1}$. Every complex number is written as the sum of a real number and another real number times i, or $a + bi$, where a and b are real numbers.

Complex numbers can be graphed using a "real" axis (for the "a" part), and an "imaginary" axis (for the "bi" part). Figure 1-9 shows how the complex number $a + bi$ can be graphed using the two axes on the complex plane. The place where the two axes meet is called the *origin*, and it is the graph of the complex number $0 + 0i$, which is the familiar zero from ordinary arithmetic.

Using the fact that $i^2 = -1$ and the ordinary rules of arithmetic, you can do arithmetic using complex numbers. For example, $(2 + 3i) + (-3 + 2i)$ is calcu-

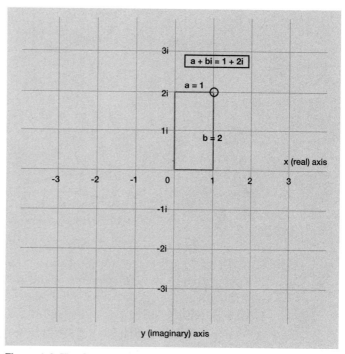

Figure 1-9 The Complex Plane

lated by adding the real parts together and the imaginary parts together, so the
answer is $((2 - 3) + (3 + 2)i)$ or $-1 + 5i$.

Multiplying is a little more complicated. The expression $(2 + 3i) * (-3 + 2i)$ is
multiplied out exactly as it would be in algebra if "i" were a variable, and then
simplified using $i^2 = -1$. (See Appendices C and D for more on complex numbers.)

Distance between Complex Numbers

The next concept we need to grasp is how to calculate the distance between
complex numbers. Imagine our map is Manhattan, New York City, U.S.A, where
the x-axis is avenue numbers and the y-axis is street numbers. Suppose you live

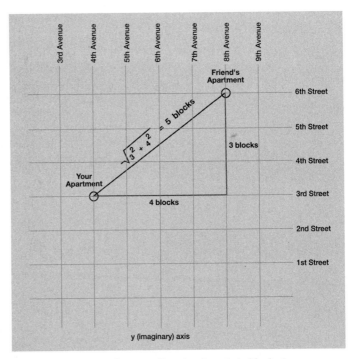

Figure 1-10 Distance between Two Apartments in Manhattan

in a high-rise apartment at 3rd Street and 4th Avenue, and a friend of yours lives
in another high-rise apartment at 6th Street and 8th Avenue. You are peeking at
your friend's apartment through a telescope, and you are curious about how far
away it is. For the sake of this discussion let's say that New York blocks are
perfectly square, so a block along the avenues is the same distance as a block

along the streets. Figure 1-10 shows the section of Manhattan where these two apartments are located.

You can see that the apartments are on the ends of the hypotenuse of a right triangle. One leg of the triangle, the leg that runs in the avenue direction, is three blocks long. The other leg is four blocks long. Using the Pythagorean theorem, we see that the distance is five blocks, because $5 = \sqrt{3^2 + 4^2}$. The formula for the distance between two complex numbers is based on the same idea. The avenues are the real part of the complex number, and the streets are the imaginary part. The distance formula is just the Pythagorean theorem applied to the distance between the two complex numbers in the x-axis (real) direction and the y-axis (imaginary) direction.

To make a Mandelbrot set, we need the distance from the complex number $a + bi$ to the origin $0 + 0i$. Again, this distance is the square root of the sum of the squares of the real and imaginary parts, or $\sqrt{a^2 + b^2}$. A shorthand way of writing the distance of a complex number $a + bi$ to the origin is $|a + bi|$, and when you see this you will know that the real meaning is $\sqrt{a^2 + b^2}$.

The purpose of using this formula in generating a Mandelbrot set is to test whether a point is inside a circle of radius 2 centered on the origin of the complex plane. If $|a + bi|$ is less than 2.0, then the point is inside the circle.

Orbits Escaping

The Mandelbrot set is a collection of points "in" the complex plane. In order to calculate it, each point is tested to determine if it is in the set. Here is how the test works. Each test point determines a sequence of points in the complex plane (you'll see how in a minute). A sequence is just a list of numbers. A subscript is used to show which is the first, the second, and so forth. This sequence is sometimes called the *orbit* of a particular test point, such as the point $37 + .4i$. Think of the sequence of complex numbers as the successive positions of an object flying through space, and you'll see why the term "orbit" is appropriate. Here is how a point passes or fails the test for membership in the Mandelbrot set. If any of the points in the orbit belonging to the test point are outside the circle of radius 2 about the origin, then that test point is *not* in the Mandelbrot set. If all of the orbit positions remain inside the circle of radius 2, then the test point is in the Mandelbrot set. Another way to put this is that the Mandelbrot set consists of all those test points whose orbits never escape the circle of radius 2, but whizz around forever inside it. A radius larger than 2 would work fine for this computation, but a smaller radius would not. A radius of 2 is the smallest radius centered on the origin that contains all of the Mandelbrot set, as you can see in Figure 1-15.

The Magic Formula

How are these orbits generated from the test point? Suppose the point to be tested is the one on the origin, $a + bi$, which we will call c. The sequence of points generated by c will be designated z_0, z_1, z_2, z_3,...,z_n,... Here, z_n is the nth member of the sequence, counting up from zero, and the little dots are mathematics-ese for "and so forth." (By the way, mathematicians often use the letter "z" to represent complex numbers.) The first element of the sequence is the origin itself, so $z_0 = 0 + 0i$, that is, $z_0 = 0$. To get the next member of the sequence, the previous member is multiplied times itself and added to c. This sequence-building process is described by the equation:

$$z_0 = 0 + 0i$$
$$z_1 = z_0^2 + c$$
$$...$$
$$z_{n+1} = z_n^2 + c$$

Let's use a real point. Suppose the test point is the complex number $.37 + .4i$. Calculating z_1 is easy, because $z_1 = z_0^2 + (.37 + .4i)$, and $z_0^2 = 0 \cdot 0 = 0$, so $z_1 = .37 + .4i$. The distance of this point to the origin is $\sqrt{(.37)^2 + (.4)^2}$, or about .545, which is well within the circle of radius 2. The orbit value z_2 is $(.37 + .4i)^2 + (.37 + .4i)$. To simplify all this we used a computer, and Table 1-3 shows the orbit sequence values for the test point $.37 + .4i$, along with the distance from the origin of each sequence member. Figure 1-11 shows a plot for the orbit formed by this table of results.

The orbit starts to swing outward, comes back in to a minimum value at z_5, and swings around outward again. The orbit member z_{12} is the first one to wander outside the circle. Notice that the distance value for z_{12} is 3.950, almost double the test circle radius. Figure 1-11 shows a plot of this escaping orbit in the complex plane.

This calculation shows that the test point $.37 + .4i$ is not in the Mandelbrot set, because its orbit escapes the circle.

Nonescaping Orbit

Now, changing this complex number just a little gives a different result. Table 1-4 shows the orbit of the point $.37 + .2i$. One hundred values were calculated, but not all are shown. Figure 1-12 shows a plot of these values. Note how nice and symmetrical this orbit is.

If we calculate the orbit sequence starting with $.37 + .2i$, we discover that the orbit values stay well inside the circle for the first 100 orbit calculations. This

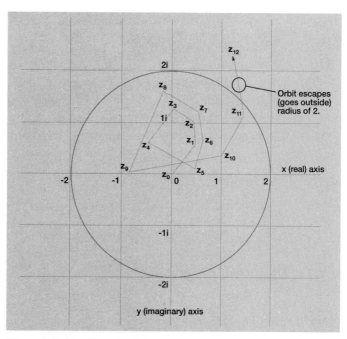

Figure 1-11 The Escaping Orbit of .37 + .4*i*

		Real	Imaginary			Distance
z_0	=	0.000	+ 0.000i	$\lvert z_0 \rvert$	=	0.000
z_1	=	0.370	+ 0.400i	$\lvert z_1 \rvert$	=	0.545
z_2	=	0.347	+ 0.696i	$\lvert z_2 \rvert$	=	0.778
z_3	=	0.006	+ 0.883i	$\lvert z_3 \rvert$	=	0.883
z_4	=	-0.409	+ 0.410i	$\lvert z_4 \rvert$	=	0.580
z_5	=	0.369	+ 0.064i	$\lvert z_5 \rvert$	=	0.375
z_6	=	0.502	+ 0.447i	$\lvert z_6 \rvert$	=	0.672
z_7	=	0.422	+ 0.849i	$\lvert z_7 \rvert$	=	0.948
z_8	=	-0.173	+ 1.117i	$\lvert z_8 \rvert$	=	1.130
z_9	=	-0.848	+ 0.014i	$\lvert z_9 \rvert$	=	0.848
z_{10}	=	1.089	+ 0.376i	$\lvert z_{10} \rvert$	=	1.152
z_{11}	=	1.415	+ 1.219i	$\lvert z_{11} \rvert$	=	1.868
z_{12}	=	0.885	+ 3.850i	$\lvert z_{12} \rvert$	=	3.950

Table 1-3 Test Orbit for .37 + .4*i*

raises a difficult point. Just because the first 100 orbit values are within the circle doesn't mean some later values might not escape. So how do we ever know a test point is in the Mandelbrot set? The answer is that we don't really know. The Mandelbrot set has to be approximated by setting an arbitrary cutoff point for how many orbit values will be tested. So for practical purposes, we will say that the test value .37 + .2i is in the Mandelbrot set, because for the 100 orbit sequence values that were checked, all were confined to the inside of the test circle. (Fractint will let you control this parameter.)

		Real		Imaginary			Distance
z_0	=	0.000	+	0.000i	$|z_0|$	=	0.000
z_1	=	0.370	+	0.200i	$|z_1|$	=	0.421
z_2	=	0.467	+	0.348i	$|z_2|$	=	0.582
z_3	=	0.467	+	0.525i	$|z_3|$	=	0.703
z_4	=	0.312	+	0.690i	$|z_4|$	=	0.758
z_5	=	-0.009	+	0.631i	$|z_5|$	=	0.631
...							
z_{96}	=	0.352	+	0.479i	$|z_{96}|$	=	0.594
z_{97}	=	0.264	+	0.537i	$|z_{97}|$	=	0.598
z_{98}	=	0.152	+	0.484i	$|z_{98}|$	=	0.507
z_{99}	=	0.159	+	0.347i	$|z_{99}|$	=	0.382
z_{100}	=	0.275	+	0.310i	$|z_{100}|$	=	0.415

Table 1-4 Test Orbit for .37 + .2i

Even though only the first 100 values were checked, this orbit looks very convincingly nonescaping. It has a definite, regular inward spiral that appears to converge to a point. Fractint lets you watch these fascinating orbits come and go while fractals are being generated.

Constrict Your Window and Your Pixels

The next problem is how to test all the points of a given set in the complex plane. This is impossible, because there are an infinite number of points to test. But it isn't really necessary to test all the points. The end objective is make a picture of the Mandelbrot set on a computer screen. The solution is to map the pixels (small dots) on the computer screen to the complex plane, and just test those complex points that correspond to a pixel. This is analogous to coloring just the street/ave-

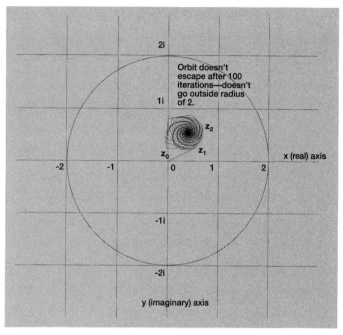

Figure 1-12 The Nonescaping Orbit of .37 + .2*i*

nue intersections of our Manhattan map. When this is accomplished, the pixels are colored one color if the test value is in the Mandelbrot set and another color if it isn't.

The Final Black-and-White Mandelbrot Algorithm

Let's summarize what has been said so far, and use a little different notation. For each pixel on the computer screen, the complex number z_{pixel} mapped to that pixel will be tested to see if it is in the Mandelbrot set or not. z_{pixel} is the test point we discussed in the above examples, and therefore it is the variable "c" in the Mandelbrot orbit formula $z_{n+1} = z_n^2 + c$, so $c = z_{pixel}$. We will define the sequence of complex numbers (called the "orbit sequence") $z_0, z_1, z_2, \ldots, z_n, \ldots$. The first member of the orbit sequence is the origin, so $z_0 = 0 + 0i$. The second member of the sequence, z_1, is $z_0^2 + c$, or c itself, since z_0 is zero. If c is already outside the circle, we are done; we'll color the pixel white.

The next member of the sequence, z_2, is the first member squared plus c, so $z_2 = z_1^2 + c$. We must plug values into z and then, after checking to see if the new value is outside the circle, the process is continued. In general, each orbit value z_{n+1} is obtained from the previous orbit value z_n by the formula $z_{n+1} = z_n^2$

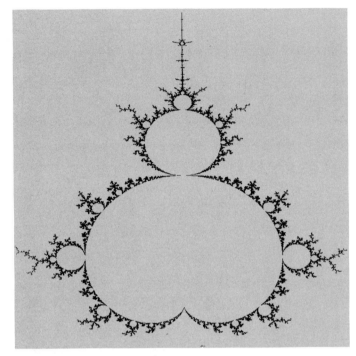

Figure 1-13 The Mandelbrot Set

+ c. Each time a new z_{n+1} is calculated, it is tested to see if it has gone outside the circle. The notation for the "in the circle test" for our Mandelbrot set is whether $|z_{n+1}| < 2$, where $|z_{n+1}|$ is the distance of z_{n+1} to the center point. If $|z_{n+1}| < 2$ is true, we calculate another iteration; otherwise, the orbit value has escaped, and it is colored white. Since we do not want the computer to calculate forever, we have a maximum iteration cutoff, and if the orbit has not escaped by the time we reach the cutoff, we quit and declare the point to be colored black.

Figure 1-13 shows the result of this little exercise, after all the points are colored. The Mandelbrot set consists of all those points we colored black—points whose orbits always stayed inside the circle (or at least, stayed inside for as long as the computer had the patience to wait). The actual edge of what appears as a lake in the figure is a fractal in the sense of the definitions earlier in this chapter. Measured with a small enough "inchstick," the coastline of "Mandelbrot Lake" can be made as long as you want, and it has a fractal dimension greater than one. The exact fractal dimension of the Mandelbrot set coastline is still an unsolved problem.

Where Did the Mandelbrot Fractal REALLY Come From?

In Figure 1-13, there are two big "bays" in the giant lake, with smaller baylets at the top and bottom. The whole "coastline" is an impossibly detailed nesting of bay within bay within bay, resulting in thin, jagged filaments shooting out like static electricity. This is a picture of a set that James Gleick called "the most complex object of mathematics."

By contrast, look at this formula, placed in a box in big, bold, type, so you can soak it in, meditate on it, and wonder about it.

$$z_{n+1} = z_n^2 + c$$

Appearances of simplicity CAN be deceiving. The innocent-looking formula $E = MC^2$ somehow encapsulates the whole theory of relativity. Not so here! The formula $z_{n+1} = z_n^2 + c$ is no more, and no less, than what it appears to be. Take a number, square it, and add a number. Nothing fancy, nothing tricky, nothing profound. No energy, no mass, no real-world stuff. Yet this is the formula which, given a few more details about repeating and checking for escaping orbits, generates the beautiful Mandelbrot set. How can such a wondrous and complex shape come from the absurdly simple formula $z_{n+1} = z_n^2 + c$?

Here is a hint of where to look for the mysterious source of fractals. The formula $z_{n+1} = z_n^2 + c$ may be simple, but it is repeated over and over a very large number of times. At the very beginning of this chapter, a fractal was described as an infinite pattern somehow compressed into a finite space. There are many different kinds of fractals, but however different they are, and however diverse their methods of generation, all of them have some kind of iterative scheme at their heart. The possible secret: formulas play a more minor role in a fractal compared to the iterative powers at work. Yet this is not enough to explain fractals completely. And while the mathematics and iterative method are logical, perhaps limitations of the human mind will never allow us to fully understand fractals. For some of us, therein lies their appeal!

Fractals Come Alive: Escape-Time Colors

Our black-and-white coloring scheme for each test point works well and provides a beautiful picture. But there is one more refinement we can make to an escape-time fractal that gives an additional and wonderous level of beauty: color.

As we have seen, the Mandelbrot set is defined as the set of points that do not escape a circle of radius 2 under iteration of the formula $z_{n+1} = z_n^2 + c$. And we have seen that a picture of the Mandelbrot set can be made with two colors, one for the points in the set, one for the points out of the set.

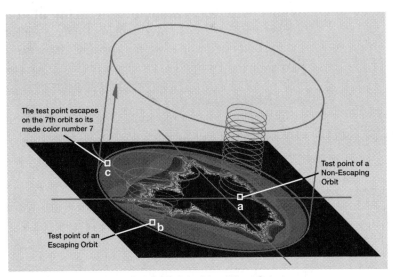

The test point escapes
on the 7th orbit so its
made color number 7

c

Test point of a
Non-Escaping
Orbit

a

Test point of an
Escaping Orbit

b

Figure 1-14 Escape-Time Coloring of the Mandelbrot Set

A brightly colored variation of this picture can be created by coloring the points *not* in the Mandelbrot set—the ones that escaped the circle—according to how long it takes for the orbit to escape, where "how long" means "how many orbits." We can use the number of iterations to control the final color of the test-point pixel. So if the test point escapes in a few iterations, the color might be red, but if it takes many iterations it might be colored blue.

Figure 1-14 shows a more graphic view of how escape-time coloring works. The bottom of the diagram shows the familiar two dimensions of the complex plane, with two points, *a* and *b*, selected for testing and coloring. The vertical axis represents the number of times the formula is iterated. You can imagine the 2" radius escape circle as a cylinder that is stretched into the third dimension, with the iteration values on the vertical scale color-coded. Therefore, the vertical level reached when the orbit escapes the cylinder is used to color the test pixel according to the color for that level. In our figure we show that test-point *a* forms a spiral that never escapes, so it is colored the "inside color" (blue in Fractint). Test-point *b* forms an orbit that escapes on the seventh iteration, so it is made of color number 7. The overall effect of this coloring scheme divides the Mandelbrot fractal into bands reminiscent of terraced rice paddies on a Chinese mountainside. Each band represents an area where the orbits begun with points in these bands escape at the exact same iteration. Near the "lake edge" of the Mandelbrot set, these bands become more and more irregular and bent. You can see these bands in full color on the back cover of this book and on the fold-out poster. See also Figure 1-15.

The spectacular stripes of the Mandelbrot set rendered with escape-time coloring should not be confused with the set itself. Mathematically, the Mandelbrot set consists of the solidly colored lake area. The colorful stripes are points *near* the Mandelbrot set. However, this distinction is not always made, and in popular fractal parlance the Mandelbrot set often refers to the whole colorful image, lake, stripes, and all.

Zooming In, or How Big Is a Fractal?

Since there are too many possible points to calculate—infinitely many, to be exact—the complete Mandelbrot set cannot be rendered in a picture. In common computer practice a rectangular grid of numbers is used for the values of *c*, using as fine a mesh as can be resolved by the particular graphics hardware. To show the complete Mandelbrot set, these numbers must span a range of approximately -2 to 2 in the *x* and *y* dimensions. However, there is no law that says that the entire Mandelbrot set from -2 to 2 must be included in the view. By picking a very small piece of the complex plane as the corners for the calculation grid, a small area of the fractal can be blown up with a zoom effect. For

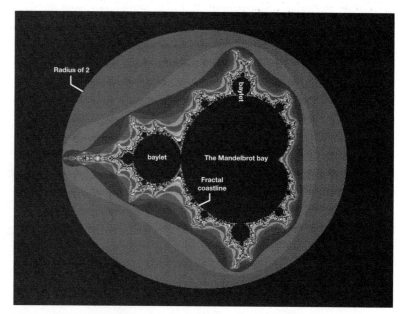

Figure 1-15 Colorized Mandelbrot Set (in Grey-Scale with Parts Identified)

example, you can look at the fractal between -.2 and +.2 or -.02 and +.02. From what we have said so far, you are undoubtedly prepared for the fact that the Mandelbrot set, being a fractal, is just as interesting in these microscopic views as it is in the large view. That is indeed the case. Even a modestly powered personal computer can reveal staggering patterns in the Mandelbrot set. Let us do a quick calculation to see just how staggering.

Fractint allows zooming in successively on a fractal ten times, magnifying the image a maximum of about twenty-five times for each zoom. The limit of ten zooms is not mathematical but is due to the computer's representation of numbers. At the most extreme magnification, a small patch of the complex plane about .000000000001 units (1.0×10^{-12}) wide fills the screen. Using the width of the Mandelbrot set of 4.0, and the width of the physical screen of about a foot, we can calculate how big the complete Mandelbrot set would be at the same scale.

Don't peek at the answer—guess! You're probably thinking that the giant Mandelbrot set would be pretty big, or we wouldn't be making much of a fuss about it, so maybe the answer is...ahhh...as big as a football field? Maybe a mile or two? Well, that's a brave answer. Indeed, if the giant Mandelbrot set were a mile wide, and because there are about twenty-five *million* different one-foot-wide patches in a square mile, you could be pretty busy charting them all.

But a mile wide is the wrong answer. A Mandelbrot set blown up to the scale of the most extreme zoomed view you can see on your PC screen with Fractint would be *one billion miles wide*. That is *ten times* the distance from the earth to the sun; almost the distance to Jupiter. Figure 1-16 shows the relative sizes of this giant Mandelbrot set and the solar system.

Figure 1-16 A Giant Mandelbrot Set Swallows the Orbit of Mars

What are the chances, then, that in your fractal explorations you will find a piece of the Mandelbrot set never before seen with human eyes? Not only pretty good, but virtually certain, as a matter of fact. You may have heard of a company that for a fee will name a star after you and record it in a book? Maybe the same thing will soon be done with the Mandelbrot set!

Mandelbrot and Julia Sets

Although the magnitude of exploration possibilities so far discussed is already of an astronomical size, you should be warned that the parade of endless fractal vistas has not even begun! The Mandelbrot set can be viewed not only as a fascinating fractal in its own right, but as an infinite "catalog" of a related class of fractals, called Julia sets. Each *point* of the Mandelbrot set may be considered an index pointing to a specific Julia set. These Julia sets are named after the French mathematician Gaston Julia, who discovered them.

Here is how Julias are formed. Consider a point c in a picture of the Mandelbrot set, and let it be inside or outside the "lake" that is the Mandelbrot set proper. Given this fixed point c, let's apply a slight modification of the escape-time algorithm for calculating the Mandelbrot set. In the calculation of the Mandelbrot set, the c in the formula $z^2 + c$ was set to the value z_{pixel}, which changes for each pixel being colored. In the Julia set calculation, by way of contrast, the value of c is kept *fixed* for the entire image and just z changes. This little trick results in a new type of fractal. Changing the value of c changes the whole Julia set to another Julia set. Thus there is no one Julia set, but rather an infinity of them, one for each value of c. That same number c corresponds to *one point* of the Mandelbrot set, so that one point may be considered as the index of the Julia set.

Figure 1-17 shows a picture of the Mandelbrot set surrounded by smaller pictures of Julia sets, with numbers connecting the Julia sets with the corresponding index points on the Mandelbrot set.

Note that Julia sets whose Mandelbrot index is inside the Mandelbrot lake have a lake themselves, whereas index points well outside the Mandelbrot lake do not have a lake. Some of the most interesting Julia sets have an index near the shore of Mandelbrot lake. As the index approaches the shore from within the Mandelbrot lake, the Julia set lake's shoreline becomes more and more convoluted, until it explodes into fragments just as the index "hits the shore." In fact, this phenomenon can be used as the definition of the Mandelbrot set (which is, you recall, just the lake part of the escape-time picture of the Mandelbrot set). The Mandelbrot set consists of exactly those Julia indices of Julia sets with lakes in one connected piece.

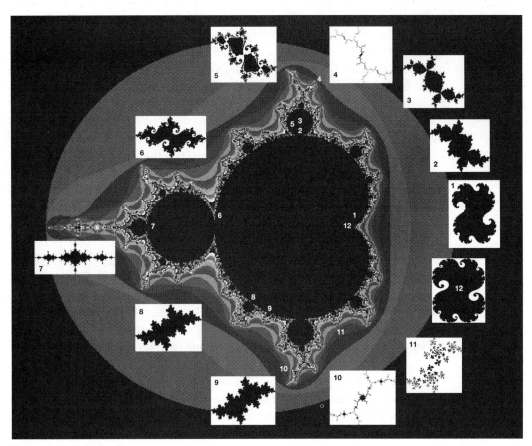

Figure 1-17 Julia Family

   This idea of one fractal being a catalog for a whole family of other fractals is a quite general idea. Later on in the book, when we are discussing other kinds of fractals, we will refer to the catalog fractal as the Mandelbrot form, and the family of fractals that correspond to the indices as the Julia form. This relationship makes sense even though the iterated formulas used to calculate the fractals are very different than the familiar $z^2 + c$ formula. When we want to make it clear that we mean the original Mandelbrot or Julias, we will speak of the "classic" Mandelbrot/Julia.

The Ubiquitous Mandelbrot Set

In physics and mathematics, there are certain numbers that appear over and over again, sometimes in completely different contexts. A good example is the number π. The definition of π comes from geometry; it is simply the ratio between the circumference and diameter of a circle. But π is ubiquitous: it pops up again and again in connection with waves, power systems, complex numbers, exponentials, and logarithms.

In a similar way, you will find the familiar bulging shape of the Mandelbrot set reappearing over and over in miniature form, both within itself and as a detail within totally different fractals. Figure 1-18 shows several "baby Mandelbrots" within a sequence of successively greater magnification zooms.

Given the fundamental nature of fractals, which has to do with the existence of infinite detail, at greater and greater magnification, it is not too surprising to find baby Mandelbrots inside the original Mandelbrot fractal. But suppose we use the same approach to fractal generation (coloring pixels by iterating a formula), but change the formula to something completely different, say, $z_{n+1} = c *$ cosine(z_n). This formula doesn't look anything like the Mandelbrot formula, and neither does the generated fractal. Yet buried within the fractal is the shape shown in Figure 1-13. Another baby Mandelbrot! This is not an isolated example—it happens again and again. The ubiquitous Mandelbrot set shape is to fractal theory what the number π is to mathematics and engineering. Indeed, the plaque on the Pioneer spacecraft should have contained a Mandelbrot set engraving!

Now that we've covered the Mandelbrot in great detail, let's take a look at some other kinds of fractals.

NEWTON'S METHOD—ESCAPE TO FINITE ATTRACTOR

The escape-time method of generating fractals we have discussed so far might be called "escape to infinity." The test for when an orbit has escaped (strayed outside a circle of radius 2) is really a test for escaping to infinity. In the case of the Mandelbrot and Julia orbit formulas, once the orbit value gets outside that circle, if you were to continue to calculate the orbit it would spiral outward forever. In this case we say that "infinity is an attractor" for the orbit. It is as if infinity were a magnet trying to attract the Mandelbrot orbit values to itself. And we can imagine that the orbit test point is trying to keep the orbit values in check.

A similar kind of fractal image is generated by measuring the escape time to a finite value rather than infinity. One example of this creates fractals using what is called Newton's method. (Newton, as you probably recall, was a famous physicist who invented—that is, discovered—a great many truths about moving objects and gravity. He also discovered some clever math techniques.) For example, every time you press the square root button on a calculator, you are using Newton's method. Newton's method is a way of doing a calculation by beginning with a guess for the answer, and repeatedly applying a formula that

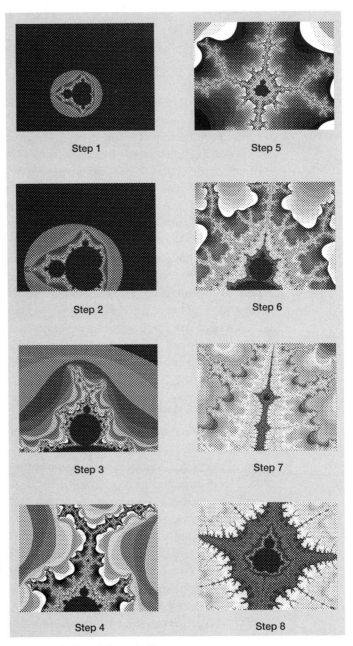

Step 1

Step 5

Step 2

Step 6

Step 3

Step 7

Step 4

Step 8

Figure 1-18 Fractal Zoom in Steps

transforms the guess into a better guess. The series of answers so generated converges rapidly to the correct answer.

Consider the problem of finding the cube root of 1. This is the same problem as finding the solution to the equation $z^3 - 1 = 0$. The solutions to this equation are the numbers that when multiplied by themselves three times ($z \cdot z \cdot z$) give 1 as an answer. You might think that this is a silly problem, because the answer is clearly the number 1, since $1^3 = 1$. What makes the problem interesting is that when complex numbers are considered (the same kind of numbers we just discussed in connection with the Mandelbrot calculation), there are actually *three* solutions to the equation. These three answers are three equally spaced points on a circle of radius 1. They are the complex numbers $1 + 0i, -\frac{1}{2} + \frac{\sqrt{3}}{2}i$, and $-\frac{1}{2} - \frac{\sqrt{3}}{2}i$. Figure 1-19 shows the three cube roots of 1 distributed on the unit circle in the complex plane, and what happens to several initial guesses when fed into the Newton's method formula.

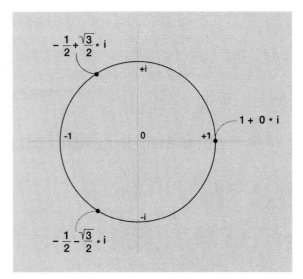

Figure 1-19 The Three Complex Cube Roots of 1

The Newton's method approach is very similar to the Mandelbrot set calculation. The pixels on the screen are mapped to complex numbers in the same way. For each complex number z_{pixel} corresponding to a pixel, an orbit sequence $z_0, z_1, z_2, \ldots z_n, \ldots$ is generated. This time the orbit sequence is generated by a slightly more complicated formula, $z_{n+1} = (2z^3 + 1) / 3z^3$. But the main difference is that with Newton's method the criterion for "escape" is different. For the Mandelbrot set, escaping meant that the orbit got outside of a circle of radius 2 centered on the origin. The orbits that got too close to the "magnet" at infinity were attracted to it. But in the case of Newton's method, there are three magnets, one located at each of the cube roots of 1 around the unit circle. Orbits escape (or perhaps we should say they die) when they are irreversibly attracted to these magnets. Each test-point pixel is colored according to the magnet that captures its orbit.

But what happens when the test point guess is *between* two of the three possible attracting values? The answer is chaos! Areas colored according to the ultimate destination of the orbit become intertwined in an infinitely complex pattern, as Figure 1-20 reveals.

Newton's method is an example of where fractals turn up in situations that engineers want to avoid. That square root button on your calculator has a purpose—to find the square root. The first guess your calculator makes before applying Newton's method is designed to be close enough to the final answer so that the algorithm will work effectively to find the square root. If the algorithm doesn't work for bad initial guesses, then it is the job of the calculator designer to avoid those values. The designer will be out of a job if he or she builds a calculator where an "ill-behaved" initial guess is used and the calculator gives the wrong answer.

Generating a Newton Fractal

Here is how to use Newton's method to generate a fractal. Start with a grid of complex numbers that more than covers the unit circle and our three cube roots of one. The corner values might extend from -2 to 2 in both the x and y direction. Assign colors to the three answers. Fractint uses dark blue, light blue, and green. For each number, z_{pixel} in the grid is used as an initial guess for the Newton's method calculation. Set $z_0 = z_{pixel}$ and successively apply the Newton formula to get a sequence $z_0, z_1, z_2, \ldots$ Each time the formula is iterated, the orbit is checked to see if it has come near one of the roots. If it does, the calculation is finished, and z_{pixel} is assigned the color of the root that captured it. The areas near the three roots end up being solidly colored with the color for that root. In between the roots, the three colors twist together in an intricate braided pattern. These solid areas are called *basins of attraction,* because they show all the starting points that end up converging to a particular attractor. Figure 1-20 shows this intriguing fractal, which might be said to be based on the applied mathematician's nightmare—the indecision of Newton's method!

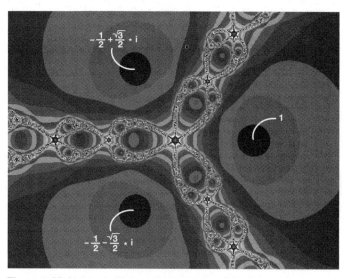

$-\frac{1}{2} + \frac{\sqrt{3}}{2} * i$

1

$-\frac{1}{2} - \frac{\sqrt{3}}{2} * i$

Figure 1-20 Newton's Method Fractal for the Cube Root of One

CHAOTIC ORBITS AND THE LORENZ ATTRACTOR

The discussion of escape-time fractals introduced the idea of an orbit as a series of points that can be imagined to be the path of a flying object. The only concern for the orbit was the time required to escape outside some radius, or the time required to be captured by an attractor (that is, the number of iterations required). The orbit itself was not the main concern but was simply a step in the calculation of a color of a single point. However, orbits can be interesting in themselves.

The idea of plotting orbits from the equations describing dynamic systems is as old as physics itself. One of the first triumphs of theoretical physics was the demonstration that the elliptic orbit of a small moon around a large planet is a consequence of the inverse square law of gravitation. The problem of determining the orbits of two objects revolving around each other is known as the "two-body problem." It has a simple and elegant solution. But adding a third body to the dynamic system greatly complicates the orbits. Three-body orbits can be complex beyond imagination.

Why is it, then, that every high school science student has the idea that planetary orbits are ellipses, when there are, to make a slight understatement, more than two objects in the universe? *No* orbit in the physical world is exactly an ellipse. If the three-body problem has a complicated solution, how about the trillion-body problem, the one that exists today in our universe!

There is, of course, a perfectly reasonable answer to this question. An ellipse is a simple geometric shape that has simple mathematical properties that make it very suitable for computational purposes, not to mention educational purposes. In science and engineering, careful simplifications and approximations can make intractable problems manageable, and they are a very important tool in the engineering tool kit.

Yet this eminently reasonable answer is unsatisfying. This propensity to imagine orbits in the simplest possible geometric terms is probably yet another manifestation of a deep cultural bias toward a classically geometric way of imagining the world. What do we find when we abandon the simple beauty of the ellipse and contemplate chaotic orbits—which is to say, virtually every *real* orbit? Fractals, of course!

Before launching into an example of a chaotic orbit, let us review a few properties of the well-behaved orbits of classical mechanics. The elliptic orbit is periodic. That is, the orbiting object describes a single path over and over. Alternatively, under different conditions the orbit might be a parabola or a hyperbola, in which case the orbit is not periodic, but the object traverses the orbit exactly once. In all of these cases the orbit is a well-defined smooth curve.

In late 1963, Edward Lorenz published a paper on deterministic chaos that included some plots of an unusual orbit. Like the Mandelbrot set, his "monster curve" had a very simple mathematical description. But the behavior of this orbit, which we will refer to as the Lorenz attractor, is far from simple.

The plot of the Lorenz attractor orbit consists of two connected spirals, in two different planes at an angle to each other (see Figure 1-21). The orbit path would swirl around inside one of these spiral areas, and then at random intervals it would switch allegiances to the other, and so on back and forth. This orbit has some bizarre properties. It is bounded, like the ellipse, and contained forever within a delimited region of space. But unlike the ellipse, the Lorenz orbit is not periodic; in fact, it never crosses itself or repeats. Its path is therefore an infinitely long thread wound around in a finite space. The combination of these three factors—bounded, infinitely long, never crossing itself or repeating—implies a complex interweaving of arbitrarily close near misses of different strands of the orbits like an air traffic controller's worst nightmare! From all that we have discussed so far, you will not be surprised to learn that such an orbit is a fractal. Figure 1-21 is a plot of the first few thousand or so turns of this chaotic orbit. You can generate the Lorenz attractor in stereo 3D using Fractint and even have it generate tones as it's being made.

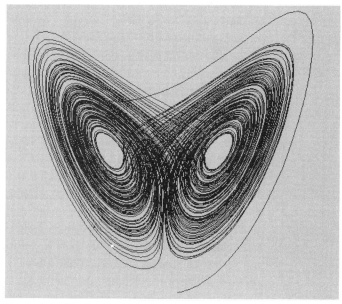

Figure 1-21 The Lorenz Attractor

Gaskets and Ferns—Iterated Function Systems

The essence of a fractal is to have detail at all scales, including the most extreme magnifications. One way to achieve this characteristic is through self-similarity. An object is self-similar if small pieces of itself are identically shaped versions of the complete object, only on a smaller scale. One method of generating fractals is to directly exploit this idea. A fractal can be defined by exactly specifying the relationship between itself and its self-similar parts.

Michael Barnsley has developed this approach and named it Iterated Function Systems, or IFS for short. An endless variety of fractals can be created in this way, some of them eerily lifelike. Fractint can create a variety of bushes, trees, and ferns using the IFS fractal type.

The Sierpinski Gasket

The Sierpinski gasket (pronounced "sear-pin-ski") is a fractal that looks as if it is made of Swiss cheese because it has so many holes. It's called a gasket because it seems to offer the structure you might find in a gasket—lots of passages surrounding each other.

The Sierpinski gasket can be exactly specified by stating the rule governing its self-similarity: it's a geometric object built within a triangle, with the property that each of the three subtriangles formed from one of its corners and the midpoints of the adjacent two sides is an exact self-similar replica of the whole triangle.

Another way to define this fractal is to use what are called affine maps. An *affine map* is a transformation of an object that preserves its shape. The transformation can rotate it, move it, enlarge it, or shrink it, but it must not distort the shape of the object. Thus you must be sure your transformations do the same operation to each point in the same way. Such a map is said to be *contractive* if it always shrinks objects. The notion of a contractive affine transformation is a formal way of saying "self-similar." In other words, if there is a contractive affine map between an object and itself, then the object contains a miniature image of itself and is self-similar.

We can easily describe the Sierpinski gasket with three affine maps. Draw the Sierpinski gasket on a graph, so that two of the sides are nestled against the x and y axes. The corners of the triangle are the points (0,0), (1,0), and (0,1). Here are three affine maps defining this Sierpinski gasket:

1. Map every point (x,y) to the point $(\frac{1}{2}x, \frac{1}{2}y)$. This maps the whole triangle to the lower left triangle by shrinking the scale by a factor of a half.

2. Map every point (x,y) to the point $(\frac{1}{2}x, \frac{1}{2}y + \frac{1}{2})$. This maps the whole triangle to the upper left corner subtriangle by shrinking the scale by a factor of a half and shifting up half a unit.

3. Map every point (x,y) to the point $(\frac{1}{2}x + \frac{1}{2}, \frac{1}{2}y)$. This maps the whole triangle to the lower right subtriangle by shrinking the scale by a factor of a half and shifting to the right half a unit.

In this particular example, the transformations are particularly simple because no rotation was involved, only shifting and shrinking. The key insight into the relationship between affine transformations and the Sierpinski gasket is to notice that there are four possible triangles with sides equal to half the sides of the original. The missing triangle is the center one, formed from the midpoints of the three sides. Why is there no transformation mapping the whole triangle to the center? Because there is nothing in the center—that is the "hole"! If the fourth affine transformation were added, mapping the whole triangle to the middle, the result would be rather boring—simply a filled-in triangle! Leaving out the center is what creates the "Swiss cheese" effect with the missing centers of the triangles.

Barnsley suggests a method of generating the fractal from these affine transformations that he calls the "chaos game." Start with any arbitrary point whatsoever. Pick one of the transformations at random and apply it to the point,

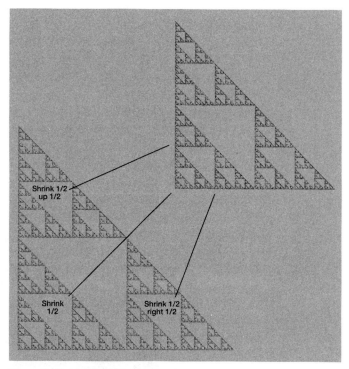

Figure 1-22 Sierpinski Gasket

plotting the result. Continue by applying a new randomly chosen transformation each time to the last point, again plotting the result. But as the process is repeated, the points generated will produce the shape of the Sierpinski gasket. The name Iterated Function Systems for this kind of fractal comes from the repeated, or iterated, application of these affine maps, or function systems.

The Sierpinski gasket is used here to illustrate IFS fractals, but it can also be generated in two other ways by Fractint: by using lsystems (see Chapter 3) and by using the escape-time methods we have discussed. The Sierpinski gasket holds the record for the number of ways that Fractint can create it.

A Fractal Fern

The Sierpinski gasket is a very unnatural-looking object, but it is just one of an endless variety of images possible with the IFS approach. Another fractal that has become almost a trademark of Barnsley's work is the fractal fern.

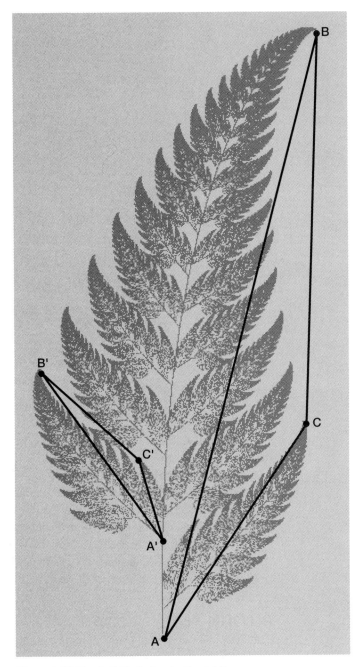

Figure 1-23 The Self Similarity of a Fractal Fern

Many plants have several levels of self-similarity because of their branching structure. Some kinds of ferns have wide fronds at the base and narrower fronds in the center, tapering to a pointed tip. If you broke off the very bottom fronds, you would end up with a smaller but still similar fern. Four iterated functions can be used to define a very natural-looking fern. Two functions define the self-similarity between the left and right fronds with the whole. One function defines the stem. Finally, another function defines the relationship between the whole fern and the fern less the bottom fronds. Figure 1-23 shows these self-similarities. As with the Sierpinski gasket, probabilities are assigned to these functions, and their repeated application seeded with an arbitrary starting point generates the image, just as we described earlier for the Sierpinski gasket.

There's Much More...

No introduction to fractals can completely cover the subject. This fractal primer was designed to give you a taste and feel of what fractals are all about, as well as a slight touch of the mathematics behind them. But since this is really more a book about exploring and creating fractals, the next chapter begins that exploration with a guided tour of the Fractint program that comes with this book.

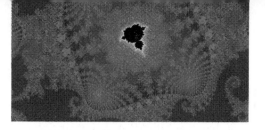

USING FRACTINT

2

$\mathbf{A}$re you ready for a wild ride into Fractal creations? You have come to the right place. To make Fractint easier to learn, this chapter includes a guided tour of the program as well as reference sections on the keystrokes and commands.

Fractint generates fractals based on any of its 68 different built-in formulas. It can save and retrieve fractals in CompuServe's Graphics Interchange Format (GIF) format. Fractint has additional capabilities for generating 3-D transformations of fractals, making stereo funny glasses images, doing color-cycle animation, changing color palettes, letting you experiment with your own fractal formulas (with no programming needed), and much more. In this chapter we will learn how to access some of these features and how to fine-tune the way the program operates.

The section called "Tour" will take you through a hands-on demo of Fractint's most basic functions. It is for readers who have never used Fractint before, but it will also show you nooks and crannies of the program that even experienced users may not have discovered. Don't feel restricted by our tour, however; you may want to jump off the tour and explore on your own at various points along the way. But do come back. Fractint is the kind of program that grows on you because it has more possibilities than you can absorb all at once. So every so often, come back and browse through the tour and reference section, and try another fractal journey.

UP AND RUNNING

We assume you have read the Installation section earlier in the book and that Fractint is installed and ready to run in a directory that is included in your DOS "path". If not, go back and read the Installation section, make sure you have the correct files in your "Fractal Creations" directory, and come back here as soon as you have Fractint running.

A FRACTINT GUIDED TOUR

To make your tour easier, a road map is shown in Figure 2-1. This figure is a simplified flowchart of the different functions of Fractint. As we go through the tour, we will be traversing the routes shown on the road map.

Here are a few conventions about how we will describe the directions to invoke commands. When we want you to type in something literally, we'll show it in monospace:

Type in the file name `altern.map`.

You type in `altern.map`.

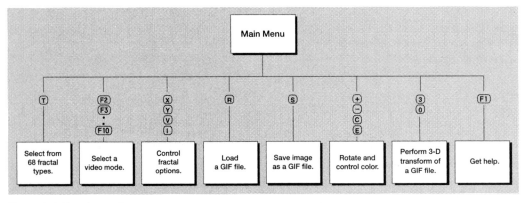

Figure 2-1 Fractint road map

Some keys or other items will be referred to by their names, as in the first example below. We will surround designations that you should *not* type in literally with the "<" and ">" characters, as in the second of these two examples.

Press (ESC) to return to the Main menu.

Type in at the DOS prompt `fractint savename=<filename>`.

In the first example, you should press the (ESC) key. In the second, you supply a file name to replace <filename>, so you would actually type in something like

`fractint savename=myfractal.gif`.

Quitting Fractint

Before we start, let's talk about the two most important commands in Fractint, the Quit command and the Help command. The Quit command key is (ESC), which is used in every context to back out of whatever mode you are in and move towards the Main menu. In fact, repeatedly pressing (ESC) will get you clear out to the "Exit from Fractint? (y/n)" prompt, which then requires typing only (Y) to return to the DOS prompt.

The Help function is accessed by pressing the (F1) key from any point of the program. The first Help screen you see is context-sensitive; it depends on where you were in the program when you pressed (F1). Pressing (F1) a second time will take you to the Help main menu, from which you can access all the Help screens. Pressing (ESC) exits the help mode.

The Credits Screen

Fractint's opening screen shown in Figure 2-2 is decidedly unconventional and comes closer than anything else to symbolizing the participatory nature of Fractint. We "Stone Soupers" (the creators of Fractint) considered giving Fractint a more fashionable face for this book, but after a little thought we realized that the opening screen has become indispensable. To our eyes, it's beautiful!

When you fire up Fractint you are presented with a scrolling list of the names of people who have made the "stone soup" tasty by contributing the odds and ends from their programming "cupboards." (Notice that the list shows the Stone Soupers' CompuServe Information Service (CIS) numbers, so you can contact any of us by electronic mail.) Fractint is truly a community project driven by the

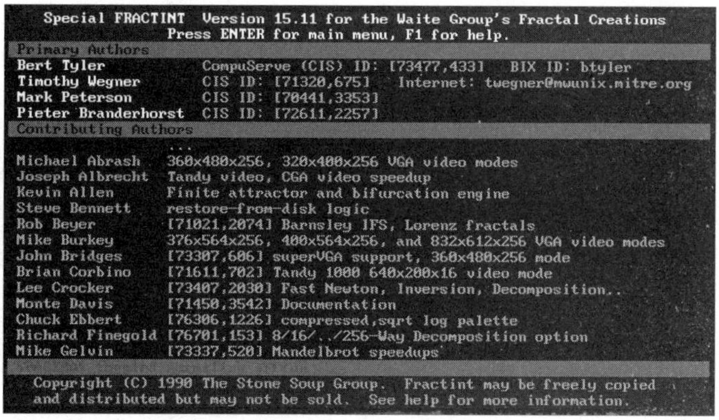

Figure 2-2 The famous Fractint credits screen

excitement and imagination of an international network of kindred souls. These people have two things in common: their fascination with fractals and their desire to share their excitement with others.

Once you have used Fractint more than a few times, you will probably get in the habit of immediately pressing (ENTER) and moving straight to the Main menu when you start Fractint.

The Main Menu

Having paid homage to the legions who have contributed to the program, go ahead and press (ENTER) to move to the Main menu, which should look like Figure 2-3.

Fractint began life as a command-driven program, which means that various keystrokes cause Fractint to execute different commands. All commands are also accessible from screens we call "menus," which you can control with the cursor keys. Throughout Fractint, just select items from the menu by moving the arrow keys to highlight different menu items, and then press (ENTER) to execute commands. Note that the menus also tell you how to select the menu items by using direct command keystrokes. For example, you can leave Fractint either by selecting "quit Fractint" with the arrow keys and pressing (ENTER), or by pressing (ESC). Note that none of the Fractint menus use the mouse (for now, at least).

Most commands can also be given at Fractint startup time using command-line options. You can, for example, specify which video mode you want Fractint to use by typing the following at the DOS prompt:

```
fractint video=F3
```

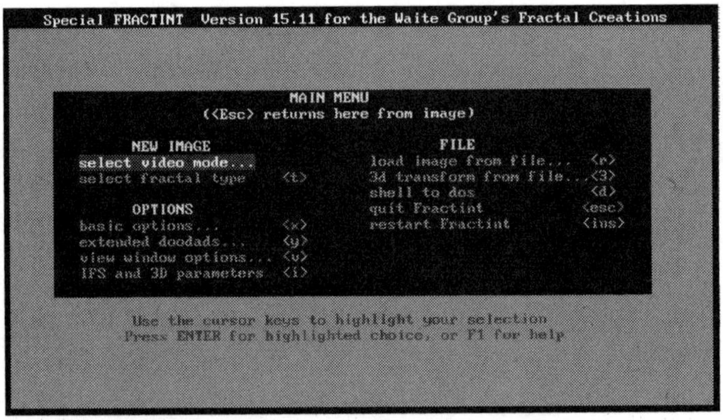

Figure 2-3 Fractint Main Menu at startup

This method can be useful when you have many specialized commands to execute and want to simply type them in instead of using the menus.

Fractint has three main modes, each with its own set of commands. These are the display mode, the color cycling mode, and the palette editing mode. Of these three modes, the display mode is the most important, because the main functions of Fractint are accessible from within this mode. Color cycling is a simple but secondary mode, while palette editing is a more advanced function. Each of the three modes has its own set of commands, so it is important for you to be clear at all times which mode is currently active. At first Fractint will be in the display mode. The other two modes will be descibed a little later.

The Fractint Main menu is divided into three sections, described in the following paragraphs.

New Image

The New Image menu category contains commands that cause the generation of a new fractal image. Fractint can calculate its images from 68 built-in formulas. But in order to create a new image, Fractint needs to know two things: what video mode you want to display and what fractal type you want to calculate (see Chapter 1 for an explanation of fractal types). The fractal type defaults to the Mandelbrot set. If Fractint is able to detect what exact video hardware your PC has, a suggested video mode will be highlighted in the list of video modes when you invoke the "select video mode" function. (A video mode is the screen resolution and number of colors supported by particular video adapter.) However, there is no universal default for the video mode; you must choose a mode in order to generate an image. But before you go ahead and choose a mode, let's discuss the other menu headings.

Options

The Options menu items give you access to a variety of settings, and special effects. You won't need these right away, except possibly the view window option. Since the time it takes to create a fractal is directly proportional to how many screen pixels have to be calculated, the view window capability allows you to specify a very small image that can be calculated very rapidly. This capability is wonderful for the intrepid fractal explorer, especially one who does not have the world's fastest computer!

File

The File menu category includes the ability to restore to the screen, or read in, previously calculated images that were saved as GIF files. (See page 275 for more about the GIF standard.) There are two ways to restore files and duplicate them on-screen: either as they were originally calculated, or by doing a 3-D transformation on the file. There are also useful commands on the File menu that let you enter DOS without exiting Fractint (you return to Fractint by typing **exit**), quit Fractint altogether with (ESC), and restart Fractint with (INS).

Let's continue this tour through each of the Main menu commands in detail.

SELECTING A VIDEO MODE

Using the arrow keys, choose "select video mode" from the Main menu, and press (ENTER). You will be presented with a list of video modes, with a choice highlighted, that should look like Figure 2-4. This list shows all the various drivers built into Fractint for a variety of video hardware, along with comments about each video mode. (A video driver is a specialized routine for accessing the features of your video hardware.) The list includes not only standard IBM-compatible modes such as the 640 × 350 EGA 16-color mode, but some highly unusual "tweaked" modes that can squeeze extra resolution out of a plain VGA.

The F3 option means that pressing function key (F3) will directly select that video mode. Each video driver has a key combination associated with it, and pressing that key combination selects the video mode. You can also select different modes by using the arrow keys to move the highlight to the mode you want and then press (ENTER). Fractint has room for up to 100 different video modes, each with a different key combination. Table 2-1 lists some examples to show how the key-naming scheme works:

Video Mode Label	Equivalent Keystrokes
F2	The function key (F2)
SF2	Press (SHIFT) and (F2) together
CF2	Press (CTRL) and (F2) together
AF2	Press (ALT) and (F2) together
Alt-1	Press (ALT) and (1) together
Ctl-1	Press (CTRL) and (1) together

Table 2-1 Key-naming scheme

As an example, the mode labeled SF10 has a resolution of 360 pixels wide and 480 pixels high, with 256 possible colors. This mode results from Fractint directly programming the VGA registers, and it should work on any VGA register-compatible with the IBM VGA. It is accessed by typing (SHIFT)-(F10).

For right now, however, our main concern is to find a good video mode for getting started. If you have a CGA, EGA, or VGA adapter, Fractint will have

```
Special FRACTINT  Version 15.11 for the Waite Group's Fractal Creations

                          Select Video Mode
     key...name.....................xdot.ydot.clr.comment................
     F2   IBM 16-Color EGA            640  350  16 Standard EGA hi-res mode
     F3   IBM 256-Color VGA/MCGA      320  200 256 Quick and LOTS of colors
     F4   IBM 16-Color VGA            640  480  16 Nice high resolution
     F5   IBM 4-Color CGA             320  200   4 (Ugh - Yuck - Bleah)
     F6   IBM Hi-Rez B&W CGA          640  200   2 ('Hi-Rez' Ugh - Yuck)
     F7   IBM B&W EGA                 640  350   2 (Monochrome EGA)
     F8   IBM B&W VGA                 640  480   2 (Monochrome VGA)
     F9   IBM Low-Rez EGA             320  200  16 Quick but chunky
     F10  IBM VGA (non-std)           320  400 256 Register Compatibles ONLY
     SF1  IBM VGA (non-std)           360  480 256 Register Compatibles ONLY
     SF2  SuperVGA/VESA Autodetect    800  600  16 Works with most SuperVGA
     SF3  SuperVGA/VESA Autodetect   1024  768  16 Works with most SuperVGA
     SF4  SuperVGA/VESA Autodetect    640  480 256 Works with most SuperVGA
     SF5  SuperVGA/VESA Autodetect    640  480 256 Works with most SuperVGA
     SF6  SuperVGA/VESA Autodetect    800  600 256 Works with most SuperVGA
     SF7  SuperVGA/VESA Autodetect   1024  768 256 Works with most SuperVGA
     (more)
                 Use the cursor keys to highlight your selection
                 Press ENTER for highlighted choice, or ESCAPE to back out
```

Figure 2-4 Top of the Fractint video mode list

detected your adapter and chosen a mode for you, which you will see highlighted. If you have a VGA, for example, a good mode to use is the one labeled "F3 IBM 256-Color VGA/MCGA," because it has relatively low resolution for fast results, and because it has more colors—a decided plus. You won't immediately notice the extra colors of a 256-color mode in the default Mandelbrot image that we'll be generating shortly, but once you zoom deep inside a fractal and try cycling the colors, you'll see the value of having more colors.

Once you select a video mode, it will remain current until you change modes. Table 2-2 shows several good initial choices of video mode for different video hardware. After you have created a really spectacular image, you may want to regenerate it using a higher-resolution mode.

Graphics Adapter	Function Key	Pixels Across	Pixels Down	Colors
CGA	F5	320	200	4
EGA	F2	640	350	16
VGA	F3	320	200	256
Hercules	Alt-G	720	348	2
SVGA	Shift-F5	640	480	256

Table 2-2 Suggested Initial Video Modes

If you have a super-VGA board, try some of the "SuperVGA/VESA Autodetect" modes. It's a good idea to get out your video board documentation, find a chart of video modes, and see which modes your board supports. For this tour, though, any of the modes in Table 2-2 will be just fine.

GENERATING A FRACTAL

Go ahead and select a video mode. If Fractint's highlighted choice looks reasonable for your computer hardware, just press (ENTER) to select it. If you don't like the mode Fractint chose and you have a VGA board, use F3; for an EGA, try F2; and for a CGA, try F5. Pressing (ENTER) to select a video mode begins generating a fractal image. The default image for Fractint is type mandel, so you should now see a fractal being generated on your screen—the famous Mandelbrot set. Your screen should look like Figure 2-5. (We used the EGA mode to generate that figure.)

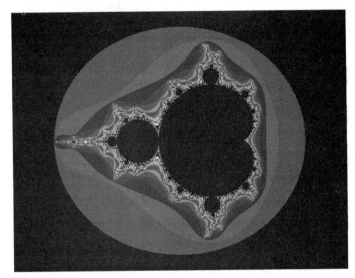

Figure 2-5 The Mandelbrot set

If you didn't get Fractint to display the Mandelbrot set, you probably selected a video mode that is not supported by your hardware. This can be disconcerting, but it does no harm. Even if your screen is black, press (ESC) to get back to the Main menu. (If the computer "locks up"—freezes the screen and keyboard—you may have to reboot.) Try again, this time selecting an appropriate video mode. If you have a color system, try (F5). That is the old IBM 4-color CGA mode, which should work on most systems.

EGA and VGA Colors

Once you get things working, try experimenting with other modes. If you have a VGA and you started off with (F3), try the EGA (F2) mode. This will give you a feel for the way resolution affects speed. Notice that the default Mandelbrot image looks almost the same with 16 colors as it does with 256 colors. In fact, the authors have had phone calls from people complaining that the 256—color modes didn't appear to work! The reason is that the colors correspond to the number of iterations of the formula used to calculate the Mandelbrot set. The outer colored area corresponds to color 1, the next stripe to color 2, and so forth. The vast majority of visible pixels in the Mandelbrot image have colors with values less than 16—which is the number of colors on the EGA, too. Try counting the stripes from the outside if you don't believe us! But after you begin zooming in, the 256-color images will begin looking very different.

To allow quick evaluation, Fractint plots its images, such as the Mandelbrot set, using multiple passes. The number of passes depends on the video mode; the higher the resolution, the more passes. For example, 320 × 200 modes have two passes, while 640 × 480 modes have three. The first pass rapidly plots the image at a coarser resolution, and the subsequent pass adds missing pixels, to make a finer image. This way you don't have to wait for the image to be completed before continuing your explorations. You can generally tell what the fractal will look like after the coarse pixels of the first pass are colored. As an added bonus, Fractint uses this multiple-pass approach to guess areas that have solid colors, greatly speeding up the calculation.

Orbits

Try the following experiment: Begin to regenerate the Mandelbrot image by pressing the mode-selecting function key that you determined works best on your machine. Without waiting for the image to finish drawing on the screen, press the letter Ⓞ. The Ⓞ key is a toggle that makes visible the orbit values generated in the Mandelbrot calculation. (See page 77 for an explanation of orbits.) Pressing Ⓞ again turns off this effect—that's what is meant by "toggle."

The Mandelbrot image is calculated by generating a sequence of points and testing whether they have escaped a circle of radius 2. The Ⓞ key plots the sequence of points on the screen. Notice that the orbits have the most structure when the "lake" points are being plotted and that the orbit path does not quickly escape to large values. (Some people feel the orbit plots are more interesting than the fractal images themselves!)

As you go through the tour, try using the Ⓞ toggle with different fractals. If the orbit display goes by too fast, try the Ⓕ toggle, which switches Fractint back and forth between fast integer arithmetic and slower floating-point arithmetic. With fractals, faster is usually better, but when you are watching the orbits, sometimes it helps to slow things down.

ZOOMING IN

Now that you have a Mandelbrot image displayed on your screen, what can you do with it? Fractals are full of interesting details that unfold as you expand them. The "zoom" function of Fractint lets you dive inside a fractal on the screen and behold its inner beauty. Pressing the (PGUP) key, for example, creates a dashed rectangle—called the zoom box—around the outer edge of the screen. Repeatedly pressing (PGUP) shrinks the zoom box. You can move the zoom box around the screen by using either the arrow keys or the mouse. Either clicking the left mouse button or pressing (PGDN) enables the zoom box. Holding the left button down while moving the mouse away from you shrinks the zoom box. Moving the mouse with no buttons pressed moves the zoom box within the screen's x-y plane.

Zoom Box Exploration Technique

It's fun to locate some interesting detail in a fractal and place the zoom box around it. Then, pressing (ENTER) (or double-clicking the left mouse button) will cause Fractint to calculate and fill the entire screen with the smaller image that was in the zoom box, so the zoom box acts as a magnifier. The (PGDN) key is used to make the zoom box larger. Repeatedly pressing (PGDN) will make the zoom box disappear. To do the same thing with the mouse, hold the left button down and pull the mouse toward you. You can use keys and mouse together, too. On some machines, you can speed up the movement of the zoom box with the cursor keys by holding down the (CTRL) key while pressing the cursor keys.

You can also zoom out by creating a small zoom box and then press (CTRL)-(ENTER). The effect of this is to zoom out so that the previous image is shrunk to the size of the zoom box and the surrounding area is filled in. The equivalent mouse command is to double-click the right mouse button.

Try zooming in on the upper peninsula between the two lakes of the Mandelbrot image. Press (PGUP) until the zoom box is quite small, move the box over the peninsula, and either press (ENTER) or double-click the left mouse button to generate the magnified image.

COLOR CYCLING

The second Fractint mode is called color cycling. In this mode, Fractint rapidly alters displayed colors of an image, giving an effect of animation. This works because most graphics adapters create colors by using color palettes. There are as many palette entries as the number of colors your computer's hardware video adapter can display at one time. So, a palette for an EGA has 16 entries, and a VGA has as many as 256. But—and this is a big "but"—the colors assigned to the palette entries are drawn from a much larger selection. For example, the VGA

320 × 200 mode can display 256 colors on the screen at one time, but these 256 can be selected from 262 thousand possible colors! (Understand that in Fractint, different shades of the same color are considered different colors. Some fractals, for example, may have only 2 colors with 128 shades.) What Fractint can do is rapidly change which colors are assigned to which palette numbers. As you'll see, this simple technique creates a magical effect.

Most fractal images have more information in them than the mind can comprehend. By assigning colors differently, you can make different details visible in the same image. By cycling the colors, areas that make up the fractal are revealed by color moving between them. Since the areas are connected in a highly organized fashion, there is a high degree of animation potential. Playing with the colors is at least half the fun of Fractint. Alas, this feature only works if your video hardware supports at least 16 colors (EGA), and works best in the VGA and super-VGA 256-color modes. If you have a CGA or Hercules monochrome graphics adapter, we suggest you skip on to the next section, or go out and buy an EGA monitor—or, better yet, get a super-VGA with 1024K of RAM.

Press the ⊕ key to see your fractal color cycle. Showtime! The colors of your fractal will now start wildly gyrating! (If the cycling is too fast on your machine, you can slow it down with the ⊙ key.)

Color Cycling Features and Experimenting

Earlier in this chapter we discussed the three modes of Fractint—the display mode, the color cycling mode, and the palette editing mode. As soon as you press ⊕ (or ⊖ or ©), Fractint enters the color cycling mode, and a whole new set of command keys takes effect. The ⊕ and ⊖ keys reverse the direction of the color rotation: the ⊕ key makes it radiate outward, the ⊖ key makes the colors move inward. To freeze the color scheme, press (BACKSPACE). The outside border of the screen will now be white to remind you that Fractint is still in the color cycling mode even though the colors aren't moving.

When you first enter the color cycling mode, Fractint rotates the existing colors in the current color palette. The original color scheme will repeat periodically (every 256 colors if you have VGA, every 16 colors if you have EGA). Pressing any of the function keys (F2) to (F10) causes Fractint to randomly create new colors in the existing palette, so the color schemes never repeat (or at least not any time soon). Indeed, the number of color schemes obtained by pressing the function keys is astronomical! The lower function keys ((F2),(F3),...) cause the colors to change abruptly. The higher function keys ((F8), (F9), (F10)) cause the colors to change more smoothly and continuously between more widely spaced random colors. Pressing (ENTER) while the colors are cycling causes the color scheme to be completely and randomly altered.

Slow-Motion Color Cycling

Often you'll want to slow down or speed up the color cycling. There are two ways to do this in Fractint. The first way is to use the ⊕ and ⊕ keys while colors are cycling. This feature was originally added to control "flicker" on machines with slower graphics adapters. On these machines, slowing down the cycling with the ⊕ cleans up the flicker. But if you have one of the new breed of faster computers (such as a 286, 386, or 486), you may find the color cycling is just too fast for enjoyment; use the ⊕ to slow it down. The other way to change the color cycling speed is to press any of the number keys, ① through ⑨ . These keys cause certain colors in the palette to be skipped, effectively increasing the rotation speed. The higher-numbered keys cause colors to rotate faster. Fractint defaults to the ① key.

Suppose, for example, you have a markedly striped fractal, and you wish to see more smoothly changing colors. You would press ⒡⒑. The new colors will be added to the end of the 256-color palette, and will take a little time to "flush out" the old colors. To speed things up, press ⑨ , wait until you see the smoother color changes have taken effect, then press ① to slow things down again.

Assuming your fractal type is still set for the Mandelbrot image, at first the image you are color cycling will have a strongly striped appearance. As you use the higher-numbered function keys, the colors of the stripes will start to blend, and your attention will be drawn more to the lake outline than to the stripes. When you see the image the way you want it, press (BACKSPACE) or (SPACE) to freeze it, and (ESC) to exit the color cycling mode and return to the regular display mode.

SAVING A FILE

Between creative zooming and color cycling, by now you should have created a few beautiful fractals. Chances are very good that your creation is unlike any other. If you save it as a GIF, it can be opened again and experimented with, or uploaded to CompuServe. (See Appendix B for details about the GIF format.)

The command to save a fractal image to a file is ⓢ. You must be viewing your fractal, and you must *not* be in the color cycling mode. Press ⓢ to save. You will see two multicolored stripes moving down the right and left sides of the screen like a bar as the saving progresses. Fractint saves images as GIF files, so when done, a window will appear on the screen with the message "File saved as FRACT001.GIF." The number "001" will increment as you save more images. These files will not be overwritten, so watch out for your disk filling up with too many images! A typical 640 × 480 256-color image can use 100 kilobytes or more of storage. If you already have a fractal saved as FRACT001.GIF, the next time you start Fractint and do a save it will increase the number and save it as FRACT002.GIF.

THE EXPANDED MAIN MENU

Assuming that you have saved your fractal creation, press (ESC) to return to the Main menu. What you will notice is that the Main menu is no longer the same. Since you have created a fractal image, there are more functions Fractint can perform, so the menu is expanded. These additional menu functions will always show whenever there is a graphics image that has been calculated or read in from a disk. Figure 2-6 shows the expanded Main menu. The next sections will tell you a little about the additional items in the Main menu.

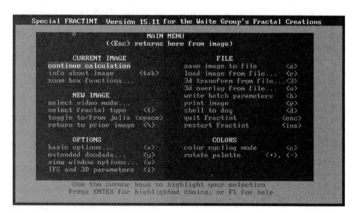

Figure 2-6 Expanded Main menu

Current Image

There are three additional functions listed that have to do with the current image. Fractint can move back and forth nondestructively between menu or information screens and fractal graphics screens. The menu item "continue calculation" returns you to the graphics screen, and if the calculation was interrupted when you returned to the Main menu, it will be resumed where you left off. The "info about image" selection gives you a screen of status information about the current image. This is particularly useful if you want to find out whether an image has been completed. The (TAB) key allows access to this status information screen directly from an image. The remaining item, "zoom box functions," takes you to the Help screen describing keystrokes for manipulating the zoom box.

New Image

There are two new items listed under "New Image," one allowing the recalculation of the previous image and one allowing toggling to and from Julia sets. The ⓋV key goes back and recalculates the previous image you created before you zoomed or changed fractal types. If you began with the Mandelbrot image, pressing Ⓥ several times will get you back to the full image. Try this now.

The command initiated by the (SPACE) key exploits the relationship between Mandelbrot and Julia fractals that was discussed in Chapter 1. Recall that the Mandelbrot fractal is a *catalog* of Julia fractals. Each point of the Mandelbrot fractal corresponds to the Julia fractal with its parameters equal to that point. The (SPACE) key automates that relationship and makes it easy to go back and forth. Once you have the Mandelbrot image back on the screen, make a small zoom box by pressing the (PGUP) key several times or by holding down the left mouse button and moving the mouse away from you. Using the cursor keys or the mouse, move the zoom box over a point right on the Mandelbrot coastline and press the (SPACE) key. Fractint will generate the Julia set corresponding to the point that was at the center of the zoom box when you pressed (SPACE). Pressing (SPACE) again will return you to the Mandelbrot image.

With a little experience, you will be able to predict the appearance of the Julia set from the characteristics of the Mandelbrot image at the point you selected. If the selected point is in the lake, the corresponding Julia set will have a lake. If the point is "on land," the Julia set will not have a single connected lake. Some of the most interesting Julia sets are created with parameter values that are right on the Mandelbrot shoreline.

There are many types in Fractint that have this Mandelbrot-Julia relationship. The (SPACE) toggle works with any of them. Table 2-3 shows all of these Mandelbrot-Julia pairs.

Options

The Option part of the Main menu is the same as before you generated an image. It allows you to set parameters that affect how images are calculated.

File

The File menu covers different ways of getting information into and out of Fractint. The Save Image command (Ⓢ key) creates a file in CompuServe's GIF format. These images can be viewed on a variety of different machines using any software that can decode the GIF89a format, and they can be read back into Fractint with the Load Image from File function. When a Fractint GIF file is read back in, all system settings are returned to the values that created the image. Another way to save all the Fractint settings is to use the Write Batch Parameters

((B)) command, which saves these settings in the file named FRABATCH.BAT. The information in this file is in the form of command-line options. You can modify the FRABATCH.BAT file with a text editor. For more information on the command controlled by the (B) key, see the reference section later in this chapter.

Colors

This menu item covers the controls for color cycling that we have already discussed. You will see this only if you are in a graphics video mode that allows color cycling, such as EGA or VGA 16- or 256-color modes.

A 3-D MANDELBROT SET

Let's continue the Fractint tour. What we are going to do next is perform some 3-D transformations on the Mandelbrot fractal you last created. For the mathematically curious, the result will be a 3-D plot of the escape times of the Mandelbrot formula. Be sure to try color cycling using the (+) key with these 3-D examples. Also, note that the zooming feature does work in the 3-D mode.

From the Main menu, select "restart fractint," or press the (INS) key, which accomplishes the same thing. This command reinitializes almost all settings to their default values, with the same result as exiting and restarting Fractint.

"Mandelbrot" Variant	"Julia" Variant
barnsleym1	*barnsleyj1*
barnsleym2	*barnsleyj2*
barnsleym3	*barnsleyj3*
cmplxmarksmand	*cmplxmarksjul*
manfn+exp	*julfn+exp*
manfn+zsqrd	*julfn+zsqrd*
mandel	*julia*
mandel4	*julia4*
manzpower	*julzpower*
manzzpwr	*julzzpwr*
mandelfn	*lambdafn*
mandellambda	*lambda*
magnet1m	*magnet1j*
magnet2m	*magnet2j*
manowar	*manowarj*
marksmandel	*marksjulia*

Table 2-3 Mandelbrot-Julia Pairs in Fractint

Press the ⓧ key, and set "inside color" to "maxiter." To do this, use the ⓓ key to move the highlight down to "inside color" and type in **maxiter**. While you're at it, have a look at the odd assortment of things that the ⓧ key (extended options command) allows you to set. Don't worry—you don't have to understand them all at once. In fact, you need never touch most of these settings to get a tremendous amount of enjoyment out of Fractint.

Moving the Lake

The "inside color" represents the palette number of the color used to color the lake areas of fractals—locations where the orbit never escapes and the maximum iterations limit is reached. This inside color value defaults to 2, which is the color blue in the standard IBM color palette on both EGA and VGA adapters. This setting is a Fractint tradition begun by the original author, Bert Tyler. Many other fractal programs favor the color 0, which is black, but Bert preferred to see a blue "lake." Setting the inside color to maxiter has the effect of setting the inside color to the maximum iteration value, which devaults to 150.

Normally the choice of inside color is purely aesthetic, but not for what we are about to do. The reason is that for interpreting fractals for 3-D purposes, Fractint treats the color as a number, and the color number is interpreted as the height above the plane. A color number of 2 means a low point, while a high color number means a mountain or high place. The setting of the inside color to maxiter has the effect of making the lake float at the top of the 3-D surface. This makes mathematical sense because the resulting image is a graph of the iteration count of the escape-time calculation, and when the lake occurs the iteration value is at the maximum, or 150, unless you change it with the ⓧ command. The important point is that setting the inside color affects the height of the lake when you are doing a 3-D transformation, and we have jammed it to the maximum height so it hangs above the plane of our fractal. Set the inside color to maxiter now.

When you are done with the ⓧ command screen, press ⎡ENTER⎤ to accept the values and return to the screen where you'll generate the fractal image. If you have a VGA, press the ⎡F3⎤ key to generate a Mandelbrot image in the 320 × 200 256-color mode. Note that the lake area is no longer blue but rather gray. If you don't have a VGA or other adapter with a 320 × 200 × 256 mode, then use the "Alt-M Disk/RAM 'Video' 320 200 256" mode. This mode is buried way down the list. You can either cursor down to it, highlight it, and press ⎡ENTER⎤ , or just press ⎡ALT⎤ and Ⓜ together to select it. (The Disk/RAM video isn't really "video" at all. Rather, it is a way of creating images using your disk, or, if you have enough memory, your extended or expanded memory.) Later we'll be able to display the disk video file.

When the image is complete (you'll hear a little whistle), save the image by pressing the ⓢ key. Make a mental note of the file name that was reported at the top of the screen—it was probably something like FRACT003.GIF, depending on how many images you have already saved. Return to the Main menu with (ESC). Select "3D transform from file" from the File menu, or press the ③ key. You will·now be presented with a list of files. Use the arrow keys to move the highlight to the file you just created with the save operation, and press (ENTER) . Next you will see a list of video modes. The video mode you used to generate the Mandelbrot image should be highlighted. If you have a VGA, you can use the same (F3) mode. Press (ENTER) to select it. If you have a CGA, use the "F5 IBM 4-color CGA 320 200 4" mode, and if you have an EGA, use the "F9 Low-Rez EGA 320 200 16" mode. In all cases, try to use a mode as close as possible to 320 pixels wide and 200 pixels high.

Setting the 3-D Parameters

Fractint is now going to lead you through some screens that allow setting all manner of parameters and effects for 3-D. The good news is that the default values almost always make sense—you do not have to understand what all of them mean. The screens are documented in detail a bit later in the chapter.

The first screen is entitled "3D Mode Selection." Here is where you can turn on what's known as funny glasses stereo (stereo using red/blue glasses) or use the sphere mode to create a fractal planet. But not yet! This time around, press (ENTER) to accept all the values. The next screen is entitled "Select 3D Fill Type." Here you will find the Fractint light source options, which let you illuminate your fractal and create shadows. The "just draw the points" option will be highlighted, which is just fine for now, so press (ENTER).

The next somewhat imposing screen, entitled "Planar 3D Parameters," presents numerous options for these three-dimensional rotations and scale factors. You can view your fractal from different angles, spin it in space, stretch it, shrink it, and move the viewer's perspective right into the middle of it! When making fractal landscapes, you can control the roughness of mountain ranges and the height of floods in the valleys. For this tour, the default values are all okay, so press (ENTER) to accept them. After the tour you can come back and experiment.

If you have a slower XT- or AT-compatible PC, you may wish to get up from your chair, stretch your legs, and grab a quick cup of coffee or beverage of choice. The 3-D transformation takes a few minutes. You will see the blue background of the Mandelbrot image appear just as you saw it on the screen a few moments before, but laid at an angle like a piece of paper on a desk. As the image develops, you will see that the colored stripes of the Mandelbrot image are raised like Chinese terraces on a mountainside. Floating above everything is the dark blue Mandelbrot lake, raining a sparkling mist down to the terrain below. You should now understand why we set inside=maxiter. If we had left the default inside=2, the lake would have been at the same level as the blue background, instead of floating mysteriously above it.

Figure 2-7 shows what your 3-D fractal should look like. For the final touch, press ⊕ to launch color cycling, and try the higher function keys to create some smoothly changing colors. When you are done playing with the colors, exit color cycling mode with (ESC).

Variations on a Theme

Let's try a few variations. For each variation, start with the ③ command. Fractint will remember your previous settings, and you can move from screen to screen by pressing (ENTER), pausing only to make the indicated changes. If you over-shoot a screen, you can back up with (ESC). The one setting that will **not** be remembered is the video mode for you CGA and EGA owners who used Disk/RAM video. When asked for the video mode, each time you should press (F5) (CGA) or (F9) (EGA). If you have a VGA and used (F3) to generate the original image you will not have this minor complication, because in your case the video list will come up with the (F3) mode highlighted. You can accept it by pressing (ENTER) just as you do for the other screens that do not require changes.

Variation #1: Make solid cliffs. Start with the ③ command, and move through the screens with (ENTER). When you come to the Select 3D Fill Type screen, select "Surface Fill (colors interpolated)", but otherwise leave the settings unchanged, pressing (ENTER) until the image regenerates. This option definitely slows things up, so take another break! This time the floating Mandelbrot image will become the top of a mountain with precipitous cliffs hanging under it.

Variation #2: Add a perspective viewpoint. Start with ③, and move through the screens with (ENTER). When you come to the Planar 3D Parameters screen, look for "Perspective distance [1 - 999, 0 for no persp]" about halfway down. Type in **150**. Smaller numbers provide the more extreme perspective of a closer viewpoint, while higher numbers create a flatter perspective such as photographers obtain through a telephoto lens. Press (ENTER) to regenerate the image. As a side effect the image edges will look a little bit rougher. But you are now closer to the scene, with closer features expanded! Figure 2-8 shows the "Mandelbrot cliffs" in perspective.

Variation #3: Make the mountain into a lake. Throughout this book we have referred to the classic Mandelbrot shape in the center of the Mandelbrot fractal as a lake, but then we turned around and made it into a mountaintop in 3-D.

Figure 2-7 Mandelbrot lake floating in space

We'll show you how to remedy that. Start with ③, and move through the screens with (ENTER). When you come to the Planar 3D Parameters screen, look for "Surface Roughness scaling factor in pct," which should have the default value of 30. We want you to depress the mountaintop and make it a lake, so

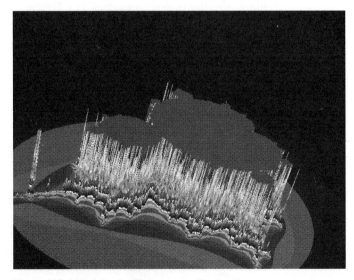

Figure 2-8 Mandelbrot cliffs in perspective

change the surface roughness value to -5. That's right, the new value is *negative* 5, which means that the z-coordinate will be scaled by negative 5 percent—depressing the mountaintop below the surrounding plain. Press (ENTER) to re-generate the image. You have turned the mountain into a lake-bottomed canyon!

And Now, Images in Stereo!

Let's try one more bit of magic and plot this Mandelbrot image in red/blue stereoscopic 3-D. For this you'll need your trusty red-and-blue glasses—the ones that came with this book. Here's how these images work: A number of different cues tell you that a scene has depth. Distant objects appear smaller than nearer objects. As you move your head, nearer objects get in the way of farther objects. Mist obscures distant objects. Because of these cues, a person with one eye can still perceive depth. Those of us with two good eyes have another depth cue: binocular vision. Our brain fuses the images coming from our two eyes and gives a sense of depth.

Red/Blue Glasses

Fractint is capable of performing the perspective transformations necessary to simulate the viewpoints of two eyes. The problem is how to get the left image to the left eye and the right image to the right eye. One solution would be to rapidly alternate the left and right images on your screen and have the user wear special glasses with liquid crystal shutters synchronized to the monitor. High-end workstations can be purchased with this capability, but it is expensive, costing in the thousands of dollars. For Fractint we have opted for a simpler approach that has cost you just the price of this book: red/blue glasses. These are the very same kind of glasses that kids of a bygone era eagerly retrieved from cereal packages in order to view stereo scenes on the box.

The idea is simple. Fractint puts a left view of a fractal on the screen in red and a right view of the image in blue. You put on the glasses, which have filters that block the incorrect view from reaching your eyes: blue blocks red, and red blocks blue. Note that some 30 percent of the population cannot see these binocular effects for one reason or another, and we hope you are not one of them! And alas, even if your eyes are perfect, you are still going to need a color monitor that can display red and blue. That rules out all monochrome setups as well as CGA which cannot show red and blue. If you have EGA or VGA with color, you are in business.

Press (ESC) to return to the main menu, and then press (3). Select the same GIF file from the File Selection screen that you created before (follow the instructions above to make it if you haven't already). Set the video mode to (F3) for VGA or (F9) for EGA. At the 3D Mode Selection screen, cursor down to the bottom option labeled

"Stereo (R/B 3D)? (0=no,1=alternate,2=superimpose,3=photo)" and press ② and then (ENTER). This is the superimpose option, which describes how the red and blue colors will be combined on the screen. The superimpose method combines colors red and blue to make magenta and pink, giving sharper results but fewer color shades. The alternate option alternates red and blue dots on the screen, sacrificing resolution but allowing more color shades. The "photo" mode is for photographing the screen and making stereo slides. The reference section later in this chapter explains all this in more detail.

Under "Select 3D Fill Type," select the top option, "make a surface grid." Press (ENTER). Note that (ESC) lets you back up to previous screens if you want to change something. You will then come to the Funny Glasses Parameters screen, which you did not see in the previous examples. The defaults are OK, so press (ENTER). If you changed the surface roughness parameter on the Planar 3D Parameters screen in the previous examples, change it back to 30 and press (ENTER).

This time you will see a grid approximating the solid Mandelbrot image you generated a moment before. First a red image is generated, then a blue image. These images should look like the Mandelbrot cliffs image of the previous example, shown in Figure 2-8. Put on the red/blue glasses that came with this book and view the image, making sure the red lens is over the left eye. There you are in living 3-D—a Mandelbrot mountain outlined in a grid!

VGA People

If you have a VGA or other adapter that can display 256 colors, you can redo the stereo Mandelbrot cliffs with solid colors rather than a wire grid. Repeat the same steps in the previous paragraph, except that in the Select 3D Fill Type screen, select "surface fill (colors not interpolated)." The result will be solid Mandelbrot cliffs in red/blue stereo.

Clouds, Mountains, and Plasma

Until now we have restricted this tour to the Mandelbrot fractal type, except for a brief interlude with the Julia types. Many hours of fascinating fractal explorations are possible with this type, especially given the options of zooming, color cycling, and 3-D transformations. There are, however, other kinds of fractals that produce radically different images and effects. One such fractal that is particularly interesting is the plasma type. This fractal allows the creation of both cloud and mountain range images. Who would have guessed that mountains and clouds are so closely related? The plasma type makes a random pattern of smoothly changing colors that look like clouds. This type works best with a 256-color mode. If you have an EGA, you can follow along, but the results will be somewhat different.

Select Plasma

Just to make sure we are on the same track, press the (INS) key to reinitialize Fractint, and then select a video mode. The (F3) mode is a good choice for VGA, (F9) for EGA. This will generate the Mandelbrot image again! (The plasma type will not work with modes with fewer than 16 colors, which rules out CGA and Hercules adaptors). After you have selected a video mode (and pressed (ENTER) if you selected the mode from the mode list), press (T) to display the type screen. You don't have wait for the Mandelbrot image to finish before pressing (T).

The Select a Fractal Type screen has a speed key feature. You can select "plasma" by moving the highlight with the cursor keys, or you can just start typing the word **plasma**. Since plasma is the only type that begins with "pl," as soon as you have typed these two letters, the highlight will jump to the plasma type. Now press (ENTER) to select the highlighted fractal type. After selecting a type, Fractint prompts you for any parameters that affect the appearance of that particular type. In the case of the plasma type, the "graininess" factor parameter affects how gradually the colors on the screen merge with one another. For now, press (ENTER) to accept the default value of 2.0. You might want to come back later and experiment. To do so, start with the (T) command and reselect type plasma, which will get you back to the plasma parameter screen.

As soon as you have pressed (ENTER) to accept your parameters choice, the plasma calculation will have begun. What you are seeing on the screen is a fascinating algorithm that recursively subdivides the screen, randomly choosing colors with values between surrounding colors. No two plasma images are quite the same, because of the random element of the calculation. When the image is complete, start color cycling with the (+) command. *Now* you understand why this type is called "plasma"! The screen colors ooze and writhe in graceful undulations of ethereal plasma waves. Be sure to try the function keys while color cycling. The lower-numbered function keys ((F2) , (F3),...) give detailed paisley patterns, while the higher ones ((F8), (F9), (F10)) result in larger, flowing patterns.

Turning a Cloud into a Mountain

Take a good long time playing with the plasma type, which is certainly one of the more colorful and dramatic fractals that you can create with Fractint. Be sure to press the (ENTER) key occasionally while it's color cycling; this instantly changes the colors. We should have convinced you that Fractint can make clouds, but what about mountains? To create mountains you have to first save a plasma image. If you are still in the color cycling mode (as visually indicated by either moving colors or a white screen boundary) then you should exit to the display mode by pressing (ESC). Press (S) to save the plasma screen, once again making a note of the file name that is reported on the screen. You are probably up to file FRACT022.GIF by now, right?

We can turn a cloud into a mountain by doing a 3-D transformation on the colors of the cloud. A cloud image can be considered a color-coded contour map of a mountain, where areas of equal color are the same height. By performing a 3-D transformation, we are transforming the contour map back into the mountain it represents.

Press the ③ key to invoke the 3-D function, and select the just-saved file from the file list. At the Video Mode Selection screen, select the same video mode used to generate the plasma in the first place (F3 for VGA, F9 for EGA.) Accept the default values of the 3D Mode Selection by pressing ENTER. At the Select 3D Fill Type screen, select "surface fill (colors interpolated)" and press ENTER. This will bring you to the Planar 3D Parameters screen. If you have an EGA and are reading in a 16-color plasma file, set surface roughness to 500. VGA users reading in a 256-color plasma file can leave the default value of 30 unchanged. Press ENTER, and watch a mountain emerge before your eyes!

Variations

Variation #1: Make the mountain emerge from water. Repeat all the instructions for making a mountain from a saved plasma cloud in the previous paragraph, until you reach the Planar 3D Parameters screen. Then set the "Water Level (minimum color value)" item to 47. This will cause all color values less than 47 to be mapped to a flat lake surface. You can begin to see why George Lucas developed Pixar to use computers to simulate real terrain. After the mountain landscape has been created, enter the color-cycling mode by pressing ©. You will be in color-cycling mode, but the colors will not be moving. Then press ⓛ (for "load map"). This color cycling command allows you to load various color maps.

There is a special map called TOPO.MAP that has color values tailored to plasma mountains, complete with water, rocks, greenery, and snow. Select TOPO.MAP from the file list. If it is not in the list, type in the drive letter and directory where you put the Fractint files, for example, if your Fractint files are in c:\fractint type **c:\fractint** ENTER. Then the map file screen will be refreshed and you should see topo.map. Select it, and press ENTER. Exit color cycling mode by pressing ESC. You should then see a plasma mountain with more realistic landscape coloring—blue water, green hillsides, brown fields, and snow-capped mountains. Figure 2-9 shows an example.

Variation #2: Make a red/blue 3-D glasses plasma mountain. Repeat the plasma mountain instructions above, beginning with the ③ command, selecting the

Figure 2-9 A "plasma" mountain rising from a lake

same plasma file, and using the (F3) video mode. At the 3D Mode Selection screen, cursor down to the bottom option labeled "Stereo (R/B 3D)? (0=no,1=alternate,2=superimpose,3=photo)," type (2), and press (ENTER). Under "Select 3D Fill Type," select the top option, "make a surface grid." Press (ENTER). Continue to press (ENTER), accepting all the defaults for the remaining screens. The result is a wire-frame mountain, which makes an excellent red/blue 3-D glasses stereo image. The "grid" fill type has the virtue of being very fast, so it is an excellent means to play with 3-D parameters. When you have an image the way you want it, you can apply a slower fill type.

Variation #3: Make a plasma planet. Repeat the plasma mountain instructions above, beginning with the (3) command, selecting the same plasma file, and using the (F3) video mode. At the 3D Mode Selection screen, cursor down to the "Spherical Projection" item and type **yes**. Set the option "Stereo (R/B 3D)? (0=no, 1=alternate,2=superimpose,3=photo)" back to 0, and press (ENTER). Continue to press (ENTER), accepting all the defaults for the next screens. The plasma image will be projected onto the surface of a sphere, making a plasma planet. You can project any GIF image onto a sphere in this way, whether or not it originated in Fractint.

At this point we shall leave you to your own devices. You can press (3) again and try some of the other 3D options—a good strategy for learning. One piece of advice, though: just change one or two things at a time so you get an idea of what you are doing! For instance, try combining your plasma landscape with your planet by first creating the landscape, and then adding the planet, using the (O) key instead of the (3). The (O) key is just like (3) except the previous image is not erased.

FRACTINT COMMANDS

Fractint's commands are your way of controlling the operation of the program. The remainder of this chapter is a reference section for Fractint commands and Fractint options.

KINDS OF FRACTINT COMMANDS

Fractint provides six ways to enter the commands that control its operation. These different methods allow you to interact with Fractint in the way that is most comfortable to you. After getting familiar with the program, you will want to use a mixture of these methods for the most effective use of Fractint. The six mechanisms are the arrow-key controlled menu interface, the keystroke commands, the mouse, command-line options, indirect file commands, and SSTOOL.INI file commands. Let's look briefly at each of these in turn.

The Arrow-Key Controlled Menu Interface

The arrow-key or cursor-key interface uses a series of full-screen menus that display options. You select an option by moving the highlighted area with the arrow keys to the desired option and then pressing (ENTER). Some screens have input fields for entering various parameters that control how the program operates. Screens used to select files also have directory navigation capabilities; by selecting subdirectories, the directory displayed is changed. On these screens, selecting the directory ".." moves the listed directory up the directory tree. The special capabilities of some of these screens are documented later in this chapter.

Keystroke Commands

Using keystroke commands is the most effective way to interactively control the operation of Fractint. Most menu selection items display the keystroke that achieves the equivalent effect as the menu items, and this can help you learn the basic commands rapidly. The most important thing to understand about keystroke commands is that the effect of a keystroke depends on the mode Fractint is in. We'll discuss this in more depth a little later on.

The Mouse

Fractint uses the mouse for only two purposes: controlling the zoom box and moving the pixel-selection cursor in the optional palette editing mode. The mouse is not used in the cursor-key controlled interface. Even if you are not an enthusiastic fan of the mouse, if you have one we recommend its use for working with the zoom box. But if you don't have a mouse, don't worry; a mouse is not required for any Fractint operation.

Command-line arguments

Fractint accepts command-line arguments that allow you to load it with your own choice of video mode, starting coordinates, and just about every other parameter and option. This is a powerful feature that is useful when there are many settings to make and you want to submit them all at once in a list when you start Fractint. The syntax is as follows:

```
fractint argument argument argument...
```

where the individual *arguments* are Fractint settings and are separated by one or more spaces (an individual argument may *not* include spaces). Either upper- or lowercase may be used, and arguments can be in any order. Keep in mind that all command line options are either typed at the DOS prompt or placed in an indirect file. A typical command might be

```
fractint type=mandel video=F3 inside=10
```

Table 2-4 lists terminology we will use throughout the rest of this chapter as the commands are documented:

Command	Meaning
COMMAND=<nnn>	*Enter a number in place of "nnn."*
COMMAND=<filename>	*You supply the file name.*
COMMAND=yes|no|whatever	*Type in exactly* **one** *of "yes," or "no," or "whatever." The "|" here means "or."*
COMMAND=1st[/2nd[/3rd]]	*The slash-separated parameters "2nd" and "3rd" are optional. You do type in the slashes.*

Table 2-4 Terminology used for commands and documents

Commands in Indirect Files

An extension of the command-line invocation to Fractint is the *indirect* file. If @filename appears in the command line right after typing Fractint, it causes Fractint to read the filename for any arguments that it contains. When it finishes, it resumes reading its own command line. For example, the command line:

```
fractint maxiter=250 @myfile passes=1
```

is legal. The statement sets the maximum iterations to 250, opens the file MYFILE, reads and executes the commands in it, and then sets the number of passes to 1. The indirect file option is valid only on the command line, as Fractint is not clever enough to deal with multiple indirection. You cannot put the indirect file @filename commands within other indirect files.

Indirect files do not have to have all the commands on just one line, although you can do it that way. For clarity, you may prefer to put each command on one line. For example, if the contents of myfile is:

```
corners=-4/4/-2/2
type=manowar
biomorph=yes
```

then the effect of starting Fractint with:

```
fractint @filename
```

is exactly the same as starting it with:

```
fractint corners=-4/4/-2/2 type=manowar biomorph=yes
```

You can build indirect files by hand, but a much easier way is to use the Ⓑ command from within Fractint. This sets up a sort of "recorder," so that each time you press Ⓑ during the operation of Fractint, a line is added to the file FRABATCH.BAT with all the command-line options needed to recreate the state of Fractint's options at the time the Ⓑ was pressed. You can take a text editor and make an indirect file out of each line of FRABATCH.BAT.

Commands in the SSTOOL.INI File

When Fractint is first started, it always looks along the DOS path for any file called SSTOOL.INI (which stands for Stone Soup Tools) and reads start-up variables and commands from that file. Then, it looks at its own command line; arguments there will override those from the .INI file. If you are familiar with Microsoft's TOOLS.INI or WINDOWS.INI configuration files, the SSTOOL.INI command file is used in the same way. Why use a convention like that when Fractint is the only program you know of that uses an SSTOOL.INI file? Because there are sister Stone Soup Group programs, such as Lee Crocker's Piclab, or Bert Tyler's Fractint for Windows, that now use the same file. In particular, you designate a section of SSTOOL.INI as belonging to a particular program by beginning the section with a label in brackets. Fractint looks for the label [fractint] and ignores any lines it finds in the file belonging to any other label. For example, if an SSTOOL.INI file looks like this:

```
[fractint]
sound=off                        ; (for home use only)
printer=hp                       ; my printer is a LaserJet
[startrek]
Aye, captain, but I dinna think the engines can take it!
[fractint]
inside=0                         ; using "traditional" black
```

Fractint will use only the second, third, and last lines. The fifth line is for a ficticious program called Startrek.

You can place any sort of Fractint command you like in SSTOOLS.INI, just as you can in a @myfile indirect file. But the intent is to place commands there that you want to *always* take effect. For example, if you wish to use the FRACTNNN.GIF files as scratch files and are in the habit of copying them to files with meaningful names after each session to save them, then you could place the command "overwrite=yes" in your SSTOOL.INI file. This will cause the FRACTNNN.GIF files to be overwritten each time you use Fractint.

THE FRACTINT OPERATING MODES

Fractint has three main modes, each with its own set of commands. These are the **display** mode, the **color cycling** mode, and the **palette editing** mode. Of these three modes, the display mode is the most important, because the main functions of Fractint are accessible from within this mode. The color cycling mode is a simple mode to use and understand, while the palette editing mode is a more advanced function. Figure 2-10 diagrams the relationship between the modes and how to move between them. The display mode is the default mode that Fractint enters on startup. The Ⓔ command switches to the palette editing mode, and the Ⓒ, ⊕, or ⊖ commands switch to the color cycling mode. In both cases ⒺⓈⒸ returns to the display mode. Each of these three modes—display, color cycle, and palette edit—has its own set of commands, so it is important for you to be clear at all times which mode is currently active.

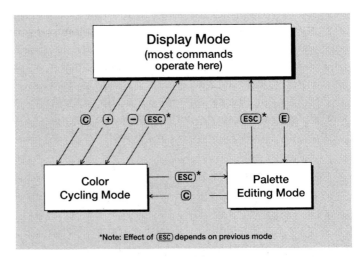

Figure 2-10 The Fractint operating modes

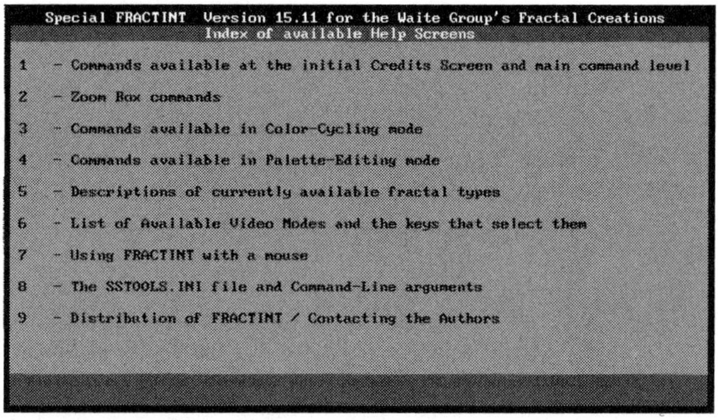

Figure 2-11 The main Help screen

There is one command that works in all modes. That is the Help command. The Help screens are accessed by pressing (F1). Help is context sensitive, so the Help screen you see when you press (F1) depends on the particular mode. Pressing (F1) a second time sends you to a main Help menu, which is shown in Figure 2-11. When in the main Help menu you select from one of nine help areas using the number keys (1) to (9) . Be sure and read the material accessed by (F1)-(9) which tells you how to contact the Fractint authors.

From the main Help screen, you can get help on any of the listed topics by typing in that topic's number. For example, typing (8) takes you to a series of screens on all the commands that work in the SSTOOL.INI file or on the command line. In many cases there is more than one Help screen on a topic. You can cycle through them by pressing (ENTER) or (PGDN). You can exit the Help screens by pressing (ESC).

The rest of this chapter documents all the Fractint commands. It is organized by mode, since different commands take effect in the different modes. Commands are listed with the function they perform first. Then the alternative means of accessing that function using the menus, keystroke commands, command-line options, and the mouse are given.

DISPLAY MODE

You are in the display mode as soon as Fractint is started up, although some of the commands are not accessible until after you have created your first image. The most basic commands may be executed either using an arrow key menu or by entering a keystroke. The mouse is used only for manipulating the zoom box in the display mode and as the pixel selection cursor in the palette editing mode; it is not used for the arrow-key interface. Some commands have *only* keystroke forms. Keystroke commands are not case-sensitive; you may enter them in either upper- or lowercase. Most commands can also be entered as a command-line option.

The Fractint Main menu deals exclusively with display mode commands. The following section is organized according to the major headings of the Main menu.

CURRENT IMAGE COMMANDS

The Current Image commands all deal with the current paused or completed graphics images. These commands include returning from the menu back to the graphics image, getting information about the image, and controlling the zoom box. Since most of these deal with zooming, we'll say more about that here.

The zoom box is the mechanism in Fractint for selecting small pieces of fractal images and recalculating them to fill the screen. These commands apply only when an image is on the screen. You do not need to wait for an image to complete before creating and manipulating the zoom box. There are no menu equivalents for the Current Image commands.

Fractint allows extraordinary control of the zoom box, including such functions as rotating and skewing. If your screen does not have a 4:3 aspect ratio (that is, if the visible display area on it is not 1.333 times as wide as it is high), rotating and zooming will have some odd effects—angles will change, including the zoom box's shape itself, circles (if you are so lucky as to see any with a nonstandard aspect ratio) become noncircular, and so on. The vast majority of PC screens do have a 4:3 aspect ratio.

Zooming is not implemented for the plasma and diffusion fractal types, nor for overlaid and 3-D images. A few fractal types support zooming but do not support rotation and skewing—nothing happens when you try it.

The effect of manipulating the zoom box is the same as resetting the "corners=" value from the command line.

CONTINUE CALCULATION

COMMAND FUNCTION

Continue calculation—resume a fractal calculation that was interrupted by (ESC)

MENU ACCESS

"continue calculation" under the Current Image section of the Main menu

COMMAND-LINE ACCESS

COMMENTS

This command switches Fractint from the Main menu to the current image, resuming the calculation if was not complete, continuing where it left off. If the image was complete, it restores the image to the screen and then waits for your next command.

FIND IMAGE STATUS

(TAB)

COMMAND FUNCTION

Find the status of your current image

MENU ACCESS

"info about image" under the Current Image section of the Main menu

COMMAND-LINE ACCESS

COMMENTS

This command displays an information screen about the current image, including fractal type, whether complete or not, corner parameters, time of calculation, parameters values, maximum iterations, and current bailout value used to test when an orbit has escaped. Pressing any key returns to the displayed image and resumes the calculation. The exact content of this screen varies with the options in effect at the time. This command is particularly useful for checking the completion status of an "all-nighter" 1024×768 image by telling you whether the image is complete and, if not, which of the multiple passes has been reached.

DEFINE ZOOM REGION

(PGUP)

COMMAND FUNCTION

Define the region in the complex plane within which to carry out a fractal calculation

MOUSE ACCESS

Clicking the left mouse button creates a zoom box. See the mouse zoom box functions below.

COMMAND-LINE ACCESS

```
fractint corners=xmin/xmax/ymin/ymax[/x3rd/y3rd]
fractint center-mag=[Xctr/Yctr/Mag]
```

COMMENTS

When you specify four values (the usual case), this defines a rectangle: x-coordinates are mapped to the screen, left to right, from xmin to xmax, y-coordinates are mapped to the screen, bottom to top, from ymin to ymax. Six parameters can be used to describe any rotated or stretched parallelogram: (xmin,ymax) are the coordinates used for the top-left corner of the screen, (xmax,ymin) for the bottom-right corner, and (x3rd,y3rd) for the bottom-left corner. Figure 2-12 shows the relationship of the "corners=" parameters and the zoom box.

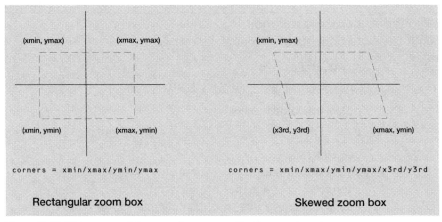

Figure 2-12 The corners of the zoom box mapped to the complex plane

Including "center-mag=" on the command line, indirect file, or in SSTOOL.INI is an alternative way to enter corners as a center point and a magnification. This approach is popular with some fractal programs and publications. Entering just "fractint center-mag=" tells Fractint whether to use this form rather than corners when creating a batch file with the ⒷB command, which adds a line of all the currently effective command-line parameters to a file called frabatch.bat. The ⓉAB status display shows the corners in both forms. Note that an aspect ratio of 1.3333 is assumed; if you have altered the zoom box proportions or rotated the zoom box, this form can no longer be used. A magnification is relative to a zoom box of width 2. The center-mag form of specifying the zoom box is particularly useful for creating a series of zooms. For example, make a file called zoom.bat with the following lines, replacing F3 with an appropriate video mode for your setup:

```
fractint type=mandel center-mag=-0.1049/0.9278/.12  maxiter=1000
savename=zoom1 batch=yes video=f3
fractint type=mandel center-mag=-0.1049/0.9278/.63  maxiter=1000
savename=zoom2 batch=yes video=f3
fractint type=mandel center-mag=-0.1049/0.9278/3.17 maxiter=1000
savename=zoom3 batch=yes video=f3
fractint type=mandel center-mag=-0.1049/0.9278/15.8 maxiter=1000
savename=zoom4 batch=yes video=f3
```

```
fractint type=mandel center-mag=-0.1049/0.9278/79.2 maxiter=1000
savename=zoom5 batch=yes video=f3
fractint type=mandel center-mag=-0.1049/0.9278/396  maxiter=1000
savename=zoom6 batch=yes video=f3
fractint type=mandel center-mag=-0.1049/0.9278/1980 maxiter=1000
savename=zoom7 batch=yes video=f3
fractint type=mandel center-mag=-0.1049/0.9278/9900 maxiter=1000
savename=zoom9 batch=yes video=f3
```

This table was made by zooming in on a baby Mandelbrot set, using the ⒷB command to make a frabatch.bat file, and duplicating the single line and changing the magnification.

ZOOM IN

(PGUP)

COMMAND FUNCTION

Resize the zoom box (zoom in)

MOUSE ACCESS

Click the left mouse button to create a zoom box. To zoom in, hold the left button down and move the mouse up (away from you).

COMMENTS

This action both creates and shrinks the zoom box. Each time you press (PGUP) the box shrinks in size.

ZOOM OUT

(PGDN)

COMMAND FUNCTION

Expand the zoom box (zoom out)

MOUSE ACCESS

Hold the left button down and move the mouse down (toward you).

COMMENTS

If the zoom box is expanded to fill the whole screen, the zoom box settings are reset (useful if you have rotated the zoom box or altered the aspect ratio accidently). Each time you press (PGDN) the box enlarges in size.

MOVE ZOOM BOX

(↓)(↑)(→)(←)

COMMAND FUNCTION

Move ("pan") the zoom box to various screen locations

MOUSE ACCESS

Move the mouse without pushing either button.

COMMENTS

It is possible to move the zoom box partially off the screen, so that the redrawn image includes points not in the original image.

DRAW ZOOM BOX AREA

(ENTER)

COMMAND FUNCTION:

Redraw the area inside the zoom box as a full-screen image

MOUSE ACCESS

Double-click the left mouse button.

COMMENTS

Do this when you have the zoom box framing the area you want to magnify.

ZOOM OUT AND REDRAW

(CTRL)(ENTER)

COMMAND FUNCTION

Zoom out, so that the screen fills the current zoom box, and redraw the image

MENU ACCESS

"select fractal type" under the File section of the Main menu

MOUSE ACCESS

Double-click the right mouse button

ROTATE ZOOM BOX

(CTRL)(KEYPAD-)
(CTRL)(KEYPAD+)

COMMAND FUNCTION

Rotate the zoom box

MOUSE ACCESS

Move the mouse left or right while holding down the right button.

COMMENTS

(CTRL)(KEYPAD-) means holding down (CTRL) and pressing the numeric keypad's ⊖ key. Rotating the zoom box works with all types except bif+sinpi, bif=sinpi, biflambda, bifurcation, diffusion, julibrot, and lsystem.

ZOOM BOX ASPECT RATIO

(CTRL)(PGUP)
(CTRL)(PGDN)

COMMAND FUNCTION

Alters the zoom box aspect ratio by shrinking or expanding its vertical size

MOUSE ACCESS

Move the mouse away from you or toward you while holding both buttons (or the middle button on a three-button mouse).

COMMENTS

There are no commands to directly stretch or shrink the zoom box horizontally–the same effect can be achieved by combining vertical stretching and resizing.

**ZOOM
BOX
SKEW**

(CTRL)(HOME)

(CTRL)(END)

COMMAND FUNCTION

"Skew" the zoom box, moving the top and bottom edges in opposite directions so it forms a parallelogram. (CTRL)(HOME) moves the edges right, (CTRL)(END) moves the edges left.

MOUSE ACCESS

Move the mouse left or right while holding both buttons (or the middle button on a three-button mouse).

COMMENTS

There are no commands to directly skew the left and right sides of the zoom box—the same effect can be achieved by using these functions combined with rotation.

**ZOOM
BOX
COLOR**

(CTRL)(INS)

(CTRL)(DEL)

COMMAND FUNCTION

Change zoom box color. Each time you press (CTRL)(INS) the box will change to the next higher color number. The (CTRL)(DEL) command changes the color to the next lower color number.

MOUSE ACCESS

Move the mouse away from you or toward you while holding the right button down.

COMMENTS

Changing the zoom box color is useful when you're having trouble seeing the zoom box against the colors around it. For example, if you zoom into an area with very light colors, the white zoom box will blend in. Changing the zoom box color to any dark color will make it visible again.

**SHOW
ORBITS**

(O)

COMMAND FUNCTION

Show the orbit paths of fractal computations as the fractal is drawn

MOUSE ACCESS

COMMENTS

This command shows the trajectories of the calculation orbits of each pixel used to create a fractal as the fractal is being drawn. These orbits appear as small spiral-like figures.. Escape-time fractals work by repeatedly iterating a formula and generating a sequence of complex numbers, while testing whether each number has exceeded a threshold as the sequence is generated. Normally once a pixel is colored, the orbit values are no longer needed. The (O) command shows you these orbit values, which are interesting in their own right. To best see this effect, press Ⓧ and set passes to **1**. The multiple-pass guessing mode that Fractint normally uses makes it hard to see what pixel is being calculated because it fills the screen's black areas with color very quickly; orbits show up best on a black background and so are much easier to see in one-pass mode.

Next, press a function key to start a Mandelbrot fractal calculation. Now press Ⓞ to see the orbits. In the beginning, you will see white pixels flitting somewhat randomly around the screen. But when the Mandelbrot calculation reaches the lake area, lovely spiral patterns will emerge. If the orbit display is too fast, use the Ⓕ key to turn on the slower floating-point math.

Note that there are two separate and completely different Display Mode commands for the Ⓞ key. Which one takes effect depends on whether or not a calculation is currently progressing. During a calculation, pressing Ⓞ turns on the orbit feature discussed here. If the calculation is completed, Ⓞ activates the "overlay" 3-D function under the File menu and therefore has some ambiguity. Just remember that if you want to see the orbits, the image calculation must be occurring.

New Image Commands

These commands are accessible under the New Image section of the Main menu. From this collection of commands you can select a new video mode, change the current fractal type, toggle between Mandelbrot fractals and the equivalent Julia fractals, and regenerate images you previously made in the same session. All of these commands result in the calculation of a new image.

**SELECT
VIDEO MODE**

Ⓕ1-Ⓕ10
SHIFT
ALT
CTRL

COMMAND FUNCTION
Select the video mode that the fractal will be displayed in

MENU ACCESS
"select video mode" under the New Image section of the Main menu

COMMAND-LINE ACCESS
`fractint video=<mode>`
where <mode> is the keystroke exactly as listed in the Video menu. For example, the popular VGA 320 × 200 × 256 VGA mode can be accessed with the command-line option video=F3.

COMMENTS
In Fractint the selection of a video mode triggers the recalculation of an image and changes the image resolution. Higher resolutions show more detail but take longer to calculate. A good strategy is to explore using a low-resolution mode

such as 320 × 200 ((F3)), and recalculate the image later at a higher-resolution mode if you like the image. Only certain modes work for any particular adapter; you should check your graphics adapter documentation or just try different modes and see what works. Don't be dismayed if you try a mode and get a blank screen; pressing (ESC) will get you back to the Main menu.

You can create a custom set of keys for invoking the video modes if you don't like the defaults that Fractint offers. To do this, you create a list of legal video modes for your adapter by invoking Fractint with the batch=config command-line option. Just type:

```
fractint batch=config
```

This creates a file called FRACTINT.CFG, which contains a list of all the modes built into Fractint, the same exact modes you see when you go to the "select video mode" Main menu item. Once these modes are all listed in a file, you can edit out illegal modes with a text editor. Then, when you run Fractint, it will only display and allow the choices in your edited FRACTINT.CFG file. This edit operation will change the keystrokes that select particular modes. Keep in mind that keystrokes are assigned to the video modes in the order they appear in the FRACTINT.CFG file, starting with (F2). Table 2-5 explains the scheme for labeling video modes by keystroke combinations:

Video Mode Label	Equivalent Keystrokes
F2	*The function key* (F2)
SF2	*Press* (SHIFT) *and* (F2) *together*
CF2	*Press* (CTRL) *and* (F2) *together*
AF2	*Press* (ALT) *and* (F2) *together*
Alt-1	*Press* (ALT) *and* (1) *together*
Ctl-1	*Press* (CTRL) *and* (1) *together*

Table 2-5

Most users will want to keep their favorite video modes at the top of the list so they are accessible using the function keys (F2) to (F9). If Fractint discovers the FRACTINT.CFG file in a directory listed in the path statement, and if the askvideo=no option is set, then when loading in files with the (R) command, the video mode prompt will be bypassed.

DISK/RAM VIDEO MODES

Certain video modes are labeled "Disk/RAM Video." These are simulated video modes that do not display on your screen but use extended, expanded, or disk memory, as it is available, to store your image. These modes allow you to create images at higher resolutions than your video equipment supports and then view them in a lower resolution. For example, the cover of this book has images created with the super-resolution 2048 × 2048 mode, using a PC with an EGA display. Keep in mind that these modes need memory—the 2048 × 2048 mode needs over 4 megabytes of expanded, extended, or disk memory free! These disk video modes are also useful because they allow you to produce fractals in the background under multitasking environments such as Windows or DeskQView. In the regular video modes if you switch to another program the calculations stop. Disk video modes have disadvantages: Besides the fact that you can't see a fractal while it is being calculated, disk video modes are slower than normal video modes, especially if Fractint can't find extended or expanded memory to use and has to use disk space.

If you have a 512K or 1024K super-VGA board such as a Video 7 or OrchidProDesigner, the "SuperVGA/VESA Autodetect" modes should work. Some of the super VGA resolution modes require video boards with more than the standard 256K memory, and therefore not every board supports all the modes. The 640 × 400 256-color mode is the highest resolution using 256 colors that works with 256K of memory. Following the Autodetect modes are some less standard resolutions that work on various adapters. You should try the ones for your brand of graphics adapter. Don't overlook various "tweaked" modes if you have a VGA. You won't find these listed in your graphics board documentation, because they are achieved by Fractint accessing and directly programming the VGA registers. A favorite mode for many VGA users is the F10 320 × 400 256-color mode. This mode has better resolution than the F3 320 × 200 mode, and despite being nonstandard, it will work on virtually any VGA.

SELECT FRACTAL TYPE
(T)

COMMAND FUNCTION
Presents a list of fractal types from which a fractal can be generated

MENU ACCESS
"select fractal type" under the New Image section of the Main menu

COMMAND-LINE ACCESS
`fractint type=<type>`
where <type> is the fractal type exactly as listed under the interactive type list. Example:
`fractint type=newtbasin`

COMMENTS
After selecting a type, you will be prompted for any needed parameters. The types formula and lsystem read in a complete list of subtypes from files you can

edit, allowing you to create new types. See Chapter 3, "Fractal Pages," for more about the fractal types available in Fractint.

TOGGLE MANDELBROT/ JULIA
(SPACE)

COMMAND FUNCTION
Toggle between Mandelbrot and Julia fractal types

MENU ACCESS
"toggle to/from julia" under the New Image section of the Main menu

COMMAND-LINE ACCESS
none

COMMENTS
As explained in Chapter 1, each point of a Mandelbrot set corresponds to a Julia set. Fractint allows you to see this connection very clearly, as follows. Create an image of a Mandelbrot set. This can be type=mandel (the "classic"), or any of the types that have "man" in their names. Zoom in on a detail near the lake shore of the image, where blue meets the multicolor shore, but don't press (ENTER). Instead, press (SPACE). Fractint will display the Julia set corresponding to the point of the Mandelbrot set that was at the center of the zoom box. Remember that each Julia type is in fact an infinite collection of quite different fractals, depending on the values of the parameters. The characteristics of each Julia set can be inferred from the appearance of the Mandelbrot set near the point that generates the Julia set. For example, if the selected point of the Mandelbrot set is deep in the lake, the corresponding Julia will have a large lake. Conversely, if you pick a point on land, the Julia will not have a large lake. The most interesting Julia sets may be found from points near the lake edge of the corresponding Mandelbrot set, where the chaos is the greatest.

REDRAW IMAGE
(\)

COMMAND FUNCTION
Redraw the previous image

MENU ACCESS
"return to prior image" under the New Image section of the Main menu

COMMAND-LINE ACCESS
none

COMMENTS
As you make a series of images Fractint remembers the zoom coordinates and fractal types of up to your last 25 images. The (x) command causes the zoom parameters and type to be set to the previous fractal that you generated. Repeat-

edly pressing Ⓛ causes Fractint to back through the list and recalculate your previous images. Use this when you have made an ill-advised zoom into a boring area and don't want to start over, but just want to retreat to an image previously attempted.

OPTIONS

The Options section of the Main menu allows many of the features of Fractint to be accessed interactively. These cover a wide gamut of different effects and alternatives. We'll cover them here in the order they are encountered in the menus.

ACCESS OPTIONS
Ⓧ

COMMAND FUNCTION

Access basic options

MENU ACCESS

"basic options" under the Options section of the Main menu

COMMAND-LINE ACCESS

various (see below)

COMMENTS

The distinction in Fractint between "basic" and "extended" options is somewhat arbitrary. The Ⓧ option "basic" input screen is shown in Figure 2-13 below, with the default values showing.

SET PASSES OPTIONS
Ⓧ

COMMAND FUNCTION

Set the passes algorithm options

MENU ACCESS

"Passes (1, 2, g[uessing], or b[oundary tracing])" on the Basic Options (Ⓧ) menu

COMMAND-LINE ACCESS:

`fractint passes=1|2|guess|btm`

Remember that "1|2|guess|btm" means to use *one* of those four possibilities. Example:

`fractint passes=btm`

COMMENTS

The passes option selects single-pass, dual-pass, solid-guessing mode, or the boundary tracing algorithm. The single-pass mode draws the screen pixel by pixel and is the slowest. The dual-pass mode generates a "coarse" screen first as a preview using 2 × 2-pixel boxes, and when the screen is filled it generates the rest of the dots with a second pass. The effect is to quickly get a coarse view of the fractal so you can exit early. Solid-guessing is the fastest mode, because it attempts to avoid calculations by guessing the color of pixels surrounded by pixels of one color. It performs from two to four visible passes—more in higher-resolution video modes. Its first visible pass is actually two passes—one pixel per 4 × 4, 8 × 8, or 16 × 16 pixel box (depending on number of passes) is generated, and the guessing logic is applied to fill in the blocks at the next level (2 × 2, 4 × 4, or 8 × 8). Subsequent passes fill in the display at the next-finer resolution, skipping blocks that are surrounded by the same color. The multiple passes are for two reasons. The first is to give you a quick preview of the image in case you don't want to wait for it to complete. The second reason is that the guessing algorithm works in stages, starting with a rough approximation. Solid-guessing can guess wrong, but it guesses wrong quickly.

Boundary tracing is a completely different approach from the others. It only works with fractal types that do not contain "islands" of colors, such as the Mandelbrot set, but not the Newton type. Boundary tracing works by finding a color boundary, tracing it around the screen, and then filling in the enclosed area. The idea of this algorithm is to speed up calculations, but in Fractint solid-guessing is almost always faster. We have included boundary tracing anyway because it is fun to watch! Boundary tracing does not work when the inside color is set to 0 (black), because it uses 0 to determine if a color has been written to the screen already.

To select one of these options from the ⊗ screen, at the "Passes (1, 2, g[uessing], or b[oundary tracing])" prompt, type in **1** for one pass, **2** for two passes, **g** or **guess** for guessing, and **b** or **btm** for boundary-tracing method.

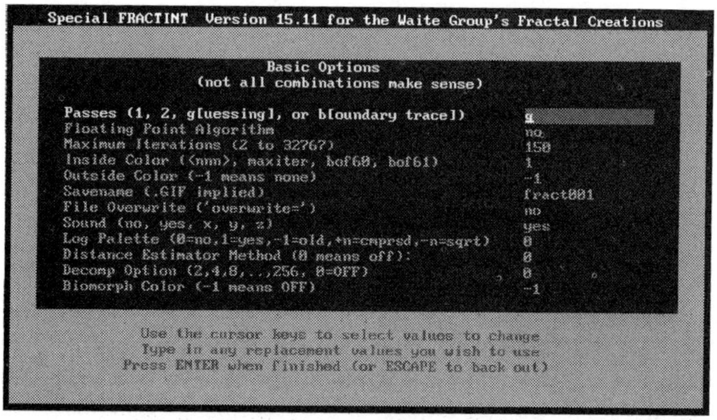

Figure 2-13 The Basic Options input screen

Understand that the single- and dual-pass mode result in exactly the same image and take the same amount of time. They work best for fractal purists who do not want to risk the occasional inaccuracies of the default guessing mode. Most of the time, the solid-guessing mode is the one to use, and it's usually the default. If you are the type who is fascinated by watching intriguing algorithms at work, by all means try the boundary tracing option.

FLOATING-POINT/ INTEGER TOGGLE

Ⓣ

COMMAND FUNCTION

Change between floating-point and integer math for calculating fractals

MENU ACCESS

"Floating-point Algorithm" under the Basic Options (Ⓧ) menu

COMMAND-LINE ACCESS

`fractint float=yes`

COMMENTS

Most fractal types have both a fast integer math and a floating-point version. The much faster, but sometimes less accurate, integer version is the default. If you have an Intel 80486-based PC or other fast machine, such as an 80286 or 80386, with a math coprocessor such as the 80287 or 80387, or if you are using the continuous potential option (which looks best with high bailout values not possible with our integer math implementation), you may prefer to use floating-point instead of integer math.

To enable floating-point, you can add float=yes at the command line, or use the Ⓕ key, which toggles between integer math and floating-point. Fractint automatically changes to floating-point math when you zoom deeply into an image and the limited range of the faster integer math is encountered. This will be seen by the slowness of regeneration when zooming.

If you want to run some comparison speed tests, the ⓉAB status key reports when floating-point is being used and also reports the time taken to generate the current fractal. On a 12-Mhz 80286-based PC, the default Mandelbrot set (type mandel) using the F3 video mode takes 7.6 seconds. After pressing Ⓕ to use floating-point instead of integer math, the time increases to 42 seconds using an 80287 floating-point coprocessor, and 280 seconds without a coprocessor. These results will vary a lot depending on which CPU chip your machine is using, and their clock speed. Creating a 320 × 200 × 256 color Mandelbrot image in 7.6 seconds on a machine with no coprocessor is one of the technical achievements of Fractint that separates it from all similar programs.

**SET
ESCAPE TIME
MAXIMUM
ITERATION**

Ⓧ

COMMAND FUNCTION

Set the maximum iteration at which the fractal formula considers a point has "escaped its orbit"

MENU ACCESS

"Maximum Iterations (2 to 32767)" under the Basic Options (Ⓧ) menu

COMMAND-LINE ACCESS

`fractint maxiter=nnn`
where nnn is a number from 2 to 32767.

COMMENTS

Recall that the escape-time algorithm creates fractal images by repeatedly iterating a formula and testing whether the orbit wanders outside the bailout threshold. Since many orbits never do escape the bailout radius, Fractint must have a limit to how many iterations it will try before giving up, or the computation will go on forever. That limit is the maximum iterations value, and it has a default of 150. The limit causes some inaccuracy in the final fractal. For example, there are points near the lake shore of the Mandelbrot set whose orbits have not escaped after 150 iterations, but they would have escaped after a few more iterations if the calculation had been extended. These points might be plotted as part of the lake, when they really belong on the shore. The higher the maximum iterations cutoff, the more accurate the final image, but also the slower the calculation. As a practical matter, the default Mandelbrot image looks fine with 150 iterations. As you zoom in further, however, you will also need to increase the iteration limit when the inaccuracies become visible.

To see the effect of setting the maximum iteration limit, press Ⓧ from the Main menu or while viewing a fractal, and set the "Maximum Iterations (2 to 32767)" value to 3. (The value 2 creates a solid blue image unless the inside value is set to something other than 2.) You will see a single oval band surrounding the lake, which consists of all the points whose orbits did not escape after 3 iterations. Now press Ⓧ again and set maximum iterations to 4. You will see one more band, and the lake will be a little smaller. After trying a few higher values, you will see why the value 150 is fine for the default Mandelbrot. A higher value makes no visual difference at that magnification.

**SET MAXIMUM
ITERATION
COLOR**

Ⓧ

COMMAND FUNCTION

Set the color assigned to points that pass the maximum iterations limit (the lake color)

MENU ACCESS

"Inside Color (nnnn, maxiter, bof60, bof61)" item on the Basic Options (⊗) menu

COMMAND-LINE ACCESS

`fractint inside=<nnn>|maxiter|bof60|bof61`

COMMENTS

The inside option lets you set the color of the lake area of a fractal consisting of the points whose orbits had still not escaped when the maximum iteration cutoff was reached (see the earlier discussion of maximum iterations). For example, setting inside to 0 makes the Mandelbrot fractal interior lake black, since color 0 is black in the standard IBM palette. (If you change the palette by cycling colors, 0 might be a different color.) Setting inside to maxiter makes the inside color the same as the maximum iteration value you are using, which is useful for 3-D purposes.

Two more options reveal hidden structure inside the lake. These are inside=bof61 and inside=bof62, named after the page numbers in our copy of *Beauty of Fractals* where we first saw these plotted. If you set inside=bof61, the lake area will be broken into colored areas where the iteration number of the closest orbit approach to the origin is the same. If you set inside=bof62, you will see the lake broken into colored areas where the closest value of the orbit to the origin is the same. Don't worry if you don't understand these two "bof" options, just try them to see what they look like!

SET OUTSIDE COLOR
⊗

COMMAND FUNCTION

Set the color of escape-time points with iterations less than the maximum iterations

MENU ACCESS

"Outside Color (-1 means none)" item on the Basic Options (⊗) menu

COMMAND-LINE ACCESS

outside=<nnn>, where <nnn> is a number from 0 up to the number of colors of the current video mode

COMMENTS

Throughout this book we have often discussed the Mandelbrot "fractal" or "image" instead of the Mandelbrot "set." The reason is that the Mandelbrot set consists of just the interior lake; all the striped colors of the usual fractal image of the Mandelbrot are not part of the set at all! The "outside" option was born when the Fractint authors received a letter from a high school math teacher who wanted to see just the Mandelbrot set (the part colored with the "inside" option), and not the distracting stripes outside the set. As you might guess, this function is the opposite of the inside option. The inside option sets the color of the lake, which is to say the points of the Mandelbrot set. The outside option sets all the striped areas outside the lake to a single color. Try typing

```
fractint inside=2 outside=1
```

and you will see what we mean. Using the outside option forces any fractal image to be a two-color one: either a point is inside the set or it's outside it. Be sure to make these two colors different; if the inside and outside values are the same, the image is pretty boring! Try this with the passes=btm option; since there is only one boundary, boundary tracing works well.

SET DEFAULT SAVING FILE NAME
Ⓧ

COMMAND FUNCTION

Set the default file name for saving images with the Ⓢ command

MENU ACCESS

"Savename (.GIF implied)" item on the Basic Options (Ⓧ) menu

COMMAND-LINE ACCESS

```
fractint savename=<filename>
```

COMMENTS

When you save an image with the Ⓢ command, Fractint creates file names like "FRACT001.GIF" and increments the number automatically as more files are saved. You can change the default file name with the savename option. This is particularly useful when you are creating a collection of files at once using the batch mode and you want the file name to remind you what the fractal is. For example, make a file called SAVENAME.BAT with these lines:

```
fractint type=mandel savename=mandel video=f3 batch=yes
fractint type=manowar savename=manowar video=f3 batch=yes
```

If you don't have a VGA, use a different video mode in this example that works with your adapter, such as F2 for EGA or F5 for CGA. Running this batch file will create two files, MANDEL.GIF and MANOWAR.GIF. Fractint will replace the last letter in your savename with a number if you save several images in a single Fractint session after setting the savename.

Note that even when you specify a savename, if you save more than one image during a session an incrementing number will appear at the end of the file name. For example, if you start Fractint with:

```
fractint savename=test
```

the successive names used for saving will be TEST.GIF, TES1.GIF, TES2.GIF and so forth.

SET FILE OVERWRITE FLAG
(X)

COMMAND FUNCTION

Set the file overwrite flag

MENU ACCESS

"File Overwrite ('overwrite=')" item on the Basic Options ((X)) menu

COMMAND-LINE ACCESS

`fractint overwrite=no|yes`
The default value is "no."

COMMENTS

If overwrite=yes, the file names used in a Fractint session will overwrite existing files from previous sessions with the same names. Files created during the same session will still not be overwritten because the file names will contain incrementing numbers. If overwrite=no, files will not be overwritten.

SET SOUND EFFECTS
(X)

COMMAND FUNCTION

Disable sound effects or attach sound to an orbit coordinate to make fractal music

MENU ACCESS

"Sound (no, yes, x, y, z)" item on the Basic Options ((X)) menu

COMMAND-LINE ACCESS

`fractint sound=off|x|y|z`
Use one of "off," "x," "y," or "z." The default is "on."

COMMENTS

The off option disables the beeps that tell you that your fractal is done or that you have made an error. The sound=x|y|z options are for the "attractor" fractals, like the Lorenz fractals, which control the frequency of the sound on your PC speaker as they are generating an image, based on the x- or y- or z-coordinate the fractal is displaying at the moment. In other words, sound=y means the y-axis pixel values will control the frequency of the tone generator. The effect depends on the speed; if the sound changes too fast for your taste, use the (F) key to toggle to floating-point math and slow the "music" down.

USE LOG MAP
(X)

COMMAND FUNCTION

Map iterations to colors with a logorithmic mapping

MENU ACCESS

"Log Palette (0=no,1=yes,-1=old,+n=cmprsd,-n=sqrt)" item on the Basic Options ((X)) menu

COMMAND-LINE ACCESS

`logmap=yes|old|<nnn>`

COMMENTS

Normally escape-time iterations are mapped one-to-one to palette colors, which causes areas with a high iteration count to lose detail, because the colors change so rapidly that the "stripes" are too close together for you to see any pattern. Turning this option on causes colors to be mapped to the logarithm of the iteration, revealing structure in the featureless areas of more chaotic coloring. Entering a positive number causes a variable degree of logarithmic compression to be used; a negative number causes quadratic compression. When using a logarithmic palette in a 256-color mode, we suggest changing your colors from the usual defaults. For example, the last few colors in the default IBM VGA color map are black, which results in points nearest the lake smearing into a single dark band, with little contrast from the blue lake.

USE DISTANCE ESTIMATOR METHOD
ⓧ

COMMAND FUNCTION

Use the distance estimator algorithm when rendering Mandelbrot and Julia fractals.

MENU ACCESS

"Distance Estimator Method (0 means off)" item on the Basic Options (ⓧ) menu

COMMAND-LINE ACCESS

`fractint distest=<nnn>`

The default is 0 (distance estimator turned off).

COMMENTS

This is Phil Wilson's implementation of an alternate method for rendering the Mandelbrot and Julia sets, based on work by mathematician John Milnor and described in *The Science of Fractal Images*. While this alternative method takes full advantage of your color palette, one of its best uses is in preparing monochrome (single-color) images for a printer. Using the $1600 \times 1200 \times 2$ disk video mode and an HP LaserJet, you can generate fractals of quality equivalent to the black-and-white illustrations of the Mandelbrot set in *The Beauty of Fractals*.

The "distance estimator method" has the effect of widening the very thin strands which are part of the inside of the set. Instead of hiding invisibly between pixels, these strands are made one pixel wide. This method is designed to be used with the classic Mandelbrot and Julia types, and it may work with other escape-time fractals.

To turn on the distance estimator method, set the "distest" value on the Basic Options (ⓧ) screen to a nonzero value. If you set distest to 1, you should also set inside to something other than 1, or you will get a solid blue fractal. You should use the one-pass or two-pass mode—solid-guessing and boundary tracing can miss some of the thin strands made visible by the distance estimator method. For the highest-quality images, maxiter should also be set to a high value, say 1000 or so. You'll probably also want inside set to zero, to get a black interior.

In color modes, the distance estimator method also produces more evenly spaced contours. Set distest to a higher value for narrower color bands, a lower value for wider ones. 1000 is a good value to start with. Setting distest automatically also toggles to floating-point mode. When you reset distest back to zero, remember also to turn off floating-point mode if you want it off.

Unfortunately, images using the distance estimator method can take many hours to calculate even on a fast machine with a coprocessor. Therefore you should not use the distest option for exploration, but use it only after you have found interesting-looking fractals.

USE BINARY DECOMPOSITION METHOD
ⓧ

COMMAND FUNCTION

Use the binary decomposition method when rendering escape-time fractals

MENU ACCESS

"Decomp Option (2,4,8,..,256, 0=OFF)" item on the Basic Options (ⓧ) menu

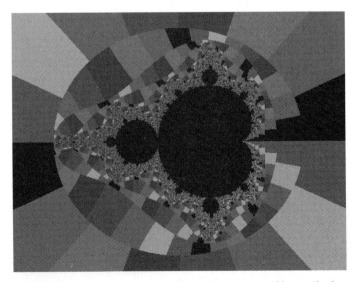

Figure 2-14 The Mandelbrot fractal using the decomposition method

COMMAND-LINE ACCESS
`fractint decomp=0|2|4|8|16|32|64|128|256`
Pick one of these values; the default is 0, which means decomposition is off.

COMMENTS
Most fractal types are calculated by iterating a simple function of a complex number, producing another complex number, until either the number exceeds some predefined bailout value, or the iteration limit is reached. The pixel corresponding to the starting point is then colored based on the result of that calculation.

The decomposition command turns on another coloring method. Here the points are colored according to which section of the complex plane the final value is in. The decomposition parameter determines how many sections the plane is divided into for this purpose. The result is a kind of warped checkerboard coloring, even in areas that would ordinarily be part of a single contour. Figure 2-14 shows what the default Mandelbrot fractal looks like with decomp=2.

ENABLE BIOMORPH RENDERING
(X)

COMMAND FUNCTION
Turn on biomorph rendering of escape-time fractals

MENU ACCESS
"Biomorph Color (-1 means OFF)" item on the Basic Options ((X)) menu

Figure 2-15 A Pickover biomorph

COMMAND-LINE ACCESS

`biomorph=<nnn>`

COMMENTS

Related to binary decomposition are the "biomorphs" invented by Clifford Pickover and discussed by A. K. Dewdney in his "Computer Recreations" column in the July 1989 *Scientific American*, page 110. These are so-named because this coloring scheme makes many fractals look like one-celled animals. Figure 2-15 shows an example of what appears to be a giant biomorph with baby biomorphs inside.

To create biomorphs, the normal escape-time coloring is modified so that if either the real *or* the imaginary component is less than the bailout, then the pixel is set to the biomorph color. The effect is a bit better with higher bailout values: the bailout is automatically set to 100 when this option is in effect. You can try other values with the bailout=nnn option. The biomorph option is turned on via the biomorph=nnn command-line option (where "nnn" is the color to use on the affected pixels). When toggling to Julia sets, the default corners are three times bigger than normal to allow one to see the biomorph appendages. This option does not work with all types; in particular it fails with any of the mandelsine family. However, if you are stuck with monochrome graphics, you should try it, as it works very well in two-color modes. Try it with the marksmandel and marksjulia types.

ACCESS EXTENDED DOODADS
Ⓨ

COMMAND FUNCTION

Access the Extended Doodads menu which contains a loose collection of fractal options

MENU ACCESS

"extended doodads" under the Options section of the Main menu

COMMAND-LINE ACCESS

various (see below)

COMMENTS

The Ⓨ option input screen is shown in Figure 2-16 with the default values showing.

LOOK FOR FINITE ATTRACTOR
Ⓨ

COMMAND FUNCTION

Invoke the basins of finite attractor option for coloring Julia lakes

MENU ACCESS

"Look for finite attractor" item on the Extended Doodads Ⓨ menu

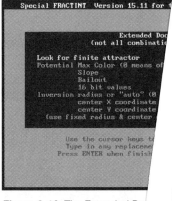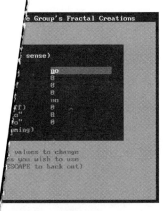

Figure 2-16 The Extended Do[...] menu

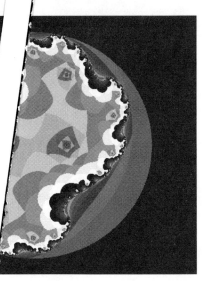

Figure 2-17 Finite attr[...]s in "Lambda Lake"

COMMAND-LINE ACCESS

`fractint finattract=no|yes`

The default value is "no."

COMMENTS

This is another option that colors s[...] Julia lakes, showing the escape time to finite attractors. It works with the [...]da and magnet types and others.

A finite attractor is a point with[...] Julia set that captures the orbits of points that come near. By "capture" we [...]n that if this option is turned on, Fractint attempts to locate such a finite at[...]or, and then to color the inside of the lake according to the time of escape of that attractor. This is an exact analogy to the way the normal escape-time algorithm colors points according to escape time to infinity. Another way to put this is that this option graphs the level sets of the basin of attraction of a finite attractor.

For a quick demonstration, select a fractal type of lambda, with real and imaginary parts of the parameter equal to .5 and .5. You will obtain an image with a large blue lake. Now set "Look for finite attractor" to "yes" with the Ⓨ menu. The image will be redrawn from scratch, this time with a much more multicolored lake. A finite attractor lives in the center of one of the resulting ripple patterns in the lake—turn the Orbits display Ⓞ on if you want to see where it is; the orbits of all initial points that are in the lake converge there. Figure 2-17 shows the result. The code and original documentation for this option was provided by Kevin Allen of Australia.

SET CONTINUOUS POTENTIAL PARAMETERS Ⓨ

COMMAND FUNCTION

Invoke the continuous potential option and control coloring (change stripes into continuously varying hues)

MENU ACCESS

The following items on the Extended Doodads Ⓨ menu:

Potential Max Color (0 means off)	*(default 0)*
Slope	*(default 0)*
Bailout	*(default 0)*
16-bit values	*(default no)*

COMMAND-LINE ACCESS

```
fractint potential=<maxcolor>[/<slope>[/<bailout>[/
16bit]]]
```

COMMENTS

Fractint's escape-time fractal images are usually calculated by the "level set" method, producing bands of color. Each of these bands consists of all points whose orbit exceeded the bailout threshold at the same iteration. The continuous potential option makes colors change continuously, rather than breaking the image into bands or stripes. A 256-color MCGA/VGA video mode is mandatory to appreciate this effect, as it is impossible to show continuous variation with only 4 or 16 colors. Non-3-D continuous potential images sometimes have a 3-D appearance because of the smoothly changing colors. Color cycling a continuous potential image with the ⊕ command gives a totally different effect than you experience with a normal striped fractal. The colors ooze rather than flash.

Max color is the color corresponding to zero potential, which plots as the top of the mountain. Generally this should be set to one less than the number of colors, for example, 255 for VGA. Remember that the last few colors of the default IBM VGA palette are black, so you won't see what you are really getting until you change to a different palette.

Slope is a number that determines how fast the colors change (try 2000 or so). If this value is too high, there will be large solid areas with the color 0; if it is too low, only a limited segment of possible colors will appear in the image. In 3-D transformations, this value determines the steepness of the mountain slopes.

Bailout is a number that replaces the normal escape-time bailout (set at 150). Larger values give more accurate and smoother potential—try 200.

16-bit values is a flag that makes Fractint save the file as a double-wide 16-bits-per-pixel GIF file. Use this flag if you wish to try a 3-D transformation of the image. The 16 bits per pixel results in a smoother 3-D image. If you do not turn on this flag but save the file in the normal way, then the potential value will be truncated to an integer, resulting in a rougher 3-D image. When this flag is turned on, saved file names will have the extension ".pot", short for "potential." You can load these files back into Fractint with the ⓡ command the same way normal GIF files are loaded back in. However, the ".pot" files will look strange when viewed with GIF decoders other than Fractint.

CREATING 3-D LANDSCAPES

Continuous potential is particularly useful when creating 3-D landscape images from fractals. When viewed in 3-D, the stripes of a typical noncontinuous-potential image turn into something like Chinese terraces; most of the surface appears to be made up of colorful horizontal steps. This effect may be interesting, but it is not suitable for use with the "illuminated" 3-D fill options 5 and 6. Continuous potential smooths the steplike terraces into a continuous surface, so that the illumination results in graduated shades of color.

Internally continuous potential is approximated in Fractint by calculating as follows:

$$\text{potential} = \frac{\log (\text{modulus})}{2^{\text{iterations}}}$$

where "modulus" is the magnitude of the iterations orbit value—the first orbit value that exceeded the bailout. The term "potential" comes from the fact that this value is related to the electrical potential field surrounding the lake that would result if it were electrically charged.

Here is a pointer for using continuous potential. Fractint's criterion for halting a fractal calculation, the bailout value, is generally set to 4, but continuous potential is inaccurate at such a low value. The integer math which makes the "mandel" and "julia" types so fast imposes a hard-wired maximum bailout value of 127. You can still make interesting images with these bailout values, such as ridges in the fractal hillsides. However, this bailout limitation can be avoided by turning on the floating-point algorithm option from the Basic Options ⓧ menu or by adding float=yes to the Fractint command line.

CREATING MTMAND USING CONTINUAL POTENTIAL OPTIONS

The following commands can be used to recreate the image that we call "MtMand." Type the following into a file called MTMAND. If you invoke Fractint from the DOS prompt as "fractint @mtmand," these options will take effect.

```
TYPE=mandel
CORNERS=-0.19920/-0.11/1.0/1.06707
INSIDE=maxiter
MAXITER=255
POTENTIAL=255/2000/1000/16bit
PASSES=1
FLOAT=yes
SAVENAME=mtmand
```

Use a 256-color video mode. (If you don't have a graphics adapter with a 256-color mode, use a disk video mode. You won't be able to see the file right away, but you can convert it to 3-D and then see it.) See the 3-D section for how to generate a 3-D image from the resulting MTMAND.POT file.

INVERT IMAGE WITH CYLINDRICAL MIRROR
ⓨ

COMMAND FUNCTION
Invert an image for viewing in a cylindrical mirror

MENU ACCESS
Use the following items on the Extended Doodads (ⓨ) menu:

Inversion radius or "auto" (0 means off)	*(default 0)*
center x-coordinate or "auto"	*(default 0)*
center y-coordinate or "auto"	*(default 0)*

COMMAND-LINE ACCESS
```
fractint invert=<radius>/<xcenter>/<ycenter>
```

COMMENTS
The invert image function has three parameters. The inversion radius must be set; the default 0 value means inversion is turned off. The center x- and y-coordinates default to 0 if not set.

Many years ago there was a brief craze for "anamorphic art": images painted and viewed with the use of a cylindrical mirror, so that they looked weirdly distorted on the canvas but correct in the distorted reflection. In other words, you could see the paintings correctly if you looked at the image in the cylindrical mirror.

Fractint's inversion option performs a related transformation on most of the fractal types. You define the center point and radius of a circle on your fractal; Fractint maps each point inside the circle to a corresponding point outside, and vice-versa. This is known to mathematicians as "everting" the plane. John Milnor made his name in the 1950s with a method for everting a seven-dimensional sphere, so Fractint still has a ways to go.

As an example, if a point A inside the circle is $1/3$ of the way from the center to the radius, it is mapped to a point A' along the same radial line, but at a distance of (3 * radius) from the origin. An outside point B' at 4 times the radius is mapped to a point B inside at $1/4$ the radius. Figure 2-18 shows the transformation that inversion accomplishes.

The Extended Options menu prompts you for the radius and center coordinates of the inversion circle. Entering **Auto** sets the radius at $1/6$ the smaller dimension of the image currently on the screen. The auto values for xcenter and ycenter use the coordinates currently mapped to the center of the screen.

The Newton fractal is a good one to try with the inversion option, because it has well-defined radial spokes that make it easy to visualize the before and after

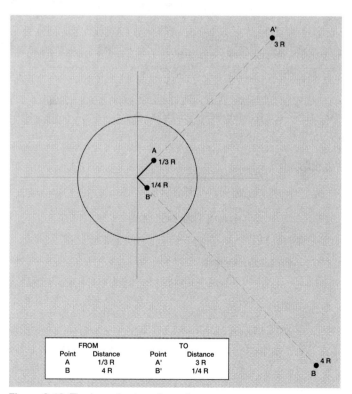

Figure 2-18 The inversion transformation

effects of inverting. Get the Type Selection menu by pressing Ⓣ, and select "newton." Then enter inversion parameters from the Extended Options (Ⓨ) menu, and use a radius of 1 with the center coordinates set to 0. The center has "exploded" to the periphery. See Figure 2-19 for an example made with an order-3 Newton fractal showing the results before and after inversion. Inverting through a circle not centered on the origin produces bizarre effects that we're not even going to try to describe. Do this by entering nonzero values for xcenter and ycenter.

Figure 2-19 Order-3 Newton fractal with and without inversion

USE SMALLER VIEW WINDOW
Ⓥ

COMMAND FUNCTION

Access view window settings so you can shrink the fractals image size for fractal calculation

MENU ACCESS

"view window options" under the Options section of the Main menu

COMMAND-LINE ACCESS

COMMENTS

The view window is the fractal explorer's best friend. It allows generating smaller size images that calculate very rapidly because there are so few pixels. You set the size of the reduction from the menu; the default is a 4.2-times reduction of the normal full-screen image size. Thus you can generate dozens of images in a fraction of the time that full-sized fractals would take. The calculation time is proportional to the number of pixels, so that if you reduce the image dimensions by a factor of four, the number of pixels is reduced by a factor of

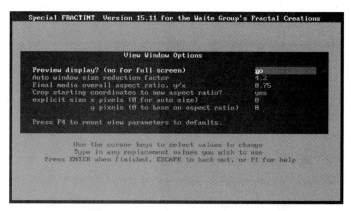

Figure 2-20 Viewing area parameters

sixteen, and the calculation time is reduced to one-sixteenth of the previous time! For experimental purposes, a small view window is just fine. When you find a promising effect, just turn off view windows, recalculate, and Fractint will make a full-screen image.

Figure 2-20 shows the input screen for the viewing area parameters accessed by the Ⓥ key. Note the message at the bottom that the F4 key will reset all parameters to the defaults. This reset feature is useful, since it is possible to get all tangled up in the settings!

Here is what each of these parameters does:

Preview display? (no for full screen) (default no)

Answer "yes" to turn on the view window feature. Most of the time this is the only setting that will be needed—the other parameters have very reasonable default values.

Auto window size reduction factor (default 4.2)

This factor is the amount the view window is scaled down. A larger value will make the view window smaller and it will calculate more quickly.

Final media overall aspect ratio, y/x (default 0.75)

Aspect ratio is the overall height divided by overall width. The default value of .75 is almost universal, so you will rarely need to change this.

Crop starting coordinates to new aspect ratio? (default yes)

If you answer "yes," and the corners parameters do not match the aspect ratio, the corners values will be changed to make the aspect ratio the value you specified. This generally will happen only if you either changed the view windows aspect ratio or altered the aspect ratio of the zoom box by stretching it in one of the dimensions.

explicit size x pixels (0 for auto size) (default 0)

y pixels (0 to base on aspect ratio) (default 0)

You may specify the exact pixel dimensions of the view window. This overrides the autosize reduction factor and aspect ratio values.

Press (ESC) to exit the View Area Parameters screen. To trigger the recalculation of the image to the new view window, reselect a video mode by pressing a function key.

LOAD IFS PARAMETERS
①

COMMAND FUNCTION

Load IFS parameters from a file

MENU ACCESS

1. Select "3D,IFS type parameters" from the Main menu.

2. Select 2-D or 3-D IFS codes (whichever desired).

3. Enter **R** (for "Restore") from the 3D IFS Parameters menu.

4. Select an IFS file from the File Selection screen.

COMMAND-LINE ACCESS

```
fractint ifs=<filename>
fractint ifs3d=<filename>
```

COMMENTS

This function allows loading Iterated Function System (IFS) parameters from a file. Each line in the file is an IFS transformation represented by seven numbers for 2-D IFS transforms, and thirteen numbers for 3-D IFS transforms. See Michael Barnsley's *Fractals Everywhere* for more information.

A 2-D IFS transformation may be represented by a 2×2 matrix and a 2-D vector:

$$F \left\{ \begin{matrix} x_1 \\ y_1 \end{matrix} \right\} = \left\{ \begin{matrix} a\ b \\ c\ d \end{matrix} \right\} \left\{ \begin{matrix} x_1 \\ y_1 \end{matrix} \right\} + \left\{ \begin{matrix} e \\ f \end{matrix} \right\}$$

The line in the IFS file corresponding to this transformation would be "a b c d e f p," where "p" is the probability assigned to that transformation.

A 3-D IFS transformation F may be represented by a 3×3 matrix and a 3-D vector:

$$F \left\{ \begin{matrix} x_1 \\ x_2 \\ x_3 \end{matrix} \right\} = \left\{ \begin{matrix} a\ b\ c \\ d\ e\ f \\ g\ h\ i \end{matrix} \right\} + \left\{ \begin{matrix} j \\ k \\ l \end{matrix} \right\}$$

The text line in the IFS file corresponding to this transformation would be "a b c d e f g h i j k l p," where "p" is the probability assigned to that transformation.

The p values of the different IFS transformations in a file must add up to 1.0. Files that can be loaded have the .IFS extension.

SAVE IFS PARAMETERS
(I)

COMMAND FUNCTION

Save IFS parameters to a file

MENU ACCESS

1. Select "3D,IFS type parameters" from the Main menu.

2. Select 2-D or 3-D IFS codes (whichever desired).

3. Enter **S** (for "Save") from the 3D IFS Parameters menu.

4. Type a file name for the IFS file and press (ENTER).

COMMAND-LINE ACCESS

COMMENTS

The saved files are in the same format specified above in the description for the "Load IFS parameters" command function.

EDIT IFS PARAMETERS
(I)

COMMAND FUNCTION

Edit current IFS parameters

MENU ACCESS

1. Select "3D,IFS type parameters" from the Main menu.

2. Select 2-D or 3-D IFS codes (whichever desired). The IFS codes are listed with one transformation per numbered row.

3. Enter the row of the desired function to edit.

4. Edit each parameter in turn, press (ENTER) when done.

COMMAND-LINE ACCESS

COMMENTS

This function allows editing of Iterated Function System (IFS) parameters. See the "Load IFS parameters" command function description above for how the IFS parameters correspond to the IFS transformation matrix and vector. Try making small changes in one number at a time and regenerating the IFS fractal to see the effect of each change.

Changing the values of an affine transformation matrix is a fairly primitive method of editing IFS transformations. For a superior method, obtain the sister Stone Soup program Fdesign by Doug Nelson. Fdesign is a freeware IFS fractal generator available from CompuServe in the COMART forum, Lib 15, and it is available on many public bulletin boards. This program requires a VGA adapter and a Microsoft-compatible mouse. It allows one to manipulate and produce IFS fractals in a visually intuitive way by moving the corners of triangles representing affine transformations with a mouse. Fdesign can load and save Fractint-style IFS files.

EDIT 3-D TRANSFORM PARAMETERS
⓵

COMMAND FUNCTION

Edit the 3-D transform parameters

MENU ACCESS

1. Select "3D,IFS type parameters" from the Main menu.

2. Select "3D Transform Parameters."

3. Edit 3-D parameter input items (see Figure 2-21).

COMMAND-LINE ACCESS

```
fractint rotation=<xrot>[/<yrot>[/<zrot>]]
perspective=<nnn> xyshift=<xshift>/<yshift> stereo=0|1|2|3
```

COMMENTS

All the 3-D capabilities in Fractint use the same variables. These 3-D parameters are also settable via the "3D transform from file" item on the Main menu. The fractal types that use 3-D are ifs3D, lorenz3d, rossler3d, kamtorus3d, and henon.

Imagine that the x-axis runs horizontally across the middle of your computer screen, with zero in the middle. The y-axis runs vertically through the computer screen with zero in the middle. The z-axis is perpendicular to the plane of the screen with the positive end toward you. Figure 2-22 shows the coordinate system (in relation to a computer screen.)

Here is what each of the 3-D parameter does:

x-axis, y-axis, and z-axis rotation

The first three parameters allow setting the rotations that cause the fractal ob-

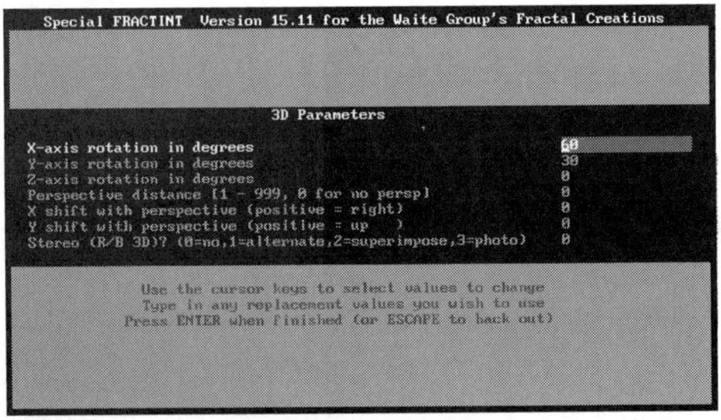

Figure 2-21 3D Parameters input screen

jects to be viewed from different angles. Refer to Figure 2-23 as you follow this example. From the Main menu, press Ⓣ ("select fractal type"), and choose type lorenz3d. Press the Ⓘ key to access the IFS and 3-D Parameter menu, select "3D Transform Parameters," and then follow the menu access sequence above to change the x-, y-, and z-axis rotation values to 0, 0, 0. Press ⒺⓃⓉⒺⓇ to accept these values, and press a video mode function key if you haven't already done so (Ⓕ❷ is a good choice for EGA/VGA). You are now seeing the Lorenz orbit as it is with no 3-D rotations. The Lorenz orbit is the path of a wildly orbiting particle under the influence of two invisible attractors. It spirals around one, then the other, back and forth, forming two flat spirals in two different planes at an angle to each other.

Repeat these steps starting with pressing Ⓘ, but change the x-axis rotation to 30. The image has rotated around the x-axis 30 degrees, with the top of the image coming toward you. One of the two spirals now looks very thin because you are viewing it end-on. Repeat these steps again, this time changing the y-axis rotation to 30, so both x and y rotations are now 30. The skinny spiral now looks fuller because the image has rotated around the y-axis and the right-hand side of the screen has moved away from you.

Repeat the steps one last time, setting all three rotation values to 30. The last rotation is the easiest to understand, because the z-axis is coming right out of the screen, and the rotation just moves the image clockwise around the screen.

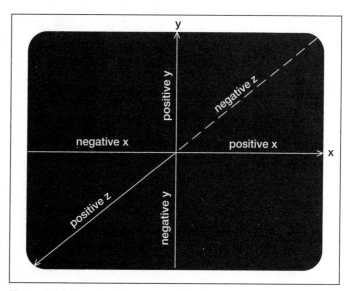

Figure 2-22 The 3-D Coordinate System

To get a little better feel, you might try repeating this whole experiment with red/blue glasses—just set the stereo option to **2**. Figure 2-23 specifically shows the first three of these Lorenz images with superimposed axes, with arrows indicating the direction of rotation. The fourth image with all three rotations set to 30 is not shown.

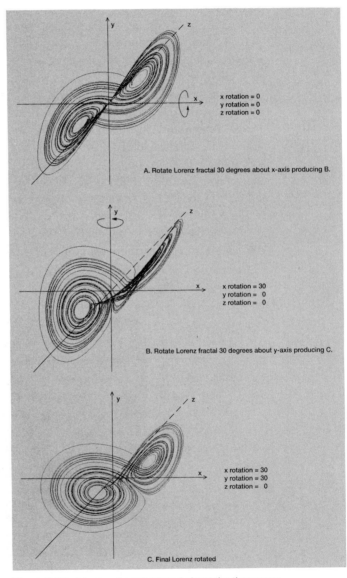

Figure 2-23 A Lorenz fractal rotated about the three axes

Perspective distance [1 - 999, 0 for no persp]

The perspective parameter causes the 3-D projection to use a viewpoint from different distances. The effect is to make closer parts of the fractal larger, and farther parts smaller, as seen by an imaginary observer. The value entered for perspective distance allows you to control how close this observer is to the fractal object. Imagine the 3-D object inside a box and just touching all the sides. A perspective value of 100 is an extreme perspective where your viewpoint is right on the near edge of the box, with parts of the object very close. This can be considered a closeup of the image. A value of 200 means that the near edge of the box is halfway between your eye and the far edge of the box. Figure 2-24 diagrams this situation. Try a value of about 120 with lorenz3d to see the effect.

X shift and Y shift with perspective

The x and y shift move the position of the observer. If perspective is also turned on, the image is not just moved on the screen, but the point of view is also changed. Shifting to the left and then to the right changes the image in exactly the same way as what you see is changed when you close your right eye and look through your left, and then look at the same scene through your right eye.

Stereo (R/B 3D)

Stereo viewing is a technique whereby two distinct views of a 3-D object are created, one as if seen by the right eye, the other a little offset and as if seen by the left eye. What is needed to reproduce stereo vision is a way to get the left and right images to the correct eye. One method of doing that is to use the red/ blue funny glasses. The red filter blocks the blue image and lets the red image through, and the blue filter does the opposite. Fractint can put the left and right images on the screen at the same time, using red and blue colors. The two images overlap, so some method of combining the two colors is needed. Fractint provides two methods, each with its advantages. The alternate and superimpose options are the two different ways that the red and blue are combined. In the alternate approach, the screen is divided so that every other pixel in each row is designated to be either a red or blue pixel. The red and blue aren't really combined except in your mind. When your eye sees red and blue pixels close together, your mind "sees" the color magenta. The alternate approach does offer less resolution, because each image is formed from only half the screen pixels, but it allows more shades of red and blue–128 shades on a VGA in a 256-color mode.

The superimpose option combines overlapping red and blue pixels in a single magenta pixel, allowing higher effective resolution but fewer shades of red and blue. Even in a 256-color mode, there are only 16 visible shades of red and blue; all the colors are taken up with combinations of these shades. Use superimpose for lorenz3d. Put on your 3-D glasses and regenerate the lorenz3d example.

Stereo option 3 makes two separate images and pauses so that pictures can be taken of the screen. The two pictures can be mounted and viewed with a stereo slide viewer. This kind of stereo doesn't use red and blue; it provides full-color stereo. But of course, you need a camera to photograph the images or else you can save the left and right views as GIF files and have slides made by a slide service.

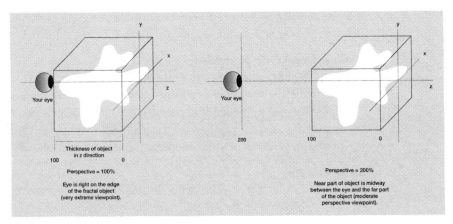

Figure 2-24 Different perspective positions

<table>
<tr><td>

**EDIT
RED/BLUE
GLASSES
PARAMETERS**

① or ③

</td><td>

COMMAND FUNCTION

Edit 3-D "funny glasses" parameters

MENU ACCESS
1. Select "3D,IFS type parameters" from the Main menu.
2. Select "3D Transform Parameters."
3. Select a "Stereo (R/B 3D)?" option 1 or 2.
4. Edit "funny glasses" parameters input items.

Funny glasses parameters are also accessible when doing a 3-D transformation on a loaded file:
1. Select "3d transform from file" from the Main menu.
2. Select a file from the "Select File for 3D Transform" list.
3. Select a video mode.
4. Fill in the items in the 3D Mode Selection input screen (specify "Stereo (R/B 3D)" as either 1 or 2).
5. Select a fill type from the Select Fill Type screen.

</td></tr>
</table>

6. Edit funny glasses parameters input items.

Figure 2-25 shows the Funny Glasses Parameters input screen.

COMMAND-LINE ACCESS

```
fractint interocular=<distance> converge=<distance>
crop=<red-left>/<red-right>/<blue-left>/<blue-right>
bright=<red>/<blue> map=<mapfilename>
```

COMMENTS

Interocular distance

The interocular distance is the distance between the left and right viewpoints measured as a percent of the screen width. It should be set small enough so that your eyes can easily converge the two images, but large enough that there is an adequate stereo effect. The default of 3 usually works quite well if the perspective value is not extremely close.

Convergence adjust

The convergence parameter adjusts the relative position of the two images in the horizontal dimension. The effect is to move the apparent image into or out from the screen. A larger value makes the image appear in front of the screen, while a smaller (possibly negative) value makes the 3-D object appear to be inside the monitor.

Left and right red and blue image crop

The red and blue images need to be clipped on the left and right differently to make a proper 3-D effect. The edge of the image should appear to be in the same place for both eyes. Setting this properly can be very tricky because it interacts strongly with the convergence parameter. The default is about right for

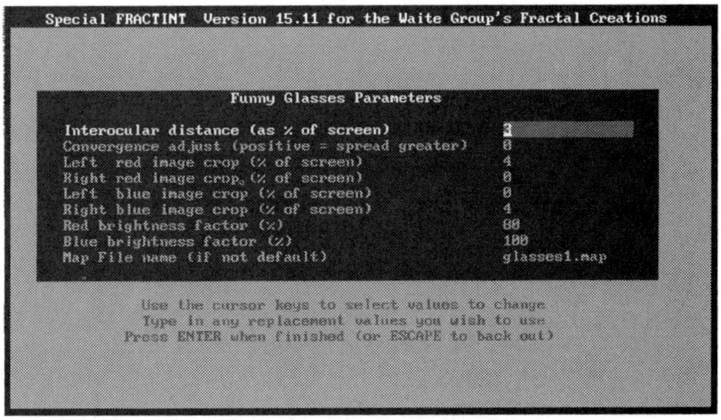

Figure 2-25 Funny Glasses Parameters input screen

images that appear near the screen surface. Cropping is only an issue when the screen edge clips the image. If a lorenz3d image is completely contained within the screen, for example, so the black background goes right up to the screen edge, then cropping is not needed.

Red and blue brightness factors

The brightness parameters allow adjustment for differences in the red and blue screen color saturation and glasses filter properties. You can adjust these values so that both the red and blue images look equally bright. The correct settings are dependent on the color properties of your monitor, the quality of your funny glasses filters, and the color sensitivity of your eyes. Try to find values that minimize the ghost image caused by bleed-through of the left (red) image through the blue lens to the right eye, and the right (blue) image through the red lens to the left eye. If you can see a faint, green, "ghost" image when you place the blue lens over the red image, it means there is too much yellow in the red image–try turning down the monitor intensity until the ghost disappears.

Map file name

The alternate and superimpose methods of displaying red and blue images on your screen each require special palette mappings. These are stored in the files GLASSES1.MAP and GLASSES2.MAP that come with Fractint. These files should be placed in a directory listed in your path. (If Fractint can't find them, it can generate the values on the fly.) The files GLASSES1.MAP and GLASSES2.MAP are designed to allow the greatest number of different shades of red and blue. If you are using superimpose, try substituting the file called GRID.MAP and see if it works any better, especially for wire frame images or other images that do not need shades of red and blue.

FILE

The File section of the Main menu is where you go to save and load images, do 3-D transformations, create batch files, print, drop to DOS, quit Fractint, or restart. We will cover the menu items in order. Keep in mind that the Main menu is modified to show more possibilities when an image has already been generated.

SAVE IMAGE
Ⓢ

COMMAND FUNCTION

Save a fractal image as a .GIF file

MENU ACCESS

"save image to file" under the File section of the Main menu

COMMAND-LINE ACCESS

`fractint batch=yes`

causes an automatic save following the completion of a calculation.

COMMENTS

Pressing Ⓢ causes the current image to be saved as a CompuServe GIF file. (See Appendix B for details on the .GIF format.) Two small vertical bars will grow down the left- and right-hand sides of the screen, they represent the progress of the save operation. When they reach the bottom of the screen, the name of the file is saved and the saved file is reported at the top of your screen. The default name, which is settable in the Basic Options menu, is FRACT001.GIF. If you save more than one time during a Fractint session, the last character of the name will be a number that is incremented, resulting in FRACT002.GIF and so forth. The saved file appears in the directory that was current when Fractint was started. You can't set the pathname from Fractint.

Normally Fractint does not overwrite existing files. If you would like to reuse existing file names to conserve disk space, set overwrite to "yes" in the Basic Options menu, or add the line "overwrite=yes" to the command line or in your SSTOOL.INI file. Even with "overwrite=yes" the file names will have an incrementing number, so that saved images made during the same session will not overwrite each other.

FRACTINT'S GIFS STORE PARTIAL STATES

Understand that Fractint remembers the state of a partial calculation when saving in the GIF file format (see the explanation of the GIF format, page 275). So although Fractint is the world's fastest fractal program, calculations with high maximum iterations in the floating-point mode, extreme resolutions, or running on a slow PC can take a long time. For example, the feather image on the cover of this book took a week to generate on a 25-Mhz 80386 machine. (The image was done using a 2048 × 2048 disk video mode with a very high maximum iteration value.) Many times throughout that week the image was saved when the computer had to be used for other purposes, and when it was restored, the calculation picked right up where it left off!

Fractint stores GIFs using the GIF89a format. If you need to make a GIF file that is viewable with software that does not support the new GIF89a standard, start the program with the option

`fractint gif87a=yes`

and then all saved images will be in the older GIF87a format. However, they will not contain any information about the Fractint parameter that created them.

You can also convert GIF89a files to GIF87a files by reading them in and then saving them. The command line

```
fractint newformat.gif gif87a=yes savename=oldformat.gif
batch=yes
```

reads in the file newformat.gif and saves it as the GIF87a format file oldformat.gif.

LOAD IMAGE
Ⓡ

COMMAND FUNCTION
Load a fractal image from a GIF file for display

MENU ACCESS
"load image from file... Ⓡ" under the File section of the Main menu

COMMAND-LINE ACCESS
```
fractint [filename=]<filename>
```
To load an image as you start Fractint so it's viewable, you can type in either **fractint myfile** or **fractint filename=myfile**. The GIF extension is assumed.

COMMENTS
GIF files created by Fractint contain not just fractal images but also information about how the fractal was generated. Thus, loading the file not only allows you to view the image, but resets Fractint to regenerate that image. Fractint is capable of being used as a GIF decoder to view files not created by Fractint, such as pictures. Since Fractint has no way of knowing how their GIFs were generated, it sets the current fractal type to "plasma."

The Ⓡ command takes you to a sophisticated file selection screen with several useful features. These features are as follows:

1. Point to file: Just use the arrow keys to move the highlight to the file you wish to select. Then press (ENTER). If you select an item that is a directory, then the current directory changes to the selected directory. Selecting ".." takes you up one directory.

2. Speed key selection: Begin typing the name of the file you wish to select. The highlight will jump to the first file name that matches what you have typed so far.

3. Path search: You can type the name of a file not in the current directory. If it is in one of the directories listed in your path statement, Fractint will find it.

4. Wild cards: If you enter a wild card template, such as t*.gif, then the list will change to show just the files matching the template, in this case, all files starting with "t" with the extension ".gif". The wild cards work the same as DOS wild cards using "*" and "?".

5. Changing drive or directory. You may enter a new drive by typing in the drive letter and a ":", or a new directory, or both at the same time. If entering a new directory, end with a "\" so that Fractint knows you want a directory rather than a file.

Once you have selected a file, the video mode list is presented and you will be prompted to select a video mode to display the selected fractal. If Fractint can locate a video mode on the list that matches the image being loaded (part of the information stored with a GIF is its resolution), that mode will be highlighted.

DISK VIDEO AND HIGHER-RESOLUTION MODES

It is possible to view an image at a lower resolution than the actual resolution of the image. For example, the image on the cover of this book was created at Fractint's highest resolution of 2048 × 2048 using the disk video mode. The same image can be viewed in Fractint at a low resolution mode such as 640 × 480 or 320 × 200; Fractint just throws out the extra pixels. This feature is extremely useful, since it allows you to create and view disk video images or other images at resolutions greater than those supported by your graphics equipment.

PERFORM 3-D TRANS-FORMATION
③

COMMAND FUNCTION
Perform a 3-D transformation of a GIF file

MENU ACCESS
"3d transform from file" under the File section of the Main menu

COMMAND-LINE ACCESS
`fractint 3D=yes`

COMMENTS
Most of the fractals created by Fractint are inherently two-dimensional, meaning they are flat in the x-y plane. A 3-D mode allows you to transform any fractal into a three-dimensional image with depth and an x-y-z-axis. The 3-D function treats a fractal's colors as the third dimension and performs various 3-D and rendering transformations on the image, so it appears on the screen projected realistically. Another feature of Fractint is that the 3-D transformations are not limited to Fractint-generated files, but they can also be performed on GIF files created by other software. Indeed some scientists use Fractint's 3-D capabilities to enhance electron microscope pictures!

Using 3-D involves several successive and somewhat complex-looking screens, but it is really quite easy to use. The ③ command leads you to the first of these screens for inputting all the parameters that affect 3-D. Do not be dismayed by the number of possibilities: usually the default values are something reasonable, and you press (ENTER) to move to the next screen. Follow the defaults at first, and then try changing the parameters a few at a time.

The ③ command begins with a file selection screen that works the same as the file selection for the ®. Select a GIF file, choose a video mode (generally the same as that of the GIF file), and then select a 3-D mode (see below).

SELECT A 3-D MODE ③

COMMAND FUNCTION

After 3-D transformation has been selected, choose a specific 3-D mode

MENU ACCESS

1. Select "3d transform from file" from the Main menu.

2. Select a file from the "Select File for 3D Transform" list.

3. Select a video mode.

4. Fill in the items in the 3D Mode Selection input screen (see Figure 2-26).

COMMAND-LINE ACCESS

```
fractint 3D=yes preview=yes|no coarse=<nnn> showbox=yes|no
sphere=yes|no stereo=0|1|2|3
```

COMMENTS

After the file name prompt and video mode check, Fractint presents a 3D Mode Selection screen as shown in Figure 2-26. Each selection will have defaults entered. If you wish to change any of the defaults, use the cursor keys to move through the menu. When you're satisfied press (ENTER) to accept your choices and move to the next 3-D screen. (ESC) allows you to back up to the previous screen.

Here are the options and what they do:

Preview Mode (yes or no)

Preview mode provides a rapid look at your transformed 3-D image by skipping a lot of rows and filling the image in. It is good for quickly discovering the best parameters. Once the 3-D parameters look good, you can turn off the preview mode and generate the full image.

Show Box

If you have selected preview mode, you have another option to consider. This is the option to show a rectangular "image box" around the image boundaries in scaled and rotated coordinates x, y, and z. The bottom of this box is the original x-y plane of your fractal, and the height is the dimension where the colors in your fractal will be interpreted as elevations. The box appears only in rectangular transformations and shows how the final image will be oriented; it doesn't draw the actual transformation. If you select light source in the next screen, it will also show you the light source vector so you can tell where the light is coming from in relation to your image.

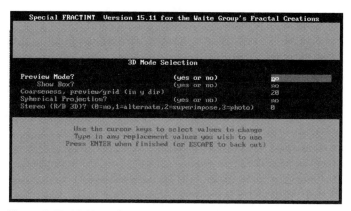

Figure 2-26 3D Mode Selection screen

Coarseness, preview/grid (in y dir)

The coarseness parameter sets how many divisions the image will be divided into in the y direction, and it is needed if you select preview mode as described above, or grid fill in the Select Fill Type screen described below. The default is 20 divisions; a larger number makes a finer (and slower) grid.

Spherical Projection

The spherical projection parameter allows you to select a sphere projection of your fractal. This maps your image onto a plane as described above if your answer is "no," or onto a sphere if you answer "yes." Thus you can take your favorite fractal, wrap it around a sphere, and turn it into a planet, an asteroid, a moon, or whatever. Fractint allows you to use any GIF image whatsoever and make a planet out of it—even a digitized photograph of your loved one! Planets can be smooth or rough, large or small, and they can be illuminated with the light from an imaginary sun.

Stereo

Fractint allows you to create 3-D images for use with red/blue glasses like those found in 3-D comic books. Option 0 turns off the stereo effect. Options 1 and 2 require the special red/blue glasses. They are meant to be viewed right on the screen or on a color print off of the screen. The image can be made to hover entirely or partially in front of the screen.

Stereo option 1 gives 64 shades of red and blue, but with half the spatial resolution you have selected. It works by writing the red and blue images on adjacent pixels, which is why it removes half the picture's resolution. In general, we recommend you use this with resolutions above 640 × 350 only. Use this mode for continuous potential landscapes where you need all those shades.

Stereo option 2 gives you full spatial resolution but with only 16 shades of gray. If the red and blue pixels overlap, the colors are mixed, and the pixel is colored magenta. This option is good for wire-frame images (we call them surface grids), lorenz3d, and ifs3d. It works fine in 16-color modes.

Stereo option 3 is for creating full-color stereo pair images for viewing with more specialized equipment. The left image is presented on the screen first. You may photograph it or save it as a GIF for later processing into a slide. Then the second image is presented, and you may do the same with it as you did with the first image. You can then take the two images and convert them to a stereo image pair.

SELECT 3-D FILL ③

COMMAND FUNCTION

Select a 3-D fill type, determining if the image is drawn with all pixels, as a wire frame image, etc.

MENU ACCESS

1. Select "3d transform from file" from the Main menu.
2. Select a file from the "Select File for 3D Transform" list.
3. Select a video mode.
4. Fill in the items in the 3D Mode Selection input screen.
5. Select a fill type from the Select Fill Type screen.

Figure 2-27 shows the Select 3D Fill Type screen as it appears in the non-sphere case. If you are doing a 3-D projection onto a sphere, the only difference is that there will be only one light source option.

COMMAND-LINE ACCESS

`fractint filltype=<nnn>`
where (<nnn> is 0 through 7)

COMMENTS

In the course of any 3-D projection, portions of the original image must be stretched to fit the new surface. Points of an image that formerly were right next to each other now may have a space between them. The "select fill type" options generally determine what to do with the space between the mapped dots.

Make a surface grid

If you select the "make a surface grid" option, Fractint will make an unfilled wire frame grid of the fractal surface that has as many divisions in the original y direction as were set in "coarse" in the first screen. This wireframe view of your image is generated very quickly and can reveal a quick approximation of what the final 3-D fractal will look like.

Just draw the points

The second option, "just draw the points," means Fractint just maps points in the 2-D image to corresponding points in the 3-D image. Generally this will leave empty space between many of the points, and this space will appear black.

connect the dots (wire frame)

This fill method simply connects the points in the hope that the connecting lines will fill in all the missing pixels. This option is rarely used, because it has been supplanted by the superior surface fill methods that were developed later.

surface fill (colors interpolated)
surface fill (colors not interpolated)

The surface fill options fill in the areas between the 3-D dots with small triangles formed from the transformed points. If the corners of the triangles are different colors, the "colors interpolated" fill colors the interior of the triangle with colors that smoothly blend between the corner colors. The "colors not interpolated" fill simply colors the whole triangle the color of one of the corners. Interpolating the colors makes the little triangles blend better but only works if the color palette is continuous, meaning that colors with near color numbers are a similar color. If the results look strange, try the "colors not interpolated" fill.

solid fill (bars up from "ground")

The solid fill method works by using a kind of bar graph approach. A line is drawn from each point to its projection in the x-y plane.

light source before transformation
light source after transformation

The two light source fill options allow you to position an imaginary sun over

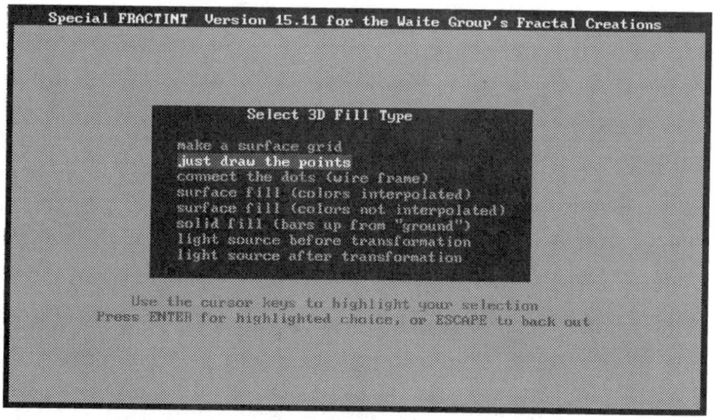

Figure 2-27 Select 3D Fill Type screen

your fractal landscape. Fractint colors each pixel of the landscape according to the angle the surface makes with an imaginary light source. This creates the appearance of shadows and can be used to create realistic mountains. You will be asked to enter the three coordinates of the vector pointing toward the light in one of the following screens.

The option called "light source before transformation" calculates the illumination before doing the coordinate transformations, and it is slightly faster. If you generate a sequence of images where one rotation is progressively changed, the effect is as if the image and the light source are fixed in relation to each other and you orbit around the image.

Light source after transformation applies the transformations first, then calculates the illumination. If you generate a sequence of images with progressive rotation as above, the effect is as if you and the light source are fixed and the object is rotating. Figure 2-28 shows the relationship between the fractal object, the viewer, and the light source for these two options.

If you select either light source fill (before or after), you will be prompted for a color map, which is a file assigning colors to the color numbers. You can try altern.map, which is a grey-scale palette that represents the light source shading as shades of grey. However, any map that has continuous shades of color works well with the light source options, although they may not look as realistic as with the grey palette in altern.map. Try color cycling with the ⊕ command and using the higher function keys such as (F8) or (F9) to get some interesting effects.

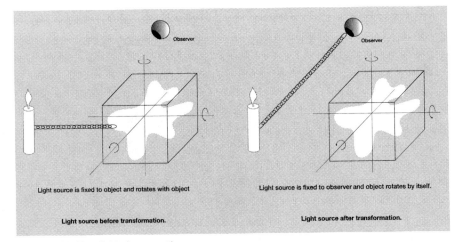

Light source is fixed to object and rotates with object

Light source is fixed to observer and object rotates by itself.

Light source before transformation.

Light source after transformation.

Figure 2-28 Two light source options

SELECT PLANAR 3-D PARAMETERS

③

COMMAND FUNCTION

Chose various planar 3-D parameters such as axis rotation, water level, etc.

MENU ACCESS

1. Select "3d transform from file" from the Main menu.
2. Select a file from the "Select File for 3D Transform" list.
3. Select a video mode.
4. Fill in the items in the 3D Mode Selection input screen with "Spherical Projection" set to "no."
5. Select a fill type from the Select Fill Type screen.
6. Fill in the items in the Planar 3D Parameters input screen.

Figure 2-29 shows the Planar 3-D Parameters input screen as it appears when the light fill option is in effect. If a light fill is not in effect, the last two items, the randomize colors and mono/color options, will not show on the screen.

COMMAND-LINE ACCESS

```
fractint rotation=<xrot>[/<yrot>[/<zrot>]]
scalexyz=<scalex>[/<scaley>[/<scalez>]] roughness=<scalez>
waterline=<level> perspective=<distance>
xyshift=<xshift>[/<yshift>] xyadjust=<xadjust>[/<yadjust>]
transparent=<startcolor>/<stopcolor> randomize=<nnn>
fullcolor=yes|no
```

COMMENTS

The number of 3-D parameters in this menu is a bit daunting; however, most have reasonable default values, so you can usually press (ENTER) to accept them all. Thus you do not need to understand all of them to get 3-D working. You'll usually change only a few of these parameters, unless you want to explore.

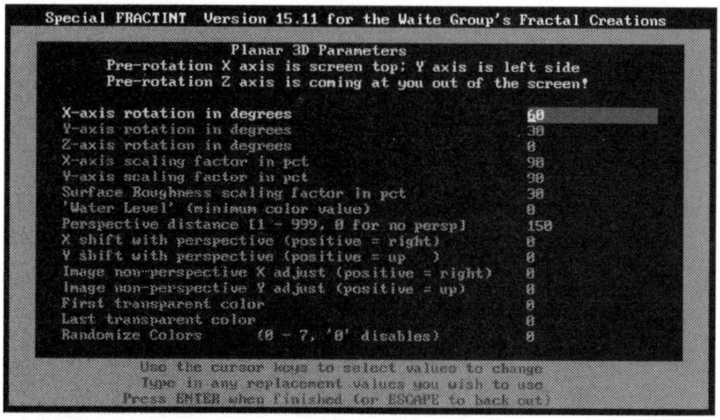

Figure 2-29 Planar 3D Parameters screen

x-axis rotation in degrees

y-axis rotation in degrees

z-axis rotation in degrees

The first entries are rotation values around the x-, y-, and z-axes. Think of your starting image as a flat map: the x value tilts the bottom of your monitor towards you by x degrees, the y value pulls the left side of the monitor towards you, and the z value spins it counterclockwise. The final result of combining rotations depends on the order in which they are done. Fractint always rotates first along the x-axis, then along the y-axis, and finally along the z-axis. All rotations actually occur through the center of the original image. Figure 2-30 shows these three rotations.

x-axis scaling factor in pct

y-axis scaling factor in pct

surface roughness scaling factor in pct

Following the three rotation parameters are three scaling factors that control the resulting size of each axis of the image. Initially, leave the x- and y-axes alone and try changing the surface roughness factor (really z-axis scaling). High values of roughness assure your fractal will be translated into steep Alpine mountains and improbably deep valleys; low values make gentle, rolling terrain. Negative roughness is legal. For example, if you're doing a Mandelbrot image and want the solid Mandelbrot lake to be below the ground, instead of eerily floating above, try a roughness of about -30 percent.

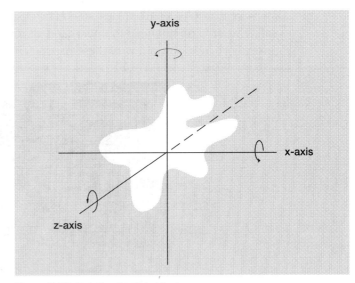

Figure 2-30: Rotating fractal objects

Water Level (minimum color value)

When a file is loaded into Fractint using the 3-D option, the colors are interpreted as elevations according to the number of the color. The water level option creates a minimum elevation in the resulting image. The result is exactly like flooding a valley. The higher the water level value, the more of the scene will be "under water." This works well with plasma landscapes.

Perspective distance [1 - 999, 0 for no persp]

Perspective distance can be thought of as the distance from your eye to the image. A zero value (the default) means no perspective calculations, which makes the image appear flat, as though photographed through a telephoto lens. If you do set perspective to a nonzero value, nearer features to the observer will be larger than farther away features. To understand the effect of the perspective number, picture a box with the original x-y plane of your flat fractal on the bottom and your 3-D fractal inside. A perspective value of 100 percent places your eye right at the edge of the box and yields fairly severe distortion, like a close view through a wide-angle lens. A value of 200 percent puts your eye as far from the front of the box as the back is behind. A value of 300 percent puts your eye twice as far from the front of the box as the back is, and so on. Try about 150 percent for reasonable results. Much larger values put you far away for even less distortion, while values smaller than 100 percent put you "inside" the box. Try larger values first, and work your way in. Figure 2-31 shows how the perspective parameter relates to the distance from the viewer to the object.

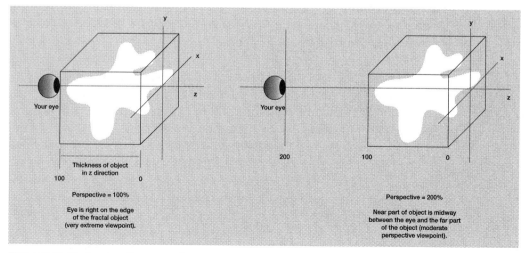

Figure 2-31 The perspective parameter

x shift with perspective (positive = right)

y shift with perspective (positive = up)

Image nonperspective x adjust (positive = right)

Image nonperspective y adjust (positive = up)

There are two types of x and y shifts that let you move the final image around if you'd like to recenter it. The first set, x and y shift with perspective, moves the image and changes the viewing perspective as well. The second set, x and y adjust without perspective, and simply moves the image without changing the perspective viewpoint. They are used just for positioning the final image on the screen.

First transparent color

Last transparent color

You may define a range of transparent colors. This option is most useful when using the Overlay command (see below) to place one image on top of another, so parts of the bottom image show through. Enter the color range (minimum and maximum value) for which you do not want to overwrite whatever may already be on the screen. The color ranges refer to the color numbers in the original image. The default is no transparency (overwrite everything).

Randomize Colors (0 - 7, '0' disables)

The randomize option will smooth the transition between colors and reduce the banding that occurs with some maps. Select the value of randomize to between 0 (for no effect) and 7 (to randomize your colors almost beyond use). A setting of 3 is a good starting point.

Color/Mono Images with Light Source (1 = Color)

This is an option for advanced users. If you selected a light source fill, you will find the color/mono option at the bottom of the screen. It is very difficult to make a convincing colorful landscape image even with the 256 colors available in VGA. If you answer **1** at the "Color/Mono Images with Light Source (1 = Color)" prompt, Fractint will create a "true color" Targa 24 bit-per-pixel file with an extension ".tga." that contains more information than is visible on the VGA screen. Fractint cannot use these files—it only creates them. The advantage of Targa files is that they can contain many more colors than GIF files can. You can manipulate the Targa 24-bit files with other software, such as the Stone Soup freeware program Piclab by Lee Crocker. Piclab is widely available on computer bulletin boards and may be found on CompuServe in the PICS forum, Lib 14. Piclab does not require a Targa graphics board to manipulate Targa files.

Here is an example of generating a Targa file based on the "MTMAND.POT" continuous-potential file. Type the following into a file called mtmand3d:

```
filename=mtmand.pot
3d=yes
filltype=6
randomize=3
fullcolor=yes
ambient=15
rotation=60/30/0
scalexyz=100/100
roughness=120
waterline=0
perspective=220
xyshift=10/-32
lightsource=1/-1/1
map=topo
```

After creating the file MTMAND3D, type in :

```
fractint @MTMAND3D savename=mtmand3D batch=yes
```

This will create a true color Targa file called MTMAND3D.TGA

You can then use Piclab to convert this file to a GIF file with dither=yes. If you don't have Piclab, you can still do a monochrome image of MtMand in regular GIF format. In the above example, remove the line "fullcolor=yes" and change the "map=yes" line to "map=altern." The result will look very much like the cover of *The Beauty of Fractals*.

SET LIGHT SOURCE ③

COMMAND FUNCTION

Set light source parameters

MENU ACCESS

1. Select "3d transform from file" from the Main menu.
2. Select a file from the "Select File for 3D Transform" list.
3. Select a video mode.
4. Fill in the items in the 3D Mode Selection input screen.
5. Select a light source fill type from the Select Fill Type screen.
6. Fill in the items in the Planar 3D Parameters input screen.
7. Fill in the items in the Light Source Parameters input screen.

   Figure 2-32 shows the Light Source Parameters input screen.

COMMAND-LINE ACCESS

```
fractint lightsource=<x>[/<y>[/<z>]] smoothing=<nnn>
ambient=<nnn> haze=<nnn> lightname=<filename>
```

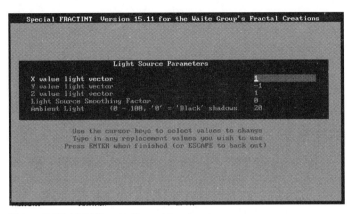

Figure 2-32 Light Source Parameters input screen

COMMENTS

The purpose of this screen is to control the details of an internal, simulated light that is shining on your fractal. You will need patience when using the light source option, because figuring out light directions can be confusing.

X value light vector

Y value light vector

Z value light vector

First, if you have selected a light source fill, you must choose the direction of the light from the light source. This will be scaled in the x, y, and z directions the same as the image. For example, the values 1,1,3 position the light to come from the lower right front of the screen in relation to the untransformed image. It is important to remember that these coordinates are scaled the same as your image. Thus 1,1,1 positions the light to come from a direction of equal distances to the right, below, and in front of each pixel on the original image. However, if the x,y,z scale is set to 90,90,30, the result will be from equal distances to the right and below each pixel but from only 1/3 the distance in front of the screen, that is, it will be low in the sky, say, afternoon or morning.

Figure 2-33 shows the coordinate system used for defining the light vectors in the two light source modes. This coordinate system is not the same for the before transformation and after transformation light source options we explained earlier. For the light source before transformation option, the positive x-axis is on the left, the positive y-axis is up, and the positive z-axis is behind the screen. A good light vector to try would be x=1, y=1, and z=-3. With this light vector and rotations of 0,0,0, the light would appear to come from the upper right. For the light source after transformation option, the positive x-axis is on the right, the positive y-axis is up, and the positive z-axis is in front of the screen. To get the

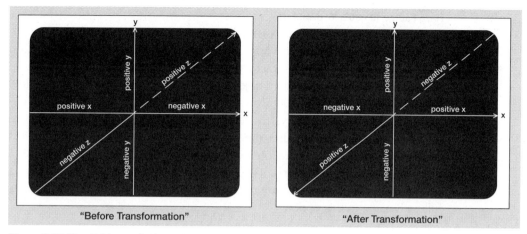

"Before Transformation"   "After Transformation"

Figure 2-33 Two light coordinate system

same effect as the above vector, the signs of the x- and z-coordinates of the light vector have to be reversed, yielding x=-1, y=1, and z=3. Confusion can be avoided by using one of the two light source options until you are familiar with the effects.

Light Source Smoothing Factor

Next you are asked for a smoothing factor. Unless you used continuous potential (see the earlier description) when generating the starting 3-D image, the illumination when using light source fills may appear "sparkly," like a sandy beach in bright sun. This is because with only 256 colors in the original image, the z-coordinate has only 256 possible values, and the transformed image surface is broken into tiny facets. With continuous potential, there are 64,000 possible z-coordinate values, so a very smooth surface is possible. The smoothing factor averages colors in each line of the original image, smearing them together. A smoothing factor of 2 or 3 will allow you to see the large-scale shapes better. If you did use continuous potential and are loading in a "*.pot" file, you should turn off smoothing. If your fractal is not a plasma cloud and has features with sharply defined boundaries (e.g., Mandelbrot lake), the smoothing may cause the colors to run.

Ambient Light (0 - 100, '0' = 'Black' shadows)

 The ambient option sets the minimum light value a surface has if it has no direct lighting at all. All light values are scaled from this value to white. This effectively adjusts the depth of the shadows and sets the overall contrast of the image.

Haze Factor (0 - 100, '0' disables)

Full Color Light File Name (if not LIGHT001.TGA)

The last two input screen items appear only if you selected the full color option to make a Targa file. The haze factor makes distant objects more hazy. Close-up objects are little affected; distant objects will be obscured by haze. The value 0 disables the function, and 100 gives the maximum effect, with the farthest objects lost in the mist. Currently, this does not really use distance from the viewer; instead, Fractint cheats and uses the y value of the original image. So the effect really works only if the y rotation (set earlier) is between +/- 30.

The last item allows you to choose the name for your light file. If you have a RAM disk handy, you might want to create the file on it for speed, so include its full path name in this option.

SELECT SPHERE 3-D PARAMETERS ③

COMMAND FUNCTION

Select the various sphere 3-D parameters for wrapping an image around a globe

MENU ACCESS

1. Select "3d transform from file" from the Main menu.

2. Select a file from the "Select File for 3D Transform" list.

3. Select a video mode.

4. Fill in the items in the 3D Mode Selection input screen with "Spherical Projection" set to "yes."

5. Select a fill type from the Select Fill Type screen.

6. Fill in the items in the Sphere 3D Parameters input screen.

Figure 2-34 shows the Sphere 3-D Parameters input screen as it appears when

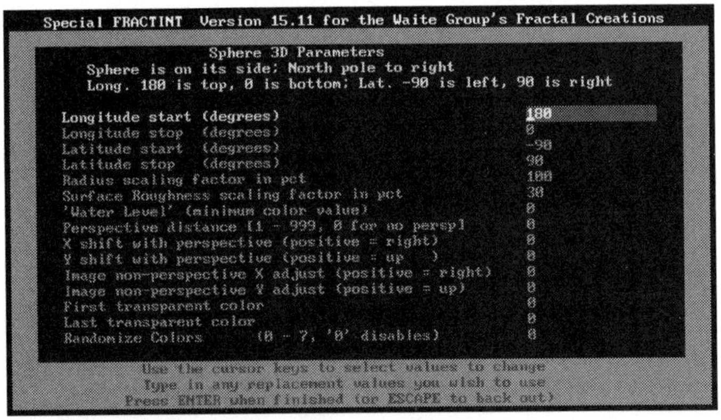

Figure 2-34 Sphere 3D Parameters screen

the light fill option is in effect. If a light fill is not in effect, the last two items, the randomize colors and mono/color options, will not show on the screen.

COMMAND-LINE ACCESS

```
fractint  longitude=<startdegree>/[<stopdegree>]
latitude=<startdegree>/[<stopdegree>] radius=<scaleradius>
roughness=<scalez> waterline=<level>
perspective=<distance> xyshift=<xshift>[/<yshift>]
xyadjust=<xadjust>[/<yadjust>] transparent=<startcolor>/
<stopcolor> randomize=<nnn> fullcolor=yes|no
```

COMMENTS

The sphere 3-D parameters function controls the wrapping of a fractal image around the surface of a sphere. In fact, you can project any GIF file image, whether from Fractint or not, onto the surface of a sphere.

Longitude start (degrees)

Longitude stop (degrees)

Latitude start (degrees)

Latitude stop   (degrees)

Picture a globe lying on its side, "north" pole to the right. You will be mapping the x- and y-values of the starting image to latitude and longitude on the globe, so that what was a horizontal row of pixels becomes a line of longitude, while what was a vertical column of pixels becomes a line of latitude. The default values exactly cover the hemisphere facing you, from longitude 180 degrees (top) to 0 degrees (bottom) and latitude -90 (left) to latitude 90 (right). By changing these values you can map the image to a piece of the hemisphere or wrap it clear around the globe. Figure 2-35 shows how this works.

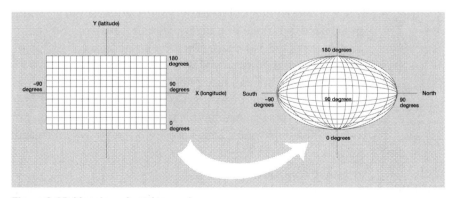

Figure 2-35 Mapping a fractal to a sphere

Radius scaling factor in pct

The radius factor controls the overall size of the globe and is the sphere analog to the x and y scale factors. Use this parameter to enlarge or shrink your globe as you wish.

Surface Roughness scaling factor in pct

The roughness factor in the sphere context controls the bumpiness of the surface of the sphere. A value of zero makes the sphere perfectly smooth.

The remaining screen items have the same meaning for a sphere transformation as they do for a plane transformation—see the Planar 3D Parameters Screen explanation.

When the wrap-around "construction" process begins at the edge of the sphere (the default) or behind it, it's plotting points that will be hidden by subsequent points as the process sweeps around the sphere toward you. Fractint's hidden-point algorithms "know" this, and the first few dozen lines may be invisible unless a high mountain happens to poke over the horizon. If you start a spherical projection and the screen stays black, wait awhile (a longer while for higher resolution or fill type 6) to see if points start to appear.

SELECT 3-D PARAMETERS AND OVERLAY
Ⓞ

COMMAND FUNCTION

Perform a 3-D transformation of a GIF file overlaid on the current image

MENU ACCESS

"3d overlay from file" under the File section of the Main menu

COMMAND-LINE ACCESS

COMMENTS

This function is identical to the normal 3-D transformation accessed with the Ⓩ command, with one important difference: the screen is not cleared prior to the drawing of the 3-D image. The new image is pasted on top of the old image. For example, if the first image is a plasma landscape, and you use the Ⓞ command to make a sphere, the sphere image will be added to the plasma landscape picture. Figure 2-36 shows an example of the kind of images that are possible with this command. This is not the same as the Ⓞ command that lets you see orbit trajectories, which applies during fractal calculations only.

WRITE BATCH FILE
Ⓑ

COMMAND FUNCTION

This command causes Fractint to write the current parameters for a fractal to a file

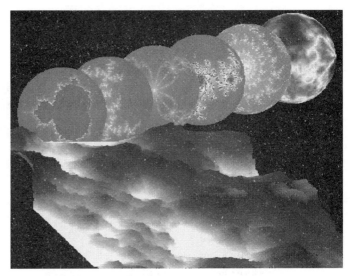

Figure 2-36 Moons over landscape

MENU ACCESS

"write batch parameters" under the File section of the Main menu

COMMAND-LINE ACCESS

COMMENTS

This command creates a batch file, FRABATCH.BAT, that will start Fractint with the command-line arguments needed to draw the current image. This is very useful when you have done a great deal of experimenting to find the correct settings and want to resume later with the same parameters. If FRABATCH.BAT already exists, a new line is appended to it. If you use the ⑧ command several times during a session, you will end up with a FRABATCH.BAT file with several lines, one line for each time you pressed ⑧.

The original intent of the FRABATCH.BAT file was that you could run it from the DOS prompt and recreate the fractal that was current at the time the ⑧ key was pressed. However, DOS does not allow more than 128 characters in a text line, and Fractint has so many options that most lines in your FRABATCH.BAT file will be longer than that. To take care of this problem, the Stone Soup authors have added the capability to run a batch file indirectly, by typing

```
fractint @frabatch.bat
```

from the command line. You should first edit the FRABATCH.BAT file so that it contains the instructions for one fractal. Commands do not have to be on one line. The Ⓑ command does not save the video mode, because the usual use of batch files is to recalculate a fractal in a higher resolution.

Let's look at a very simple example. The FRABATCH.BAT file created when the default Mandelbrot image was on the screen would contain the single line

```
fractint type=mandel corners=-2.5/1.5/-1.5/1.5
```

Suppose you want to redo that image using the F10 VGA 320 × 400 mode, and just to make it interesting, suppose you add the biomorph option. Rename the FRABATCH.BAT file to say FRACTAL1, and edit it so it looks like this:

```
type=mandel
corners=-2.5/1.5/-1.5/1.5
video=F10
biomorph=yes
savename=fractal1.gif
batch=yes
```

Adding the batch=yes and savename=fractal1.gif lines will make Fractint automatically save when done.

To run this batch file from the DOS command line, type

```
fractint @fractal1
```

Then all the options in the file FRACTAL1 will take effect. The fractal type will be type mandel, the corners values will be -2.5, 1.5, -1.5, and 1.5, the video mode will be F10, the biomorph option will be turned on, and the fractal will be saved with the file name FRACTAL1.GIF. Finally, Fractint will run in batch mode, calculating the fractal and saving it without user intervention. Using this approach, you could record the parameters of a number of promising fractals with the Ⓑcommand, and set up a batch file that looks like this:

```
fractint @fractal1
fractint @fractal2
fractint @fractal3
```

Each of the files—fractal1, fractal2, and so forth—would contain commands for a single fractal similar to the example.

PRINT A FRACTAL
Ⓟ

COMMAND FUNCTION
Print a fractal on the screen to a printer

MENU ACCESS
"print image" under the File section of the Main menu

COMMAND-LINE ACCESS

COMMENTS

The ⓟ command prints the current fractal on the screen. The default printer is assumed to be an Epson in the 75 dots-per-inch graphics mode, unless another printer is set with Fractint's "printer= " command. Most graphics printers, including the Epson, cannot represent shades of grey. The only fractals that can be properly printed on these printers are two-color fractals that use only black and white. Black and white fractals done with the distance estimator method ("distest=") option look spectacular when printed on a Hewlett-Packard LaserJet at maximum resolution. The only printers that Fractint can use to create shades of grey are those driven by PostScript. The PostScript printer driver is also the only printer driver that preserves the aspect ratio and makes the width and height come out in the right proportion. If you want to make high-quality printouts of fractals using an Epson or Hewlett-Packard printer, use a disk video mode to match the printer resolution you want to use. For example, if you want to use an Epson at its highest resolution, invoke Fractint with

```
fractint printer=epson/240
```

and use the (ALT)-ⓥ (Disk/RAM 'Video' 768 × 1920 Full-Page Epson @240dpi) mode to generate the fractal. When the fractal is done, press ⓟ to print it. You can also use a normal video mode such as 640 × 480. This is fairly close to the number of dots in the Epson low-resolution mode (768 × 480), so the result is close to what you see on the screen.

SET PRINTER INFO

COMMAND FUNCTION

Set printer information

MENU ACCESS

COMMAND-LINE ACCESS

```
fractint printer=<type>[/<resolution>[/<port#>]]
printfile=<filename> epsf=1|2|3 title=yes
translate=yes|<nnn> halftone=<frequency>/<angle>/<style>
```

COMMENTS

These commands can be typed in at the command-line when Fractint is invoked, but they are probably best placed in the SSTOOLS.INI file, since they generally will not be changed all that often.

The command "printer=<type>[/<resolution>[/<port#>]]" defines your printer setup. Table 2-6 shows the possible values for <type>.

Type	Name
HP	Hewlett-Packard LaserJet
EP	Epson-compatible
IB	IBM-compatible
CO	Star Micronix/Epson Color
PA	Hewlett Packard PaintJet
PS	PostScript portrait
PSL	PostScript landscape

Table 2-6 Printer Types

The default printer type is the Epson. The resolution is in dots per inch. Possible values are 60, 120, and 240 for the Epson/IBM; 75, 150, and 300 for the LaserJet; 90 and 180 for the PaintJet; and 10 through 600 for PostScript. The Printer port can be 1, 2, and 3 for LPT1-3; 11, 12, 13, and 14 for COM1-4. With PostScript, a negative port number can be used to redirect printing to a file. The default print-to-filename is FRACT001.PRN and is incremented after each print to file operation. The command printfile=<filename> causes printing to go to the file <filename>. The comport=port/baud/options command allows serial printer port initialization. "Port" may be 1, 2, 3, or 4 for com1 through com4. "Baud" is the baud rate, which may be 115, 150, 300, 600, 1200, 2400, 4800, or 9600. "Options" includes bits, stop bits, and parity in any order. For example,

```
fractint comport=1/9600/n81
```

sets the printer for port com1, 9600 baud, no parity, 8 bits per character, and 1 stop bit.

The next few commands are for PostScript output only:

EPSF=1|2|3|

forces print to a file with the default file name fract001.eps. The PostScript mode is turned on. Lower numbers force stricter adherence to the Encapsulated PostScript (EPS) format.

TITLE=YES

causes the printing of a title with the output.

TRANSLATE=YES|<NNN>

yes prints a negative image; nnn>0 reduces image colors; nnn<0 reduces image colors and prints a negative image.

HALFTONE=<FREQ>/<ANGLE>/<STYLE>

The halftone option is presented here for the advanced PostScript owners and those who want to experiment. This option defines the halftone screen for PostScript, which affects how colors are rendered as dot patterns. The first value, frequency, defines the number of halftone lines per inch. The second chooses the angle (in degrees) of the screen. The third option chooses the halftone spot style. Good frequencies are between 60 and 80; good angles are 45 and 0; the default style is 0. If the halftone option is not in SSTOOL.INI, Fractint will print using the printer's default halftone screen, which should have already been set to do a fine job on the printer. The halftone styles are:

0 - Dots	A circular dot pattern
1 - Horizontal Lines	Horizontal lines running the width of the image
2 - Vertical Lines	Vertical lines running the height of the image
3 - Inverted Dots	White dots surrounded by black Inverse of style 0
4 - Black Rings	Black rings with white on the inside and outside
5 - White Rings	White rings—inverse of style 4
6 - Diamond	Style consisting of black diamonds
7 - Microwaves	Horizontal lines with pronounced ripples
8 - Grid	Pattern of boxes with grid lines running horizontally and vertically
9 - Star	Mutation from a cross to a diamond to a grid pattern
10 - Alternate Lines	Vertical lines with occasional microwave type ripples
11 - Triangle	A triangular dot pattern
12 - RoundBox	Square with rounded corners
13 - Random	Different diffused style at each printing

EXIT TEMPORARILY TO DOS
Ⓓ

COMMAND FUNCTION
Use this command to leave Fractint in memory so you can exit to DOS and return to Fractint quickly

MENU ACCESS
"shell to dos" under the File section of the Main menu

COMMAND-LINE ACCESS
none

COMMENTS

This option switches to DOS, leaving Fractint stored in memory, ready to resume when you type **exit** at a DOS prompt. Be careful not to do anything that changes the video mode. If you do, upon returning to Fractint, your graphics image may not be preserved. Return to Fractint by typing **exit** (ENTER)

QUIT FRACTINT
(ESC)

COMMAND FUNCTION

Quit Fractint and return to DOS

MENU ACCESS

"quit Fractint" under the File section of the Main menu

COMMAND-LINE ACCESS

COMMENTS

You will be given the prompt "Exit from Fractint? (y/n)." Pressing either (Y) or (ENTER) exits, (N) returns to the Main menu, other keys do nothing. Since (ESC) is also used to back through the menu system, this safety feature prevents exiting by inadvertently typing an extra (ESC).

RESTART FRACTINT
(INS)

COMMAND FUNCTION

Restart Fractint

MENU ACCESS

"restart Fractint" under the File section of the Main menu

COMMAND-LINE ACCESS

COMMENTS

Pressing (INS) on the numeric keypad from the Main menu has the same effect as quitting and restarting Fractint. Use it when you have altered many Fractint settings and wish to return to the startup defaults. Since Fractint is a rather large program and takes a few seconds to load, this command avoids an irritating delay that would be experienced by exiting and restarting.

COLORS

The Colors section of the Main menu appears only if your graphics adapter supports palette manipulations. If you have a CGA- or Hercules-compatible monochrome graphics, this menu will not appear. If you do have an EGA, VGA, or higher advanced graphics adapter, this menu is your avenue to some spectacular color effects, most notably color cycling.

COLOR
CYCLE
⊕ ⊖ ©

COMMAND FUNCTION

Enter color cycling mode with or without starting cycling

MENU ACCESS

"color cycling mode"
"rotate palette <+>, <->"
under the Colors section of the Main menu

COMMAND-LINE ACCESS

COMMENTS

The purpose of the © command is to enter the color cycling mode without actually starting the color cycling. Since the © command itself does not start color cycling, a visual indicator of the mode is provided; the border area of the screen turns to white. You might want to do this if you wanted to load a map file or do some of the other functions available under color cycling.

Use the ⊕ or ⊖ key to enter color cycling mode and start color cycling at the same time. Color cycling is one of the really exciting features in Fractint. An animation effect is achieved by rapidly changing how colors are mapped to the color numbers of the orginal image. Plasma images are particularly fascinating. The plasma colors flow into each other in an endless unfolding. Here is an explanation of what is happening: Your fractal image actually assigns numbers to pixels, not colors. If your image is a 256-color image, the numbers range from 0 to 255. At any given time, your graphics adaptor assigns each of these numbers to colors selected from a much larger set—262,144 different colors for a VGA. Color cycling plays musical chairs with these colors. Think of the 256 numbers as the chairs, and the colors as the kids circling with these chairs. If the kids go one chair at a time, they are doing exactly what color cycling does. All three of these commands cause the current mode to change from display mode to color cycling mode.

Note that the palette colors available on an EGA adapter (16 colors at a time out of a palette of 64) are limited compared to those of VGA, super VGA, and MCGA (16 or 256 colors at a time out of a palette of 262,144). So color cycling in general looks a *lot* better in the VGA/MCGA modes. Also, because of the EGA palette restrictions, some color cycling commands are not available with EGA adapters.

A completely different set of keystroke commands apply while in color cycling mode. These are listed here.

(ESC)
Exits color cycling mode. Use this when you are ready to save a fractal with (S).

(C)
Toggles cycling on and off.

(F1)
Brings up a Help screen with commands specific to color command mode.

(+) or (→)
Cycles the palette forward. Each color moves to the higher color index. Colors at the last index move to the first index.

(−) or (←)
Cycles the palette backward. Each color moves to the next-lower color index. Colors at the first color index move to the last. Alternate between (−) and (+) to see the colors throb!

(↑)/(↓)
Increases/decreases the cycling speed. The original purpose of this command was to eliminate flicker experienced on some displays when color cycling. But it is also useful just to slow down the color cycling on very fast machines to a more pleasing speed. This works like the speed keys (1) to (9).

(F2) through (F10)
Switches from simple color palette rotation to color selection using randomly generated color bands of short ((F2)) to long ((F10)) duration. Pressing any function key except the help key ((F1)) during color cycling causes Fractint to add new random colors. Pressing (F2) causes a new random color to be created for each cycle. Higher function keys cause new colors to be generated at intervals and, in between, the colors smoothly merge from the last random color to the next. The higher the function key number, the more intermediate colors are calculated. To see a few colors cycled through many beautiful shades, use the higher (F) *keys*.

(1) through (9)
Causes the screen to be updated every 'n' color cycles (the default is 1), so smaller numbers give slower cycling, higher give faster cycling. Handy for slower computers.

(ENTER)
Randomly selects a function key (F2 through F10) and then updates *all* the screen colors prior to displaying them for instant, random colors. Press this over and over again to see your fractal with totally different colors.

(SPACE)
Pauses cycling and turns the screen border white as a visual indication of the continuation of the color cycling mode.

(SHIFT)(F1)-(F10)	Pauses cycling and resets the palette to a preset two-color "straight" assignment, such as a spread from black to white. (Not for EGA.) These keys allow you to access some built-in palettes and see how they look with your fractal.
(CTRL)(F1)-(F10)	Pauses cycling and uses a two-color cyclical assignment, for example, red→yellow→red (not for EGA). These are some more built-in palettes to try.
(ALT)(F1)-(F10)	Pauses cycling and uses a 3-color cyclical assignment, for example, green→white→blue (not for EGA). Still more built-in palettes!
(D) or (A)	Pauses cycling and loads an external color map from the files DEFAULT.MAP ((D)) (IBM default palette) or ALTERN.MAP ((A)) (continuous greyscale palette), supplied with the program.
(L)	Pauses cycling and prompts for the file name of an external color map. Several others are supplied with the program. (The .MAP extension is assumed.) Map files allow you to specify what colors each color number represents. They are ordinary text files. Each line in the text file determines one color; the first line is color 0, the second line is color 1, and so forth. Each line of the map file has three numbers that determine the red, green, and blue content of that color number. These numbers range from 0 to 255. The first few lines of ALTERN.MAP, a grey-scale color map, are shown in Table 2-7.

0	*0*	*0*
252	*252*	*252*
248	*252*	*252*
252	*248*	*252. (This is color 3)*
252	*248*	*248*
248	*248*	*248*

Table 2-7 The famous Peterson-Vigneau pseudo-grey sequence

For example, if you load in ALTERN.MAP, color 3 (the fourth row, because you count up from 0) would have a red component of 252, a green component of 248, and a blue component of 252. This is an almost-white shade with an almost invisible red-blue (magenta) tinge. Note that comments can be placed after the numbers. Color 0 is usually 0 0 0 because it is used for the normally black overscan border of your screen.

Ⓢ   Pauses cycling, prompts for a file name, and saves the current palette to the named file (.MAP assumed).

ENTER PALETTE EDITOR

Ⓔ

COMMAND FUNCTION

Enter palette editing mode for altering the color map in use

MENU ACCESS

"palette editing mode" under the Colors section of the Main menu

COMMAND-LINE ACCESS

COMMENTS

The palette editing mode is a sophisticated mechanism for customizing and adjusting the Fractint color palette. It requires a graphics adapter supporting 256 colors, such as a VGA or super VGA.

Skilled fractal artists spend a lot of time manipulating the colors of their fractals; this is what separates the beginners from the true artists. When the palette editing mode is entered, an empty palette frame is displayed. Use the cursor keys to position the frame, use the (PGUP) and (PGDN) keys to size it, and then press (ENTER) to display the palette in a grid. Figure 2-37 shows the palette editor grid.

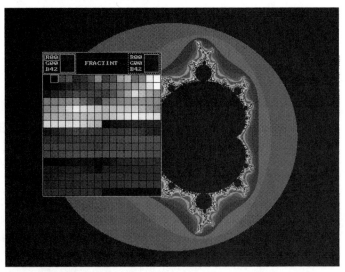

Figure 2-37 The palette editor grid

Note that the palette frame shows R(ed) G(reen) and B(lue) values for two color registers at the top. The active color register has a solid frame, the inactive register's frame is dotted. Within the active register, the active color component is framed. The mouse controls a cross hair. Once the palette frame is displayed, the following commands are available:

(ESC)	Exit to color cycling mode.
(H)	Hide the palette frame to see the full image; the cross hair remains visible and all functions remain enabled; press (H) again to restore the palette display.
(→)(←)(↑)(↓)	Move the cross-hair cursor around. In auto mode (the default) the center of the cross hair selects the active color register. Cursor-control keys move the cross hair faster. A mouse can also be used to move around.
(R),(G), or (B)	Select the red, green, or blue component of the active color register for the subsequent Insert or Delete and Select Previous or Next Color Component in Active Register commands.
(+), (−)	Increase or decrease the active color component by 1. Numeric keypad (+) and (−) keys do the same.
(PGUP) or (PGDN)	Increase or decrease the active color component by 5. Moving the mouse up or down with the left button held is the same.
(0),(1),(2),(3),(4),(5),(6)	Set active color component to 0, 10, 20, ..., 60.
(SPACE)	Select the other color register as the active one. (In auto mode this results in both registers set to the color under the cursor until you move it.)
(,), (.)	Rotate the palette one step.
(<) or (>)	Rotate the palette continuously (until next keystroke).
(C)	Enter color cycling mode.
(=)	Create a smoothly shaded range of colors between the two color registers.
(D)	Duplicate the inactive color register in active color.
(T)	Stripe-shade; create a smoothly shaded range of colors between the two color registers, setting only every nth register; after pressing (T), press a number from 2 to 9 which is used as n.

(SHIFT) (F2), (SHIFT) (F3),... (SHIFT) (F9)	Store the current palette in a temporary save area associated with the function key; these save palettes are remembered only until you exit palette editing mode.
(F2),(F3),...(F9)	Restore the palette from a temporary save area.
(\)	Move or resize the palette frame. The frame outline is drawn; it can then be moved and sized with the cursor keys, (PGUP), and (PGDN). Press (ENTER) when done moving/sizing.
(I)	Invert frame colors, useful with dark colors.
(L)	Prompt for a palette map file name (default file type is .MAP), and load the palette from that map file.
(S)	Prompt for a palette map file name (default file type is .MAP), and save the palette to that map file.
(A)	Toggle auto mode on or off. When on, the active color register follows the cursor; when off, (ENTER) must be pressed to set the register to the color under the cursor.
(ENTER)	Useful only when auto is off, as described above; double-clicking the left mouse button is the same as (ENTER).
(X)	Toggle exclude mode on or off—when toggled on, only the active color is displayed.
(Y)	Toggle exclude range on or off—when on, only colors in the range of the two color registers are shown.

MAKE STARFIELD
(A)

COMMAND FUNCTION
Make a starfield from your favorite fractal image

MENU ACCESS
"make starfield" under the Colors section of the Main menu

COMMAND-LINE ACCESS
none

COMMENTS
Once you have generated your favorite fractal image, you can convert it into a fractal starfield with the (A) transformation (for "astronomy"). The screen is filled with random-appearing distributions of individual pixels of different degrees of brightness. Stars are generated on a pixel-by-pixel basis—the odds that a particular pixel will coalesce into a star are based (partially) on the color index of that pixel.

If the screen is entirely black and the star density per pixel is set to 30, then a starfield transformation will create an evenly distributed starfield with an average of one star for every 30 pixels. Therefore if you're on a 320 × 200 screen you have 64,000 pixels and would end up with about 2,100 stars. By introducing the variable of "clumpiness" we can create more stars in areas that have higher color values. At 100 percent clumpiness a color value of 255 will change the average of finding a star at that location to 50:50. A lower clumpiness value will lower the amount of probability weighting. To create a spiral galaxy, draw your favorite spiral fractal (IFS, Julia, or Mandelbrot) and perform a starfield transformation. For general starfields we recommend transforming a plasma fractal. For starfields based on fractals with lakes, such as the Mandelbrot fractal, be sure to set inside=255 for the best effect.

Real starfields have many more dim stars than bright ones because very few stars are close enough to appear bright. To achieve this effect the program will create a bell curve based on the value of ratio of dim stars to bright stars. After calculating the bell curve, the curve is folded in half and the peak is used to represent the number of dim stars.

Starfields can be shown in 256 colors only. Fractint will automatically try to load ALTERN.MAP and abort if the map file cannot be found.

COMMAND-LINE-ONLY COMMANDS

This section documents Fractint commands that exist only in command-line or batch form and do not have associated keystrokes or menu items.

adapter=cga | ega | egamono | mcga | vga | hgc

Skip the autodetect logic, assume this kind of adapter is present. Use this only if the autodetect logic fails for your adapter. This will affect the default mode and any other Fractint features that depend on auto-detecting adapters. However, this command does not actually change what your adapter can do. (The " | " means "or"—use one of these options)

askvideo=yes | no

If "no," this eliminates the prompt asking you if a file to be restored is OK for your current video hardware. This command assumes that you have created the video mode table in the file fractint.cfg and edited out all modes that are illegal for your graphics adapter. You can create such a table by typing in **fractint batch=config** at the DOS prompt. See below or Appendix A for more information.

batch=config

Starts a quick batch-mode run that creates a default fractint.cfg file from the full internal video table. You can edit modes that don't work on your system out of this list.

exitmode=nn

Sets the bios-supported video mode to use upon exit (if not mode 3)—nn is the mode in hexadecimal. For people who like nonstandard text modes.

formulafile=<formulafilename>

Lets you specify the default formula file for type=formula fractals (the default is FRACTINT.FRM). Handy if you want to generate one of these fractal types in batch mode.

formulaname=<formulaname>

Lets you specify the default formula name for type=formula fractals (the default is no formula at all). Required if you want to generate one of these fractal types in batch mode, as this is the only way to specify a formula name in that case. Formulas are discussed in Chapter 3.

function=<fn1>[/<fn2>[/<fn3>[/<fn4>]]]

Allows setting variable functions found in some fractal type formulae. Possible values of the functions are sin, cos, sinh, cosh, exp, log, and sqr.

gif87a=yes

Backward-compatibility switch to force creation of GIF files in the GIF87a format. Fractint now creates files in the new GIF89a format, which permits storage of fractal information within the format. This switch is needed only if you wish to view Fractint images with a GIF decoder that cannot accept the newer format. The disadvantage of this option is that no fractal information will be stored with the file, and Fractint will not know how the file was created.

hertz=nnn

Sets the frequency of the sound produced by the sound=x/y/z option. Legal values are 200 through 10000.

initorbit=pixel
initorbit=<nnn>/<nnn>

Allows control over the value used to begin each Mandelbrot-type orbit. The command initorbit=pixel is the default for most types; this command initializes the orbit to the complex number corresponding to the screen pixel. The command initorbit=nnn/nnn uses the entered value as the initializer.

lfile=<lfilename>

Lets you specify the default lfile for type=lsystem fractals (the default is fractint.l). Handy if you want to generate one of these fractal types in batch mode.

lname=<lsystemname>

Lets you specify the default lsystem name for type=lsystem fractals (the default is the first type in the lfile). Required if you want to generate one of these fractal types in batch mode, as this is the only way to specify an lsystem name in that case.

periodicity=no | show | nnn

Allows control of periodicity checking; "no" turns it off, "show" lets you see which pixels were painted the inside color due to being caught by periodicity. Specifying a number causes a more conservative periodicity test (each increase of 1 divides the test tolerance by 2). Entering a negative number lets you turn on "show" with that number. Type lambdafn function=exp needs periodicity turned off to be accurate–there may be other cases.

symmetry=<symmetry>

This option forces symmetry to one of None, Xaxis, Yaxis, XYaxis, Origin, or π symmetry. Some fractals are symmetrical and have parts that are reflections of their other parts. For example, the top and bottom of the Mandelbrot fractal are reflections of each other. The Mandelbrot fractal has X axis symmetry, because the top points are the reflections of the bottom points about the x axis. Y axis symmetry means the left and right sides of a fractal are reflections of each other. XY axis symmetry is a combination of both of these. Origin symmetry reflects upper points to lower points on the opposite side. Finally, π symmetry describes the symmetry of periodic fractals that repeat themselves every π units.

This command forces symmetry whether or not the fractal really exhibits it. A portion of the fractal is calculated, and the symmetrical parts are reflections of the calculated part. The Stone Soupers have attempted to automatically use symmetry when it exists, but they have not caught every case. For example, any of the fractal types with "fn" in their name (such as "fn+fn") exhibit different symmetry depending on which functions are used to replace "fn" in the formula. If you are experimenting with a fractal and can see that it has symmetry that Fractint doesn't know about, you can set the symmetry with this command and make the fractal run faster, because fewer points have to be calculated. You can also apply symmetry just to change any fractal and see how it looks. If you type in

```
fractint symmetry=xyaxis
```

and plot the Mandelbrot fractal, you will see that it has changed. What is normally the upper left corner of the Mandelbrot image is reflected to the other three corners; the right half of the fractal is no longer the same.

textcolors=<aa>/<bb>/<cc>/...

Set text screen colors. Each value is a hexadecimal number, with the first digit the background color from 0 to 7, and the second digit the foreground color from 0 to 15. Hex color values are as follows:

0	*black*	8	*gray*
1	*blue*	9	*light blue*
2	*green*	A	*light green*
3	*cyan*	B	*light cyan*
4	*red*	C	*light red*
5	*magenta*	D	*light magenta*
6	*brown*	E	*yellow*
7	*white*	F	*bright white*

A total of 27 different colors can be specified, with their use in Fractint as follows:

Heading

1 Fractint version info

2 heading line development info (not used in released version)

Help

3 subheading

4 main text

5 instructions at bottom of screen

Menu, Selection Boxes, Parameter Input Boxes

6 background around box and instructions at bottom

7 low-intensity information

8 medium-intensity information

9 high-intensity information (e.g., heading)

10 current keyin field

11 current choice in multiple choice list

12 speed key prompt in multiple choice list

13 speed key keyin in multiple choice list

General (tab key display, IFS parameters, "thinking" display)

14 high-intensity information

15 medium-intensity information

16 low-intensity information

17 current keyin field

Disk Video

18 background around box

19 high-intensity information

20 low-intensity information

Diagnostic Messages

21 error

22 information

Credits Screen

23 bottom lines

24 high-intensity divider line

25 low-intensity divider line

26 primary authors

27 contributing authors

The default is textcolors = 1F/1A/2E/70/28/78/17/1F/1E/2F/
                                        5F/07/0D/71/70/78/0F/70/0E/0F/
                                        4F/20/17/20/28/0F/07

textcolors=mono

Set text screen colors to simple black and white. Use this if the shades of color do not show up well on your monochrome screen.

textsafe=yes no bios save

When you press (F1), (TAB), or (ESC) to switch from a graphics image to text mode, Fractint remembers the image and displays it next time you choose graphics mode. This is a fast method for saving the graphics screen, but it does not work perfectly for every graphics adapter in every video mode—especially high-resolution modes. If this method does not work on your computer, you can use the "textsafe" command to specify methods that are slower but safer. Try various "textsafe" options if you have the following display problems:

• A display image that is either garbled or overlaid with lines and dashes when you return to the graphics image after opening a menu, pressing (TAB), or pressing (F1) for help.

• A blank screen when you start running Fractint.

The following are the "Textsafe" options:

textsafe=yes

This option is the default. When you switch either to or from the graphics mode,

Fractint saves only the part of video memory that EGA and VGA adaptors are supposed to modify during the mode change.

textsafe=no

This option uses a monochrome, 640 × 200 × 2-mode to display text. It displays text quickly, but it uses characters that are chunky and, of course, colorless. If you use this option, specifying "textcolors=mono" might improve the text display.

bios

This option saves memory just as "textsafe=yes" does, but it uses the adaptor's BIOS routines to save and restore the graphics image. This option is fast, but it works perfectly on only a few adaptors

save

If all other options fail, try this one. It is slow, but it should work on all adaptors and in all modes. It directs Fractint to save and restore the entire image. Expanded or extended memory is used if enough is available; otherwise, a temporary disk file is used.

FRACTAL TYPES

3

Fractint is capable of creating a tremendous variety of fractals. If you press ⓉT, you'll see the list of the built-in fractal types that Fractint can generate. (See Figure 3-1.) You should understand that there really isn't a whole lot of rhyme or reason to this list of fractal types or to their names. Whatever fractal algorithms tickled the Stone Soupers' fancy made their way into Fractint. In fact, fractal formulas have been contributed by enthusiasts in dozens of countries all around the world, and new ones are added constantly. Some of the algorithms in Fractint have been obtained from the classic fractal books such as Peitgen and Richter's *The Beauty of Fractals*, Peitgen and Saupe's *The Science of Fractal Images,* or Barnsley's *Fractals Everywhere*. All these fractals and their sources are described in this chapter. Despite the fact that Fractint already contains over sixty built-in fractals, as sure as fractals are infinitely complex, the abundance of contributions for Fractint will continue to grow!

Some of Fractint's "types" are specific fractals based on a particular formula. (Other Fractint types allow you to custom design your own fractals by specifying your own equations for Fractint to calculate.) The first section of this chapter, Built-In Fractal Types, describes each of the types available when you press the ⓉT key. The second section, User-Defined Fractals, describes how you can use Fractint to create your own fractal types.

```
Special FRACTINT  Version 15.11 for the Waite Group's Fractal Creations

                            Select a Fractal Type

barnsleyj1      barnsleyj2      barnsleyj3      barnsleym1      barnsleym2
barnsleym3      bif+simpi       bif=simpi       biflambda       bifurcation
cmplxmarksjul   cmplxmarksmand  complexbasin    complexnewton   diffusion
fn(z*z)         fn*fn           fn*z+z          fn+fn           formula
gingerbreadman  henon           ifs             ifs3d           julfn+exp
julfn+zsqrd     julia           julia4          julibrot        julzpower
julzzpwr        kamtorus        kamtorus3d      lambda          lambdafn
lorenz          lorenz3d        lsystem         magnet1j        magnet1m
magnet2j        magnet2m        mandel          mandel4         mandelfn
mandellambda    manfn+exp       manfn+zsqrd     manowar         manowarj
manzpower       manzzpwr        marksjulia      marksmandel     newtbasin
newton          pickover        plasma          popcorn         popcornjul
rossler3d       sierpinski      spider          sqr(1/fn)       sqr(fn)
test            tetrate         unity

                 Use the cursor keys or type a value to make a selection
           Press ENTER for highlighted choice, ESCAPE to back out, or F1 for help
```

Figure 3-1 Fractint's built-in fractal types

BUILT-IN FRACTAL TYPES

In this chapter, each fractal type has a page or more describing the fractal in a common format. The following is a brief description of what you will find in these pages.

FRACTAL CATEGORY

The fractal category tells to which of the fractal families discussed in Chapter 1 this particular type belongs. Some of the possibilities are escape-time fractals, chaotic orbit fractals, bifurcation fractals, iterated function systems (IFS) fractals, L-systems fractals, and random fractals.

FORMAL NAME

The formal name is how the fractal is known to non-Fractint users.

FRACTAL TYPE

The name of the fractal as it appears in Fractint's list of types shown with the ⓣ command. You use this name when you want to identify or select the fractal and display it.

FORMULA

A mathematical description of the algorithm used to generate the fractal. For most fractals, the pixels on your computer screen are mapped to a rectangle in the complex plane, and the procedure for calculating the fractal must be repeated for each complex number located at every pixel in that rectangle. The variables z and c in these formulas appear repeatedly and refer to complex numbers. Generally, the pixel's x- and y-coordinates correspond to the real and imaginary portions for the values of z or c. For Mandelbrot sets, the screen pixel is used for the value of c, and the initial value of z is set to zero. For Julia sets, the value of c is kept constant, and the screen coordinates are used for the initial value of z.

Occasionally we will refer to the real or imaginary portions of a complex number using x and y, respectively, with a subscript denoting which variable it belongs to. For example, x_z refers to the real portion of the variable z and y_c refers to the imaginary portion of the variable c. Complex numbers enclosed in absolute value bars, such as $|z|$, mean the modulus of the complex number. The *modulus* of a complex number is the absolute distance of the number's corresponding point on the Cartesian plane from the origin. More information on complex number theory is available in Appendix D.

Some fractals, however, do not use complex numbers at all, but rather treat the screen coordinates as two separate real numbers. For these variables we will use x and y without subscripts.

With the exception of Julibrots, three-dimensional fractals do not use complex mathematics. For these fractals, the variables x, y, and z are used as real numbers referencing a position in three-dimensional space.

COMMAND LINE

This command, when typed at the DOS prompt, will generate the image shown at the top of the page. You can either use ⓣ and set parameters, or you can enter the text under the figure from the DOS command line and press (ENTER). After Fractint has started, press (ENTER) a second time and select a video mode compatible with your machine. The image generated will be in black and white with the higher iteration levels in darker shades of grey if you add the statement "map=altern" to the command line.

DESCRIPTION

The description covers facts about the fractal type. In this section you'll find out more about the math behind the fractal, where the fractal came from, hidden or subtle facts, details on how it acts or looks, and the like.

PARAMETERS

Most fractal types have numerical parameters that alter their appearance. When selecting a type from Fractint's type list, you are prompted for these. While normally you can just press (ENTER) and ignore these parameters, here we tell you the meaning of the parameters, their default values, and the effect of changing them. For example, many of the Mandelbrot fractal types accept a perturbation parameter, which is used to warp the fractal. The effect of setting this to a non-zero value is similar to viewing the fractal through a carnival mirror. Internally, this is done by adding the perturbation variable to the initial value of z, but the on-screen effect causes the fractal to be pulled, stretched, and squeezed out of its original shape.

While you can just press (RETURN) and accept the defaults, changing parameters can often create some amazing effects and in some cases generate entirely new fractals to explore.

EXPLORER

Locations in the fractal we believe are places to zoom in to for most intriguing and mysterious shapes.

SPECIAL EFFECTS

Collections of Fractint settings that give other means of viewing, such as 3-D.

WARNINGS

Problems to avoid or machine-specific restrictions. For example, the Julibrot fractal can be generated only on a 256-color machine or using a 256-color disk video mode.

ALTERNATE COLOR MAPS

Suggested color maps to try. Color maps allow you to reset the color palette to bring out or enhance different characteristics of the fractal. A few selected maps can be found on the companion disk as files with the extension ".map".

HISTORY AND CREDITS

Who discovered this fractal, who contributed it to Fractint, or how it was obtained.

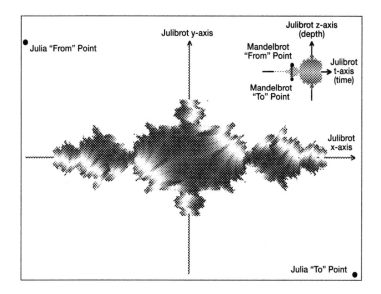

BARNSLEYJI

FRACTAL CATEGORY	Escape-time fractal
FORMAL NAME	None
FRACTAL TYPE	barnsleyj1
FORMULA	$(z-1)c,\ x_z >= 0$ $(z+1)\|c\|/c, x_z < 0$

COMMAND LINE

```
fractint maxiter=20000 inside=255 logmap=-1 type=barnsleyj1
```

DESCRIPTION

Because the formula has two cases, depending on whether the real part of the orbit value (x_z) is positive or not, the image is broken up into a patchwork quilt of colored patterns.

This fractal type is a family of Julia sets corresponding to the Mandelbrot fractal type barnsleym1.

PARAMETERS

Real part of parameter	*0.6*
Imaginary part of parameter	*1.1*
Bailout value (0 means default)	*0.0*

As with all Julia variants, the first two parameters determine the value of c in the formula, and they result in a different image. Even a small change will sometimes produce a radically different fractal. The best guide for how the parameters affect the image is to generate the Mandelbrot map of the formula (fractal type barnsleym1) and then use the space bar to toggle to the Julia set. Fractint will use the coordinates for the point in the center of the screen as the real and imaginary parameters.

EXPLORER

Interesting barnsleyj1 images can be discovered by zooming in near the lake edge in barnsleym1, which is the Mandelbrot set for this Julia family, and toggling back to barnsleyj1 using the space bar. Try this in reverse, starting with barnsleyj1 using default parameters. You will notice that the image is a multicolored island surrounded by a blue ocean. Now press (SPACE). This will show you a barnsleym1 image with the zoom box centered on the point that represents the parameters values of the barnsleyj1 you just generated. If you look closely, you will see that the zoom box is centered on a colored part of the barnsleym1 lagoon. Now center the zoom box on the edge of the lake, and press (SPACE) again. You will see the Julia set with the island reduced to disconnected colored fragments. By making a series of images with the parameters values varying smoothly from those of the default barnsleyj1 to one exploded into fragments, you can chronicle all the steps and produce the effect of a fractal explosion.

SPECIAL EFFECTS

Here are some samples of an explosion sequence, created by heading due east on the barnsleym1 "map."

At the very start of the explosion

Real part of parameter	*0.52*
Imaginary part of parameter	*1.1*

During the explosion

Real part of parameter	*0.50*

After the explosion

Real part of parameter	*0.48*

HISTORY AND CREDITS

Dr. Michael Barnsley of the Georgia Institute of Technology originated this fractal type, and it was adapted for Fractint from the description in the book *Fractals Everywhere* by Dr. Barnsley.

BARNSLEYJ2

FRACTAL CATEGORY	Escape-time fractal
FORMAL NAME	None
FRACTAL TYPE	barnsleyj2
FORMULA	$(z - 1)\, c,\; x_z y_c + x_c y_z >= 0$
	$(z + 1)\, c,\; x_z y_c + x_c\, y_z < 0$

COMMAND LINE

```
fractint maxiter=20000 inside=255 logmap=-1 type=barnsleyj2
```

DESCRIPTION

This is a family of Julia sets corresponding to the Mandelbrot fractal type barnsleym2. Unlike the classic Mandelbrot, the Barnsley fractals tend to have a lot of chaotic patterns inland from the lake. These patterns are a mixture of large and small patches that arise from the two different formulas used for the generation.

A tremendous variety of images can be created with this type, many of which have a printed shirt design quality that is less fractal-like than some other types.

PARAMETERS

Real part of parameter	*0.6*
Imaginary part of parameter	*1.1*
Bailout value (0 means default)	*0.0*

The first two parameters determine the value of c in the formula. Small changes can sometimes give you a radically different image. For example, the following settings produce an image with very large lake areas:

Real part of parameter	*-.36*
Imaginary part of parameter	*1.14*

But with a slight change in each parameter, as follows, almost all the lake region disappears:

Real part of parameter	*-.39*
Imaginary part of parameter	*1.21*

EXPLORER

Interesting barnsleyj2 images can be discovered by zooming in near the lake edge in the barnsleym2 variant and toggling to barnsleyj2 using the space bar.

This time let's try varying values along the *y*-axis of the barnsleym2 Mandelbrot map. Start with the following settings:

Real part of parameter	*0.0*
Imaginary part of parameter	*1.5*

You will see a symmetrical barbell-shaped figure. Recalculate with the imaginary part of the parameter changed to 1.35, then 1.3, 1.29, and 1.28.

For another exploration, start with the generation of a barnsleym2 fractal. Note that the image has a horizontal discontinuity along the negative *x*-axis. Barnsleyj2 images corresponding to points in the top half of the image look very different than those corresponding to the bottom half. Zoom into the middle of the bottom island and hit the space bar to generate a barnsleyj2. With a little luck you can create some very fashionable designer Easter eggs this way!

SPECIAL EFFECTS

Try the almost-exploded image from the "explorer" sequence:

Real part of parameter	*0.0*
Imaginary part of parameter	*1.295*

Now try the designer Easter egg:

Real part of parameter	*-.2*
Imaginary part of parameter	*-.8*

HISTORY AND CREDITS

See the barnsleyj1 fractal type.

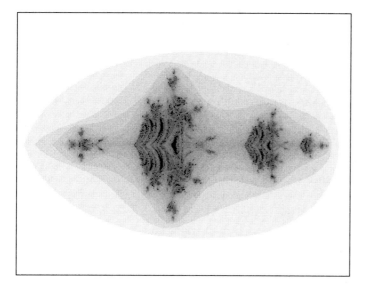

BARNSLEYJ3

FRACTAL CATEGORY	Escape-time fractal
FORMAL NAME	None
FRACTAL TYPE	barnsleyj3
FORMULA	$x_z^2 - y_z^2 - 1 + i\,2x_z y_z,\qquad\qquad x_z > 0$ $x_z^2 - y_z^2 + x_c x_z + i\,(2x_z y_z + y_c x_z),\; x_z <= 0$

COMMAND LINE

```
fractint maxiter=20000 inside=255 logmap=-1 type=barnsleyj3
```

DESCRIPTION

This is the Julia variant corresponding to the barnsleym3 Mandelbrot map. It looks very different from the other Barnsley Julia sets. The default parameter values yield an image that has several distinct islands of chaotic colors. With the right change of parameters these become lakes (see below).

PARAMETERS

Real part of parameter	*0.1*
Imaginary part of parameter	*0.36*
Bailout value (0 means default)	*0.0*

As with other Julia variants, the first two parameters determine the value of *c* in the formula, and give you a different image.

EXPLORER

Interesting barnsleyj3 images can be discovered by zooming in near the lake edge in the barnsleym3 variant and toggling to j3 using the space bar. To convert the chaotic islands to lakes, try the following:

> *Real part of parameter*   *0.1*
> *Imaginary part of parameter*   *0.2*

By creating a sequence of images with the imaginary part of the parameter moving from the default .36 to .2, you can watch the chaotic clumps explode, scatter into little islands, and then vanish into lakes. After you have created lakes with the above parameters, look closely at the right side of the image generated with the lakes parameters above. There is a nested sequence of smaller and smaller little lakes. Try zooming into the sequence for a wonderful example of fractal self-similarity, using the following command-line options:

```
fractint params=.1/.2 corners=1.57668/1.62464/-0.016723/
0.0192422
```

Because of the self-similarity of the nested lakes, it is almost impossible to tell from this image how far you have zoomed in.

HISTORY AND CREDITS

This type was originated by Dr. Barnsley. Tim Wegner modified the formula, which originally had only a real parameter, by making the parameter complex and adding the $y_c x_z$ term to take advantage of the imaginary part of the parameter.

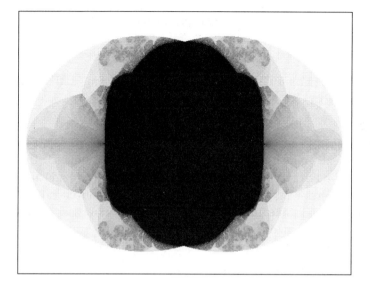

BARNSLEYM1

FRACTAL CATEGORY	Escape-time fractal
FORMAL NAME	Called "M1" by Dr. Barnsley
FRACTAL TYPE	barnsleym1
FORMULA	$(z - 1)c, x_z >= 0$
	$(z + 1)|c|/c, x_z < 0$

COMMAND LINE

```
fractint maxiter=20000 inside=255 logmap=-1 type=barnsleym1
```

DESCRIPTION

This is the Mandelbrot map for the Julia family barnsleyj1. The original Barnsleym1 is the inversion of Fractint's implementation, which means that we have turned the image inside out. Our version looks like a kind of barrier reef with a "maximum iterations" bay surrounded by a "minimum iterations" ocean. Barnsley's original was the reverse of this.

PARAMETERS

Real perturbation of Z(0)	*0*
Imaginary perturbation	*0*
Bailout value (0 means default)	*0*

As with other Mandelbrot maps, the first two parameters warp the fractal by perturbing the initialization value of z_0.

EXPLORER

See the barnsleyj1 description for explorations that involve toggling to the Julia variant with the space bar.

SPECIAL EFFECTS

Since the programmers of Fractint turned Dr. Barnsley's fractal inside out, you might try to experiment with the inversion option and restore his original. This is found as one of the advanced options accessed by the Ⓨ key command. Leave the center of inversion at (0,0), and play with the radius of inversion. Try values from about .75 to 1.5. Note that the outside of the "reef" now has gravelly detail, whereas in the uninverted version the inside has that appearance.

For an inverted barnsleym1, try typing the following at the command line:

```
fractint type=barnsleym1 invert=0.75/0/0
corners=-.835/.860/-.636/0.636
```

For two zooms in a search of wallpaper patterns, try the following:

```
fractint type=barnsleym1 invert=0.75/0/0
corners=-.686/-.486/.978/1.128
```

```
fractint type=barnsleym1 invert=0.75/0/0
corners=-1.166/-.966/.499/.649
```

HISTORY AND CREDITS

See fractal type barnsleyj1.

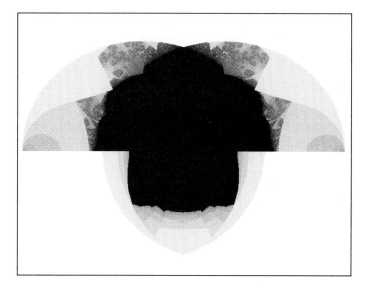

BARNSLEYM2

FRACTAL CATEGORY	Escape-time fractal
FORMAL NAME	Called "M2" by Dr. Barnsley
FRACTAL TYPE	barnsleym2

FORMULA

$$(z-1)c, \; x_z\,y_c + x_c\,y_z \quad >= 0$$
$$(z+1)c, \; x_z\,y_c + x_c\,y_z \quad < 0$$

COMMAND LINE

```
fractint maxiter=20000 inside=255 logmap=-1 type=barnsleym2
```

DESCRIPTION

This is a Mandelbrot map of the Julia family barnsleyj2. Related fractal types are barnsleym1 and barnsleym3.

PARAMETERS

Real perturbation of Z(0)	*0*
Imaginary perturbation	*0*
Bailout value (0 means default)	*0*

As with other Mandelbrot variants, the first two parameters warp the fractal by perturbing the initialization value of z_0.

EXPLORER

See the barnsleyj1 description for explorations that involve toggling to the Julia variant with the space bar.

HISTORY AND CREDITS

See the fractal type barnsleyj1.

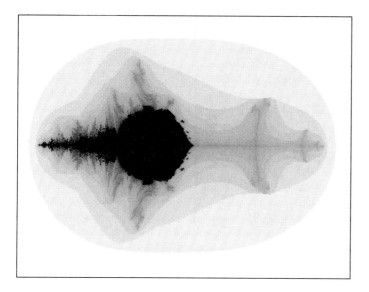

BARNSLEYM3

FRACTAL CATEGORY	Escape-time fractal
FORMAL NAME	None
FRACTAL TYPE	barnsleym3

FORMULA

$$x_z^2 - y_z^2 - 1 + i2x_z y_z, \qquad x_z > 0$$
$$x_z^2 - y_z^2 + x_c x_z + i(2x_z y_z + y_c x_z), \quad x_z <= 0$$

COMMAND LINE

```
fractint maxiter=20000 inside=255 logmap=-1 type=barnsleym3
```

DESCRIPTION

For a description and other details, see the barnsleym1 fractal type.

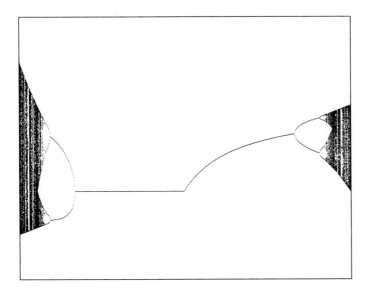

BIFURCATION: SINEPI

FRACTAL CATEGORY	Bifurcation
FORMAL NAME	None
FRACTAL TYPE	bif=sinpi
FORMULA	$x' = r\sin(\pi * x)$

COMMAND LINE

```
fractint maxiter=20000 type=bif=sinpi
```

DESCRIPTION

This fractal looks identical to the Robert May Bifurcation fractal (see the biflambda fractal type), but it is based on an entirely different formula. The related fractal type bif+sinpi looks similar to the bifurcation fractal type. The reason the fractals are identical is that recursive iterated functions have a universal relationship similar to the way circles are universally related to π. The number π is the ratio of the circumference of a circle to its diameter. Iterated functions have a similar ratio:

$$\frac{r_n - r_{n-1}}{r_{n+1} - r_n} = 4.66920160\ldots$$

where r_n is the value of x that produces a maximum value for y for a function. In other words, the ratio of the difference between successive parameters that produce a maximum is equal to a constant, known as *Feigenbaum's Number*.

This is true whether the function used is $rx(1 - x)$, $r\sin(\pi * x)$, or any other function that has a single differential maximum. Feigenbaum's Number appears in all types of situations ranging from fluid-flow turbulence to electronic oscillators to chemical reactions and even to the Mandelbrot set. As a matter of fact, the budding of the Mandelbrot set along the negative x-axis occurs at intervals of Feigenbaum's Number.

Other related fractal types are bif+sinpi, biflambda, and bifurcation.

EXPLORER

Try zooming in and finding the exact transition from stable oscillations, where you see multiple branching, to the region of chaos. Just when you think you've found it, switch to a higher iteration level and a higher screen resolution. Surprise—there is no transition point! With each zoom you will find smaller and smaller periods between the stable and chaotic regions. Chaos and stability are kept separate by an infinite period. Note that even the smallest area of chaos has areas of stability within it.

HISTORY AND CREDITS

Mitchell Feigenbaum discovered this universal number in 1976 while investigating the maximum points in Robert May's bifurcation formula (see the biflambda fractal type) at Los Alamos National Laboratory in New Mexico. The computer he used for the study was extremely slow, so to save time he guessed at the value for next using his HP-65 hand-held calculator. As time progressed, the constant he was using for his guessing became more accurate and more closely matched the numbers returned by the computer. When he changed from a bifurcation formula to one based on the sine function and came up with the same constant, he realized he was on to something big. His constant was first published in the *Journal of Statistical Physics* 19 (1978) in an article entitled "Quantitative Universality for a Class of Nonlinear Transformations."

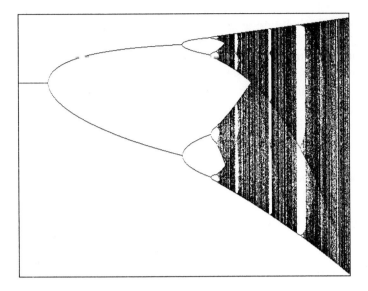

BIFURCATION: SUMMATION SINEPI

FRACTAL CATEGORY   Bifurcation

FORMAL NAME   None

FRACTAL TYPE   bif+sinpi

FORMULA $x' = x + r\sin(\pi * x)$

COMMAND LINE
`fractint maxiter=20000 type=bif+sinpi`

DESCRIPTION   See the bif=sinpi fractal type.

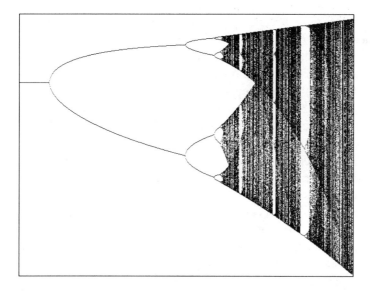

BIFURCATION

FRACTAL CATEGORY	Bifurcation
FORMAL NAME	Verhulst Bifurcation
FRACTAL TYPE	bifurcation
FORMULA	$x' = x + rx\,(1 - x)$

COMMAND LINE

```
fractint maxiter=20000 map=altern type=bifurcation
```

DESCRIPTION

This fractal models a very simplified abstract population growth. The variable x in the formula, which ranges from 0 to 1, represents the number of individuals in the population as a fraction of the total possible. Changes in the value of r can produce stable populations or chaotic ones. As the points are plotted from left to right, the value of r, or the population's growth rate, is continually increased from 1.9 to 3.0 for the initial screen (this value is varied from -2.0 to 4.0 for the biflambda fractal type). The behavior of the population numbers is plotted on the vertical y-axis, which is scaled from zero to 1.34 (-1.0 to 2.0 for biflambda).

For relatively low values of r the population remains steady. Raising the population growth (r) creates a "boom and bust" oscillation pattern, similar to many population oscillations occurring in the real world. The population will rise to a peak then crash to a low, cycling between two constant levels. This is where you see the line split in two, or *bifurcate*.

At some rate beyond this point, the oscillations split again, into a 4-level oscillation pattern. Higher still, and they split into 8- and 16-level oscillations. Then you reach the point of chaos. The population level never settles out into a regular pattern or steady level when the growth rate is at these levels. It constantly fluctuates to unpredictable levels. Two populations with the same growth rate but which differ in number by only one individual will have wildly different populations several generations later. Furthermore, you can't predict ahead of time which one will be higher!

At still higher levels of *r*, pockets of stability appear at odd period levels. The first is a 3-level oscillation. This splits into a 6-level oscillation, then 12-level, 24-level, and at some higher level chaos reappears. This alternating pattern of chaos and stability continues on for all higher growth rates.

Related fractal types are biflambda, bif+sinpi, and bif=sinpi.

EXPLORER
Try zooming in and finding the exact transition from stable oscillations to chaos. Just when you think you've found it, switch to a higher iteration level and a higher screen resolution. Surprise—there is no transition point! With each zoom you will find higher and higher periods between the stable and chaotic regions. Chaos and stability are kept separate by an infinite period.

HISTORY AND CREDITS
This equation was originally studied by P. F. Verhulst in 1845. It was later studied by Robert May in 1971. The coding for this fractal originally came from Phil Wilson and was later revised by Kev Allen.

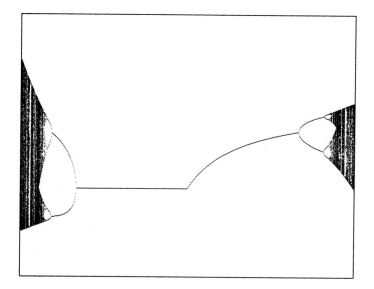

BIFURCATION LAMBDA

FRACTAL CATEGORY	Bifurcation
FORMAL NAME	Robert May bifurcation
FRACTAL TYPE	biflambda
FORMULA	$x' = rx(1 - x)$

COMMAND LINE

```
fractint maxiter=20000 type=biflambda
```

DESCRIPTION

See the bifurcation fractal type.

HISTORY AND CREDITS

This equation was originally studied by P. F. Verhulst in 1845. It was later studied by Robert May in 1971. The coding for this fractal originally came from Phil Wilson and was later revised by Kev Allen.

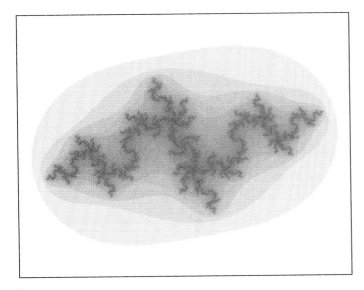

COMPLEX MARK'S JULIA

FRACTAL CATEGORY	Escape-time fractal
FORMAL NAME	Complex Mark's Julia
FRACTAL TYPE	cmplxmarksjul
FORMULA	$z^2 c^{(p-1)} + c$

COMMAND LINE
```
fractint maxiter=20000 inside=255 logmap=-1
type=cmplxmarksjul
```

DESCRIPTION

These fractals are the Julia sets associated with the different points from Complex Mark's Mandelbrot. As with other Julia set families there are an infinite number of complex Julia sets.

PARAMETERS

Real part of parameter	*0.3*
Imaginary part of parameter	*0.6*
Real part of degree	*1*
Imag part of degree	*0*
Bailout value (0 means use default)	*0*

The real and imaginary parameters define the value of c in the formula. The value of z is initialized to the coordinates of the pixel color being calculated. The real and imaginary parts of the degree are used to set the complex value of p in the formula.

EXPLORER

With an infinite number of sets to choose from, a complete exploration of this fractal type is not possible. Fortunately, the cmplxmarksmand fractal is a catalog of all the different Julia sets associated with this formula. Find an interesting spot in cmplxmarksmand and press the space bar to toggle to the Julia set associated with the point in the center of the screen.

HISTORY AND CREDITS

See Complex Mark's Mandelbrot.

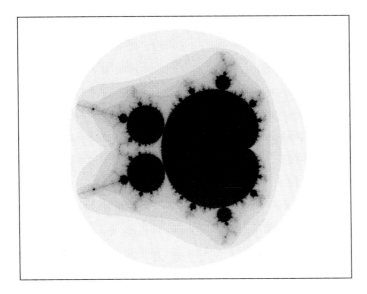

COMPLEX MARK'S MANDELBROT

FRACTAL CATEGORY	Escape-time fractal
FORMAL NAME	Complex Mark's Mandelbrot
FRACTAL TYPE	cmplxmarksmand
FORMULA	$z^2 c^{(p\text{-}1)} + c$

COMMAND LINE
```
fractint maxiter=20000 inside=255 logmap=-1 params=0/0/
1.1/0 type=cmplxmarksmand
```

DESCRIPTION

This fractal uses the traditional Mandelbrot fractal formula as a base for an even more interesting fractal. As can be seen by the formula, with the period variable p equal to $(1, 0)$, the formula reduces to the traditional Mandelbrot set, as follows:

$$z^2 c^{(p\text{-}1)} + c = z^2 c^{((1+i0)\text{-}1)} + c$$
$$= z^2 c^0 + c$$
$$= z^2 + c$$

As with the traditional Mandelbrot set, the initial value of z for each pixel calculation is zero. Other integer real values for p draw multiple Mandelbrot sets

extending outward from the origin. Using imaginary and negative periods produce some rather unexpected results. No matter how bizarre the initial drawing,
however, you can always find a tiny, undistorted Mandelbrot set somewhere in
the drawing.

The cmplxmarksjul fractals are the Julia sets associated with each point on
the drawing. The fractal type marksmandel is a faster version of this fractal.

PARAMETERS

Real perturbation of Z(0)	*0*
Imaginary perturbation of Z(0)	*0*
Real part of degree	*1*
Imag part of degree	*0*
Bailout value (0 means use default)	*0*

The real and imaginary perturbations warp the drawings. For exploration we'd
recommend using zeros for these parameters. The real and imaginary degree
values are used to set the complex value of p in the fractal formula. The default
settings produce the same old boring Mandelbrot set. Changing the real and
imaginary portions of the degree gets some action going.

> *Real part of degree*   *1.1*

Using a degree with a real value greater than 1 (such as 1.1 above) splits the
negative "tail" of the Mandelbrot set in two. Continue drawing sets with higher
values of the real part and the two tails move towards vertical. At 2.0 they are
both straight up and down. Go beyond 2.0 and a new negative tail begins to
form.

> *Real part of degree*   *0.8*

Use real values for the degree of less than one and the Mandelbrot set folds
in on itself. First the negative tail of the set is absorbed into the body of the set,
and knobs around the set move steadily towards the negative *x*-axis. At the
above settings, the knobs that were at the top and bottom of the set have moved
to 45 degree angles off the negative *x*-axis.

> *Real part of degree*   *0.55*

At these values the two knobs have merged into one, forming a new negative
tail. This drawing looks like a miniature version of the original Mandelbrot set.
Progressively lowering the real value of the degree causes more and more of the
set to absorb itself. At a value of zero there is only a point in the center of the
screen.

> *Real part of degree*   *-0.6*

With negative values for the real portion of the degree, the set is turned inside out. Using progressively more negative values causes more of the set to grow out of the negative x-axis.

Real part of degree	*1.0*
Imag part of degree	*0.1*

Using imaginary values as part of the degree causes the Mandelbrot set to skew into imaginary planes outside of the two-dimensional drawing. With degrees having a nonzero imaginary component there is always a split along the negative x-axis. The set grows smaller as you move around the circumference in a counterclockwise direction if the imaginary values are positive. With negative imaginary values the set grows larger in this direction.

EXPLORER

Whatever way you prefer to view the regular Mandelbrot set will also work well with this set. We would recommend setting inside=0 in either the command line or sstools.ini or from the Ⓧ key options menu so as to distinguish the inside of the set from the outside. This is especially important with negative real values or when the degree is part imaginary.

Setting the firestrm color map (map=firestrm) with logmap=-1 and maxiter=31000 (again, this can be done from the command line, in SSTOOLS.INI, or from the Ⓧ key options menu) also produces excellent drawings. The small amount of extra time needed to draw the image at the higher iteration value is well worth the wait.

HISTORY AND CREDITS

Mark Peterson originated the fractal formula and added the marksmandel fractal to Fractint. In a later version he added the code allowing the period to be complex.

COMPLEX NEWTON'S BASIN

FRACTAL CATEGORY	Escape-time fractal
FORMAL NAME	Newton's basin
FRACTAL TYPE	complexbasin
FORMULA	$\dfrac{(n\text{-}1)\,z^n + r}{nz^{(n\text{-}1)}}$
COMMAND LINE	

```
fractint type=complexbasin params=10/3/1/0 maxiter=20000
```

DESCRIPTION

Many colors in this fractal exist next to each other, but no color actually touches another. At every color boundary an intricately beautiful pattern forms, gently separating the two. The pattern itself is made of many colors and not one of these touches another. Each color of the pattern is kept separate by the pattern itself.

There are regions where colors may appear to touch when the value of n has an imaginary component. Then the fractal skews into imaginary complex planes along the negative x-axis that are not shown by Fractint. The skewing also appears in the smaller copies. Where the colors appear to touch, the fractal actually continues on into other complex planes.

Near the origin, and other points on the fractal, the colors seem to merge into a region of blue or black. This is where Fractint reached the maximum allowed number of iterations and gave up trying to determine the color. In this situation Fractint assigns the inside color as a way of saying, "I don't know what the solutions are here. Your guess is as good as mine." Setting a higher iteration level will push back, but not entirely remove, the "unknown" regions.

With the Newton fractal types, which includes complexbasin, complexnewton, newton, and newtbasin, Fractint uses Newton's method for finding the solutions to the equation $z = \sqrt[n]{r}$. Newton's method involves successive iterations of the equation $z' = z - \frac{p(z)}{p'(z)}$ to approximate the solution. The function $p(z)$ is the equation written as a polynomial. The symbol $p'(z)$ represents the derivative of the polynomial. Each iteration of the equation is a "guess" that rapidly converges on a correct solution. In many cases there is more than one solution.

Fractint uses a generalized equation for Newton's method applied to $z = \sqrt[n]{r}$. The equation is first rewritten as a polynomial equal to zero and then applied to the Newton's method $z - \frac{p(z)}{p'(z)}$, as follows:

$$z = \sqrt[n]{r} \;\rightarrow\; z^n = r$$
$$\rightarrow\; z^n - r = 0$$

$$p(z) = z^n - r, \quad \text{polynomial}$$
$$p'(z) = nz^{(n-1)} \quad \text{derivative of the polynomial}$$

$$z - \frac{p(z)}{p'(z)} = z - \frac{z^{(n)} - r}{nz^{(n-1)}}$$
$$= \frac{z(nz^{(n-1)}) - (z^n - r)}{nz^{(n-1)}}$$
$$= \frac{(nz^n - z^n) + r}{nz^{(n-1)}}$$
$$= \frac{(n-1)z^n + r}{nz^{(n-1)}}$$

The initial value, or "guess," of z is the screen coordinate for the pixel color being calculated. This guess is plugged into the generalized formula. The result from this calculation is used as the next value of z and run through the equation again. With each iteration Fractint determines whether the value of $p(z)$ is less than a predetermined threshold. When this happens, Fractint determines which root was found and displays the corresponding color. The value of n can also be a complex number. Rather than thinking of Fractint as solving complex roots, it is sometimes easier to think of Fractint as finding the values of z that satisfy the equation $z^{(x+iy)} = r$.

The fractal type complexnewton is similar to this fractal except it displays the number of iterations performed rather than the solution. The fractal types newton and newtbasin are faster versions of this fractal that work strictly with the integer roots of the number 1.

PARAMETERS

Real part of degree	*3*
Imag part of degree	*0*
Real part of root	*1*
Imag part of root	*0*

The default parameters tell Fractint to look for the solutions to the equation $x = \sqrt[3]{1}$. The real part of degree and imag part of degree set the value of n in the formula. The variables real part of root and imag part of root set the value of r in the formula. An odd integer value for the degree produces one fractal arm along the negative x-axis and n-1 evenly spaced arms extending outward from the origin. The actual solutions to $x = \sqrt[3]{1}$ are $(1 - i0)$, and $-(\frac{1}{2} + i\frac{\sqrt{3}}{2})$ and $-(\frac{1}{2} - i\frac{\sqrt{3}}{2})$.

The fractal arms are always found between the actual solutions to the equation.

Real part of degree	*3*
Imag part of degree	*0*
Real part of root	*10*
Imag part of root	*0*

These parameters tell Fractint to look for solutions to $z^3 = 10$. Raising the value of the real portion of the root enlarges the fractal arms.

Real part of degree	*3*
Imag part of degree	*0*
Real part of root	*1*
Imag part of root	*1*

These parameters set the equation to $z^3 = (1 + i)$. Adding an imaginary component to the root rotates the fractal arms slightly in the counterclockwise direction.

Real part of degree	*3.5*
Imag part of degree	*0*
Real part of root	*1*
Imag part of root	*0*

These parameters instruct Fractint to find the values of z that satisfy the equation $z^{3.5} = 1$. Fractional values above an odd integer split the arm along the negative x-axis and rotate the other arms towards the positive x-axis.

Real part of degree	*4*

Real even integers for the degree produce n evenly spaced arms extending out from the origin with no arm on the negative x-axis.

Real part of degree   *4.75*

Raising the Real part of degree to fractional real values above an even integer causes a new fractal arm to form along the negative x-axis. The fractal arms above and below the negative x-axis are rotated towards the positive x-axis.

Real part of degree   *10*
Imag part of degree   *3*
Real part of root   *1*
Imag part of root   *0*

These parameters tell Fractint to look for values of z that satisfy $z^{(10+i3)} = 1$. The hitch is there are an *infinite* number of solutions! These solutions fall along an exponential spiral around the origin. This is best seen in the drawing of the complexnewton fractal using the same parameters. The blue areas of the complexnewton fractal surround the actual solutions to the equation. If the imaginary portion of the degree is positive, the spiral is counterclockwise. Negative imaginary portions produce a clockwise exponential spiral of solutions.

Fractint clips the solutions to those existing on the imaginary plane based between $-\pi$ and $+\pi$. The spiral of solutions both above and below the negative axis continue on in other imaginary complex planes based on positive and negative multiples of 2π. The remaining solutions are skewed into other complex planes. For a more detailed explanation of the reasons why there are an infinite number of solutions, see "More Exotic Operations: Complex Transcendentals" in Appendix D.

Real part of degree   *-5*

Negative real values for the degree effectively turn the fractal inside out.

EXPLORER

Zoom in on any section of a Newton fractal and you will find a repetition of the same overall pattern. No matter how high a zoom level, so long as you stay within the accuracy limits of the Fractint calculation algorithm, the pattern will repeat itself.

WARNINGS

This fractal is very slow if your machine does not have a floating-point co-processor.

ALTERNATE COLOR MAPS

Alternate maps that use a smooth palette are not recommended with this fractal type. The colors are numerically too close together to differentiate in a smooth palette such as firestrm.map or grey.map.

HISTORY AND CREDITS

The actual fractal characteristics of Newton's method for roots was first discovered by John Hubbard in Orsay, France. The first fractal types newton and newtbasin were coded into Fractint by Tim Wegner. Lee Crocker wrote a more efficient algorithm using FPU-specific assembly language. Mark Peterson wrote the complexnewton and complexbasin fractal type variations.

COMPLEX NEWTON

FRACTAL CATEGORY	Escape-time fractal
FORMAL NAME	Newton
FRACTAL TYPE	complexnewton
FORMULA	$\dfrac{(n\text{-}1)\,z^n + r}{nz^{(n\text{-}1)}}$

COMMAND LINE

```
fractint maxiter=20000 inside=255 logmap=-1 params=10/3/1/
0 type=complexnewton
```

DESCRIPTION

This fractal is identical to the fractal type complexbasin except the colors represent the number of iterations Fractint required to find the solution. As with complexbasin the iteration formula above is a generalization of Newton's method for finding solutions to $z = \sqrt[n]{r}$, where z, n, and r are complex numbers. The fractal description for complexbasin has a detailed explanation of Newton's method.

The fractal types newton and newtbasin are faster versions of the complexnewton and complexbasin that restrict the variable n to positive integers greater than or equal to 3 and restrict the variable r to a value of 1. The closer a pixel is to the solution of $z = \sqrt[n]{r}$, the more rapidly Newton's method converges. Consequently, the color that represents the numerical value of 1, which is blue if you are using the default palette, marks the pixels that are closest to the actual solution. Color cycling this type of fractal is like moving through an infinitely long tunnel.

PARAMETERS

Real part of degree	*3*
Imag part of degree	*0*
Real part of root	*1*
Imag part of root	*0*

The default parameters tell Fractint to look for the solutions to the equation $x = \sqrt[3]{1}$. The real part of degree and imag part of degree set the value of n in the formula. The variables real part of root and imag part of root set the value of r in the formula. An odd integer value for the degree produces one fractal arm along the negative x-axis and n-1 evenly spaced arms extending outward from the origin. The actual solutions to $x = \sqrt[3]{1}$ are $(1 + i0)$, and $(-\frac{1}{2} + i\frac{\sqrt{3}}{2})$, and $(-\frac{1}{2} - i\frac{\sqrt{3}}{2})$.

The fractal arms are always found between the actual solutions to the equation.

The effects of variations on the parameters for the complexnewton are identical to those for the complexbasin.

EXPLORER

Zoom in on any section of a Newton fractal and you will find a repetition of the same overall pattern in different colors. Higher zooms may require the use of higher maximum iteration levels and use of logarithmic color to prevent overflowing the number of colors available on your machine.

ALTERNATE COLOR MAPS

Alternate maps that use a smooth palette work well with this fractal type.

HISTORY AND CREDITS

See the complexbasin fractal type.

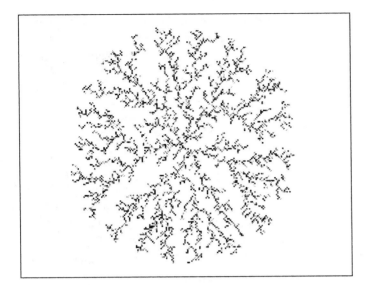

DIFFUSION LIMITED AGGREGATION

FRACTAL CATEGORY	Random Fractal
FORMAL NAME	None
FRACTAL TYPE	diffusion

COMMAND LINE

```
fractint type=diffusion params=1 map=altern
```

DESCRIPTION

This fractal type begins as a single point in the center of the screen. Fractint then randomly generates points around the pixel until it finds a point adjacent to a point already assigned a color, at which time its location is fixed and the next sequential color is assigned. This process continues until the edges of the screen are reached. This process is best understood by watching the orbits as the fractal is generated (use the ⓞ key to toggle on and off the orbits).

PARAMETERS

Border size   10

The border size limits how the point is allowed to wander away from the colored pixel region. Lowering the number reduces the generation time but results in more densely packed branches. Higher numbers take much longer to generate but result in more delicate structures.

ALTERNATE COLOR MAPS

Continuous palette maps, such as firestrm.map or grey.map, work best with this fractal type.

HISTORY AND CREDITS

Diffusion was inspired by a *Scientific American* article a few years back. Adrian Mariano provided the code and documentation for Fractint.

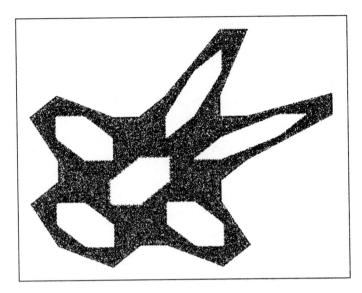

GINGERBREADMAN

FRACTAL CATEGORY	Orbital fractal
FORMAL NAME	Gingerbreadman
FRACTAL TYPE	gingerbreadman
FORMULA	$x' = 1 - y + |x|$ $y' = x$

SCREEN DUMP

```
fractint type=gingerbreadman maxiter=20000
```

DESCRIPTION

Hot from the mathematical oven—a cookie fractal. We tried to think of something intelligent to say about this fractal type, but it's hard to be serious about a fractal that looks like something you'd find in your Christmas stocking. The orbit traces out a gingerbreadman lying on his side. Just when you think he is finished baking, you will see some new pixels being added to his outline. Don't wait for him to finish—he bakes forever!

EXPLORER

Zoom in on the "skin" section of the gingerbreadman and you'll find smaller copies of the fellow. The gingerbreadman is a good fractal to use to practice the rotating zoom box feature. Reveal the zoom box by pressing (PGUP) or clicking on the left mouse button. You can rotate the zoom box by using the (CTRL) (KEYPAD +) and (CTRL) (KEYPAD -) keys or moving the mouse left or right while holding down the right button. After rotating the zoom box, press (ENTER) or double-click the left mouse button to redraw the image. Can you make the gingerbreadman stand up?

HISTORY AND CREDITS

The gingerbreadman is from Robert L. Devaney's description in *The Science of Fractal Images*.

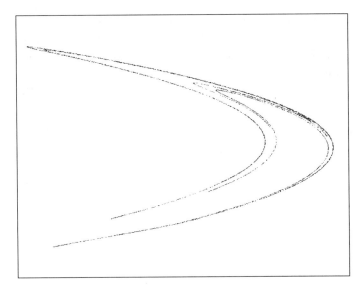

HENON FRACTALS

FRACTAL CATEGORY	Orbital fractal
FORMAL NAME	Henon
FRACTAL TYPE	henon
FORMULA	$x' = 1 + y - ax^2$
	$y' = bx$

COMMAND LINE

`fractint type=henon maxiter=20000`

DESCRIPTION

This fractal type, named after its founder, Michael Henon, came from an investigation into the orbits of astronomical objects. The Henon fractal is an example of a very simple dynamic system that never settles into a stable, periodic cycle. With each iteration of the two equations, the new x and y positions are plotted. The orbit tracings form a characteristic banana shape. On closer inspection of any line, you will find it composed of many thinner lines. Each of these lines is made up of even thinner lines. Every line in the fractal is composed of a cluster of infinitely thin lines. The fractional dimension of the henon fractal type is somewhere between 1.0 and 2.0.

PARAMETERS

a	*1.4*
b	*0.3*

The *a* and *b* parameters are used as the constants in the formula. Changing them to other values will usually result in the iterations falling into a periodic loop.

EXPLORER

Zoom in on any line section and you'll see a collection of thinner lines. You may have to wait a considerable time at high zooms for enough of the iteration points to fall inside your zoom box and form the lines.

HISTORY AND CREDITS

Michael Henon, of Nice Observatory in France, discovered this fractal in 1976.

ITERATED FUNCTION SYSTEMS

FRACTAL CATEGORY	Iterated Function Systems (IFS)
FORMAL NAME	Iterated Function Systems
FRACTAL TYPE	ifs
FORMULA	$\left(\dfrac{x'}{y'}\right) = \left(\dfrac{ab}{cd}\right)\left(\dfrac{x}{y}\right) + \left(\dfrac{e}{f}\right)$
COMMAND LINE	

```
fractint type=ifs
```

DESCRIPTION

IFS is another Fractint universe disguised as a humble fractal type. There is no limit to the variety of fractals you can make with this one type alone. Iterated Function Systems are directly inspired by the idea of self-similarity. Self-similarity is the quality an object possesses when its parts are miniatures of the whole (see Chapter 1). Each IFS fractal is defined by several equations that specify different self-similarities that exist in the fractal. You can change those equations and create new fractals using the Ⓘ command.

The default IFS fractal in Fractint is a delicately curved fern. There are four transformations that define this fern. The first maps the whole fern to the fern that remains after cutting off the bottom two fronds. This transformation is the source of the curling fern tip. Two more transformations define the relationship between the whole fern and the two bottom fronds. If you look closely, you can see that these are indeed copies of the whole fern. The last transformation isn't what you would really think of as self-similarity—it maps the whole fern to the stem at the bottom.

Fractint uses the random form of IFS generation. This means that any point can be used to start, and each point is plotted and then transformed by the random choice of one of the transformations. You will see a collection of points appearing on the screen like raindrops on a window which slowly build up to the fractal shape. When new colors start to overlap older points, the next sequential color in the palette is assigned.

PARAMETERS

2D IFS PARAMETERS

#	A	B	C	D	E	F	PROB
1	0.00	0.00	0.00	0.16	0.00	0.00	0.01
2	0.85	0.04	-0.04	0.85	0.00	1.60	0.85
3	0.20	-0.26	0.23	0.22	0.00	1.60	0.07
4	-0.15	0.28	0.26	0.24	0.00	0.44	0.07

Enter the number of the line you want to edit or R to start from another (.IFS) file, or S to save your edits in a file, or ENTER to end ==> __

Parameters are accessed by pressing ⓘ (for "IFS") and selecting "2D IFS Codes." The above shows the resulting screen, which allows editing the IFS transformations, saving them to a file, or restoring from a file. Each line in the parameters matrix is a separate transformation. The values a, b, and so forth refer to the position in the matrix formula for the fractal.

EXPLORER

It is devilishly hard to figure out what these parameters do, but you can make some headway by experimenting. Go to the parameters screen by pressing ⓘ and then selecting "2D IFS Codes." Enter 4, which means you want to edit the bottom transformation. This is the one that creates the right-hand fronds. Let's move these fronds up so they connect with the stem at the same place as the left-hand fronds. Keep pressing (ENTER), which accepts the values without change, until you come to the f value, which is .44. Change this to 1.60, and keep pressing (ENTER) until you have backed out and are regenerating the image. Behold the now-symmetrical fern! The matrix values a, b, c, and d generally rotate and shrink the transformation, while the d and e values shift it.

Try this experiment. Look at the values of transformation #2. The b and c values are .04 and -.04. These values control the fern curl. Try bumping them up to .06 and -.06 to increase the curl.

There are quite a number of other IFS example files on the disk. To try them out, press Ⓡ from the 2D IFS Parameters screen and Fractint will display a list of files in the current directory ending with the .ifs extension.

ALTERNATE COLOR MAPS

Try the map file green.map to color the fern green. When viewing the fern, press Ⓒ to get in color cycling mode, then Ⓛ to load a map file, and select or type in green.map.

HISTORY AND CREDITS

The originator of Iterated Function Systems is Michael Barnsley. His book *Fractals Everywhere* is an excellent reference. Many of the sample IFS files provided with this book came from the program Fdesign, by Doug Nelson, a freeware IFS fractal generating program that works well with Fractint.

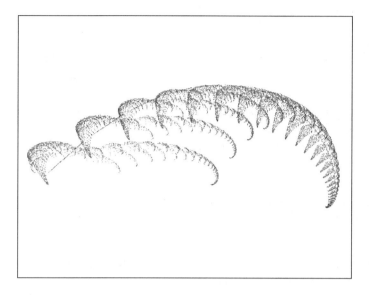

ITERATED FUNCTION SYSTEMS 3D

FRACTAL CATEGORY   Iterated Function Systems

FORMAL NAME   Iterated Function Systems

FRACTAL TYPE   ifs3d

FORMULA
$$\begin{bmatrix} x' \\ y' \\ z' \end{bmatrix} = \begin{bmatrix} abc \\ def \\ ghi \end{bmatrix} \begin{bmatrix} x \\ y \\ z \end{bmatrix} + \begin{bmatrix} j \\ k \\ l \end{bmatrix}$$

COMMAND LINE

```
fractint type=ifs3d map=altern corners=-2.6/2.6/-2.6/2.6
maxiter=20000
```

DESCRIPTION

The ifs3d type is identical to the ifs type, except that the transformations are 3-D, resulting in a fractal with three dimensions. Fractint's 3-D capabilities allow viewing the resulting fractal from all angles, with or without a perspective viewpoint.

PARAMETERS

3D IFS PARAMETERS

#	A	B	C	D	E	F	G	H	I	J	K	L	PROB
1	0.00	0.00	0.00	0.00	0.18	0.00	0.00	0.00	0.00	0.00	0.00	0.00	0.01
2	0.85	0.00	0.00	0.00	0.85	0.10	0.00	-0.10	0.85	0.00	1.60	0.00	0.85
3	0.20	-0.20	0.00	0.20	0.20	0.00	0.00	0.00	0.30	0.00	0.80	0.00	0.07
4	-0.20	0.20	0.00	0.20	0.20	0.00	0.00	0.00	0.30	0.00	0.80	0.00	0.07

Enter the number of the line you want to edit or R to start from another (.IFS) file, or S to save your edits in a file, or ENTER to end

==> __

Access the parameters the same way as you do for type ifs, only select "3D IFS Codes" instead of "2D IFS Codes."

EXPLORER

After viewing the default 3-D fern fractal, try manipulating the 3-D parameters. Starting with the Ⓣ command, select "3D Transform Parameters," after which you will have one or more screens of 3-D controls that can be changed. Try altering the rotation values to view the fern from different angles. To see the fern in stereo, type **2** at the "Stereo (R/B 3D?)" prompt for viewing with the red and blue 3-D glasses.

ALTERNATE COLOR MAPS

Try the green.map.

HISTORY AND CREDITS

Michael Barnsley (see credits for the IFS fractal type).

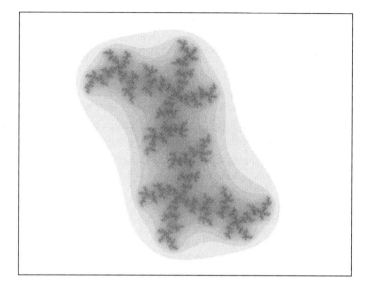

JULIA SETS

FRACTAL CATEGORY	Escape-time fractal
FORMAL NAME	Julia set
FRACTAL TYPE	julia
FORMULA	$z^2 + c$

COMMAND LINE
```
fractint maxiter=20000 inside=255 logmap=-1 type=julia
```

DESCRIPTION

"You obtain an incredible variety of Julia sets: some are a fatty cloud, others are a skinny bush of brambles, some look like the sparks which float in the air after a firework has gone off. One has the shape of a rabbit, lots of them have sea-horse tails."—Adrien Douady, *Julia Sets and the Mandelbrot Set*, p. 161

For every x, y point on the Mandelbrot set you can generate a unique Julia set. And since there are an infinite number of points there is an infinity of Julias. Each Julia is different and yet eerily the same. All are symmetrical and all have a self-symmetry that gives an overall pattern repeated in infinitely smaller scale.

Julia sets use the exact same formula as the Mandelbrot set, only in a different way. The Mandelbrot set uses a different value of c for each pixel and starts every iteration loop with the value of z equal to zero. The Julia sets, on the other hand, are calculated using the same value for c throughout the drawing and varying the initial value of z with each pixel. Julia sets have an overall symmetry around the origin. If you cut the set in half at any angle through the origin you will find that each half is a reverse image of the other. This self-symmetry and reversed symmetry are the signatures of a Julia set.

Julia sets are not limited to the classic formula described in this fractal type. *Any* complex function that is differentiable (analytic) has a Julia set. And whenever there is a collection of Julia sets where the derivative of the formula can be set to zero, there is one associated Mandelbrot set for the whole collection.

PARAMETERS

Real part of parameter	*0.3*
Imaginary part of parameter	*0.6*
Bailout value (0 means use default)	*0*

The real part of parameter and imaginary part of parameter are used to set the real and imaginary portion of the variable c in the formula. The bailout value is the variable that determines when Fractint should stop the iterations and assign the pixel a color. The default value is 4.

EXPLORER

Starting with the Mandelbrot set is the best method of finding interesting Julia sets. It is, after all, a catalogue of Julia sets. Whatever colorful pattern you find in the Mandelbrot set will be the self-symmetrical pattern drawn in the associated Julia set.

Some sets to view include the following:

```
fractint params=.28261/-.01077 maxiter=20000 logmap=-1
map=firestrm type=julia inside=255

fractint params=.16894/-.65747 maxiter=20000 logmap=-1
map=firestrm type=julia inside=255

fractint params=-.74527/.12475 maxiter=20000 logmap=-1
map=firestrm type=julia inside=255
```

If the Julia set variable c is close to the Mandelbrot lake, large areas of blue will be splotched in various places on the screen. If the value of c isn't actually in the Mandelbrot lake, there is more to see inside that blue! Set the iteration level higher (indicate maxiter on the command line or select it from the "x" options menu) and drive the blues back into the lake from whence they came. If the iteration level exceeds the number of colors available on your machine, you should try using a logarithmic color map.

SPECIAL EFFECTS
Continuous potential produces the best viewing!

ALTERNATE COLOR MAPS
All the color maps will work well with the Julia sets.

HISTORY AND CREDITS
Julia sets are named after the mathematician Gaston Julia. With the aid of Pierre Fatou, Julia studied complex dynamic systems for fifteen years between 1910 and 1925. Unfortunately, there were no computers around at the time, making the calculations arduous and extremely time-consuming. We had to wait until 1979 for Dr. Mandelbrot to revive Fatou's and Julia's work and, with the aid of modern computers, create a science out of chaos.

JULIBROT

FRACTAL CATEGORY	Four-dimensional escape-time fractal
FORMAL NAME	Julibrot
FRACTAL TYPE	julibrot
FORMULA	$z^2 + c$

COMMAND LINE
fractint type=julibrot

DESCRIPTION

The Mandelbrot set is a catalog of all the various Julia sets. Every point on the two-dimensional drawing of the Mandelbrot set intersects with a unique two-dimensional Julia set. Thought of as a whole, the Mandelbrot and Julia depictions are different aspects of a single four-dimensional mathematical object called the *Julibrot*. If you were to draw a vertical line on the Mandelbrot depiction and draw all the Julia sets that intersect with that line, layered one on top of another, you would have a snapshot of a moment in the life of a Julibrot. Move the line horizontally in the negative direction along the *x*-axis and you move backwards in time. Move the line in the positive direction and you move forwards in time. The 3-D transformations in Fractint generally take a two-dimensional fractal and plot the iteration levels as the third dimension. These three-dimensional fractals are hollow and similar to a relief drawing stamped out of a sheet of copper. If you turn over the copper, all you see is the underside of the same drawing.

Julibrots are solid. They have Julia fractal characteristics in both the horizontal and vertical directions and Mandelbrot fractal characteristics along their depth. Peel away the outer layers like an onion and reveal different fractals underneath.

Julibrots are really four-dimensional objects. In order to visualize a four-dimensional Julibrot, think of it as a solid 3-D crystal changing with time, where time dimension is the Mandelbrot x-axis (see the parameters below). You can show the Julibrot changing with time by generating a sequence of Julibrot images and changing the Mandelbrot x parameter a little with each image. Some Julibrots are born, live hectic lives, then die. Others are reincarnated again and again in an endless cycle. They even have fractal characteristics along their time lines—they *behave* like fractals! Fractint is the *only* program that allows you to explore the existence of this dynamic, solid fractal type.

Some people feel that since the Julibrot is an abstract object any of the 4 axes can be used as the time axis. This is not the case. Consider using either the Julia x- or y-axis for time. If you depict the Julibrot at a particular point before time zero you will find a mirror image of the Julibrot at the same point on the other side of time zero. Using the Mandelbrot y-axis as the time axis produces a similar situation, but the images before and after time zero are identical instead of mirrored. Any one of these three axes used for time produces a symmetry of Julibrots about time zero. Time, however, is not symmetrical. Objects from the past cannot suddenly appear as mirrored or identical images in the future. Use of the Mandelbrot x-axis as time prevents this from happening—all objects along the time-line are then unique.

Any mathematical formula that has both a Mandelbrot set and a family of Julia sets can be displayed as a Julibrot. However, Fractint currently draws the Julibrot based on the equation $z^2 + c$ only. This Julibrot, though, has a fascinating existence. Born out of the void as a single speck of dust, it grows slowly at first in spits and sputters, alternating between expansions and sudden explosive contractions. With each spurt of growth it is larger than before. Soon it starts curling in on itself. Eddies form into massive swirling vortexes. In one final heave it coagulates into a twisting, wriggly mass. Then, like a star going supernova, it collapses one last time and explodes into fragments. The fragments themselves explode into smaller fragments and these explode in turn, again and again, until only the void remains.

PARAMETERS

JULIBROT PARAMETERS

Julia from x	*1.99999*
Julia to x	*-2*
Julia from y	*1.5*
Julia to y	*-1.49999*
Mandelbrot from x	*-0.83*
Mandelbrot to x	*-0.83*
Mandelbrot from y	*0.25*
Mandelbrot to y	*-0.25*
Number of z pixels	*128*
Penetration level	*30*
Location of z origin	*8*
Depth of z	*8*
Screen height	*7*
Screen width	*10*
Distance to screen	*24*
Distance between eyes (0 for Greyscale)	*0*
Blue:Red ratio (0 for Greyscale)	*0*

The default parameters for the Julibrot provide an absolutely gorgeous view of the Julibrot just before it reaches its maturity and turns into a wriggly lump. The first four Julia parameters set the corners of the drawing the same as other fractal drawings. Changing the Julia parameters zooms in or out of the drawing. Using the mouse or keyboard zoom box will automatically change these parameters for you and also keep the aspect ratio of the image proportional.

Figure 3-2 shows part of the Julibrot's relationship to the Mandelbrot set. The shading of this figure is somewhat different than the rendering of the Julibrot in Fractint. The darker shades of the Mandelbrot set in the upper right-hand corner correspond to the darker shades of the Julibrot. The line through the Mandelbrot set is the z-axis of the Julibrot. The x-axis of the Mandelbrot set corresponds to the time, or t-axis, of the Julia set. This drawing is shown at t = -1.098. Moving the line in the positive direction along the Mandelbrot x-axis shows the Julibrot at later points in time.

The Mandelbrot parameters form the end points for a line of Julia sets. The two "from" parameters draw the Julia set associated with the Mandelbrot point in the foreground. The Julia set associated with the "to" Mandelbrot point is drawn at the rear. Fractint draws the foremost Julia sets in the brightest shades with progressively dimmer shades used to the rear. The dimmest shade is used to draw the Julia set associated with the "to" endpoint of the Mandelbrot line.

Remember that we are thinking of the Mandelbrot x parameter as a time dimension. To keep each level of the Julibrot display in the same time reference, the two Mandelbrot x parameters should be identical. Then each Julibrot image is a snapshot of the Julibrot at time x. Setting the Mandelbrot "from x" parameter different from the Mandelbrot "to x" parameter will skew the depiction along the time line, and make the time metaphor break down. Each layer of Julia sets would then be in a different time frame. Skewing the time frame produces some interesting effects, though! It amounts to slicing the 4-D Julibrot with the knife at a different angle. Setting the Mandelbrot y parameters equal and varying the x parameters depicts the evolution of a cross section over time. In this case the z-axis of the drawing represents time rather than depth. The deeper levels of the drawing show the cross section at later points in time (or earlier if you draw the Mandelbrot line from a positive x to a negative x).

The Number of z pixels parameter determines how many Julia sets will be layered. With the above settings, 128 of the Julia sets along the Mandelbrot line will be layered to make up the drawing. Setting this number higher will give the drawing better depth resolution. Since there are only 256 shades of grey available, depth resolutions above 256 provide little improvement in the quality of the image.

The penetration level parameter is equivalent to the maxiter parameter used for the Mandelbrot and Julia set fractals. Setting maxiter higher in these fractals

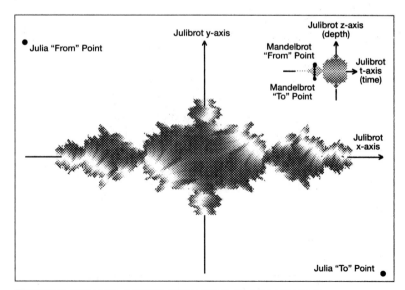

Figure 3-2 Part of the Julibrot's relationship to the Mandelbrot set

sharpens the areas closest to the lakes (areas of periodic orbits). With the Julibrots, as the name penetration level implies, the higher values take you deeper into the Julibrot and remove the outer layers to let you see what lies beneath. The deeper layers of the Julibrot have more details but take much longer to draw.

The screen height and screen width parameters are used to determine the aspect ratio of the drawing and also provide a frame of reference for other parameters. You can use any units of measure you wish—inches, feet, meters, and so on—so long as you use the same units for all parameters requiring a distance measure.

If you want the Julibrot drawn for viewing without the red/blue 3-D glasses, then set the parameters for distance between eyes and blue:red ratio both to zero. Fractint will automatically load the grey.map file to use for drawing. For grey-scaled drawings the remaining parameters are not used.

EXPLORER

You can zoom in on any of the Julibrot drawings—even the ones in red/blue 3-D! This has the effect of looking at the Julibrot through a 3-D magnifying glass. You should definitely try at least one zoom and experience it for yourself. To find the more interesting Julibrots, you should use the Mandelbrot set as a guide. Pick a straight line anywhere on the Mandelbrot set that looks interesting and plug the end points into Mandelbrot x and y parameters.

SPECIAL EFFECTS

Setting the blue:red ratio parameter to a value other than zero will instruct Fractint to load the glasses1.map file to use for drawing. This map draws alternating blue and red pixels needed for use with the red/blue glasses. These are called *anaglyph* 3-D drawings. Since the eye is more sensitive to blue light than red, the anaglyph would appear on the bluish side if equal intensities for red and blue were used to draw the image. The blue:red ratio determines how much brighter the red image will be than the blue. A good setting for the blue:red ratio is 0.8. If the image appears on the reddish side then use a higher number. Likewise, if the drawing appears bluish in the glasses you are using, the number should be lowered.

Anaglyphic drawings need more information than the grey-scaled drawings to place the image at the proper depth in the monitor and draw it with an accurate perspective. The distance between eyes parameter should be a measure of the distance between your pupils. For most people three inches is a good number. Another parameter used as a reference is distance to the screen. This should be a measure of how far your eyes are from the screen.

The location of z origin parameter determines how far beyond the screen into the monitor the center of the image will appear to the viewer. Setting this value to a negative distance will place the center of the image in front of the screen out in open space. Many 3-D enthusiasts consider this practice of "breaking the viewing plane" as vulgar, but others get quite a kick out of it. Try it both ways and see which one you prefer!

The final parameter, depth of z, determines how thick the image will appear. If you use the default settings of location of z origin and depth of z (both equal to 8), then the front part of the image will appear 4 inches into the monitor (8 - 8/2), and the rear edge of the image will appear at 12 inches into the monitor (8 + 8/2).

WARNINGS

With this particular fractal, the screen may be blank for a period of time before anything is actually drawn onto it. Also, Fractint will only attempt to draw the fractal in 256 colors. Trying to use 16 colors simply does not provide adequate depth resolution for the 3-D effect. If you are running on an EGA or CGA machine you will have to use a disk video option with 256 colors.

It takes a *long* time to draw a portion of the Julibrot, even using Fractint on a 386! Indeed, for a 320 × 200 with a z resolution of 128 it may take as long as an hour to draw. The amount of time required is directly proportional to the resolution product of all three axes. If it takes 1 hour to draw a 320 × 200 × 128 image, then it would take 15 hours to draw an 800 × 600 × 256 image. You can reduce the amount of time by keeping the penetration level to a reasonably low number.

ALTERNATE COLOR MAPS

The only color maps available for the Julibrot are grey.map and glasses1.map, both of which are loaded automatically when needed.

HISTORY AND CREDITS

The Julibrot algorithm and code were both originated by Mark Peterson. Mark coined the name Julibrot by combining "Juli-a" with "Mandel-brot." At about the same time Mark developed the Julibrot algorithm, Dr. Pickover independently published an article on an identical fractal type, which he referred to as "Repeller Towers" in *Computers in Physics*, "A Note on Rendering Chaotic Repeller Distance Towers," May/June 1988 (Vol. 2 No. 3).

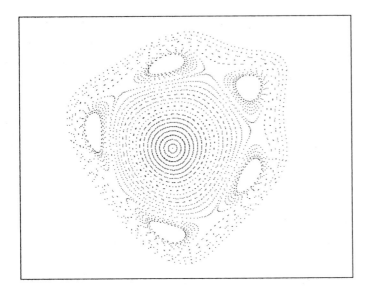

KAM TORUS

FRACTAL CATEGORY	Orbital fractal
FORMAL NAME	Kam Torus
FRACTAL TYPE	kamtorus and kamtorus3d
FORMULA	$x' = x\cos(a) + (x^2 - y)\sin(a)$ $y' = x\sin(a) - (x^2 - y)\cos(a)$

COMMAND LINE
```
fractint type=kamtorus map=altern
```

DESCRIPTION

Initially this fractal generates concentric circles. As it progresses, smaller concentric circles are generated inside the outer edges of the previous circles. When the fractal reaches maturity, it grows "whiskers" extending outward perpendicular to the radius. These whiskers eventually curl in on themselves.

At the start of each orbit calculation the initial values of x and y are set to the orbit level divided by 3 (the number 3 is hard-coded into Fractint). As the fractal is drawn, a point is plotted at the screen coordinates given by the values of x and y. After the calculations reach a stop value, the orbit level is incremented and a new set of initial values for x and y are calculated.

PARAMETERS

Angle (radians)	*1.3*
Step size	*0.05*
Stop value	*1.5*
Points per orbit	*150*

The angle parameter is used as the setting for the variable *a* in the formula. Lowering this value will create a smaller fractal and cause it to enter the mature "whisker" stage more quickly.

The step size parameter is used as the increment for the orbit. Lower values will generate tighter concentric circles. Higher values produce more widely spaced circles.

The stop value parameter determines when to stop the fractal generation and call it quits. Higher values produce larger, more detailed fractals.

The points per orbit parameter determines how many points will be plotted before Fractint moves on to the next orbit. High values produce more solid circles. Lower values produce a scattering of points in the circle. Some of the lower values produce some interesting interference patterns when they overlap.

EXPLORER

Angle (radians)	*0.5*
Step size	*0.01*
Stop value	*1.5*
Points per orbit	*500*

These settings will produce a fractal "eye." Try to use a high screen resolution around 800 × 600 pixels.

Angle (radians)	*4.712*

Changing the value of the angle to half π will produce a four-legged starfish.

SPECIAL EFFECTS

The 3-D variant of this fractal type is kamtorus3d. This fractal plots each new orbit as occurring at a different depth.

HISTORY AND CREDITS

The term "KAM" is from the three people who studied this equation: Kalmogorov, Arnold, and Moser. The code used by Fractint came from Stone Souper Scott Taylor, who found it in E. Reitman's book *Exploring the Geometry of Nature.* The 3-D representation was coded by Tim Wegner.

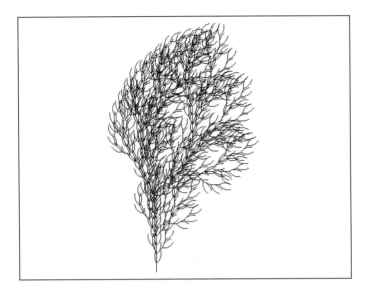

L-SYSTEM FRACTALS

FRACTAL CATEGORY   L-System fractal

FORMAL NAME   None

FRACTAL TYPE   lsystem

COMMAND LINE
`fractint type=lsystem params=4 map=altern lname=bush`

DESCRIPTION
See the User-Defined Fractals section in this chapter.

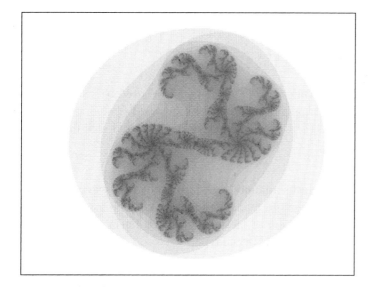

LAMBDA

FRACTAL CATEGORY	Escape-time fractal
FORMAL NAME	The Logistic Equation
FRACTAL TYPE	lambda
FORMULA	$cz(1 - z)$

COMMAND LINE

```
fractint maxiter=20000 inside=255 map=altern logmap=-1
type=lambda
```

DESCRIPTION

This fractal type calculates the Julia sets for the Lambda formula, where the variable c is the *lambda* of the equation. This formula can also be written in quadratic form as $-cz^2 + cz$.

The fractal type mandellambda is the Mandelbrot set associated with this Julia family. Pressing the space bar toggles to the mandellambda fractal type. Pressing the space bar from the mandellambda fractal type toggles to the Julia set associated with the point in the center of the screen.

PARAMETERS

Real part of parameter	*0.85*
Imaginary part of parameter	*0.6*
Bailout value (0 means use default)	*0*

The real and imaginary portions of the parameter are used to set the value of the variable c in the formula. At the start of each pixel's iteration loop the value of z is initialized to the Cartesian coordinates associated with the pixel's location.

EXPLORER

Since this fractal type produces a family of Julia sets, the best way to find the most interesting sets is to use the mandellambda fractal type as your guide. Zoom in on an interesting section of the mandellambda fractal type and then press the space bar to toggle to this fractal type.

Some places to try are the following:

```
fractint map=firestrm logmap=-1 params=-0.2393/1.0507
type=lambda maxiter=20000 inside=150

fractint map=firestrm logmap=-1 params=-0.6091/0.8117
type=lambda maxiter=20000 inside=150
```

HISTORY AND CREDITS

The lambda equation comes from the very same population modeling equation used in bifurcation and is discussed on pages 139 and 211 of *The Science of Fractal Images*. Tim Wegner wrote the code for this fractal type and the corresponding Mandelbrot mapping, fractal type mandellambda.

LAMBDA FUNCTION FRACTALS

FRACTAL CATEGORY	Escape-time fractal
FORMAL NAME	None
FRACTAL TYPE	lambdafn
FORMULA	$c\mathrm{fn}(z)$, $\mathrm{fn}(z) = \sin(z), \cos(z) \sinh(z), \cosh(z), e^z, \ln(z), z^2$

COMMAND LINE

```
fractint maxiter=20000 inside=255 map=altern logmap=-1
type=lambdafn
```

DESCRIPTION

These are variants of the classic Julia set families. Instead of the traditional z^2, we've substituted a transcendental function multiplied by c. As with all Julia sets, associated with any of the function fractals is a Mandelbrot set (see the mandelfn fractal type).

PARAMETERS

Real perturbation of z(0)	*0*
Imaginary perturbation of z(0)	*0*
First function	*sin*
Bailout value (0 means use default)	*0*

Setting the real perturbation of $z(0)$ and the imaginary perturbation of $z(0)$ to a nonzero value will warp the original fractal. The first function parameter accepts any one of these seven parameters to generate a fractal:

sin	*cosh*	*log*
cos	*exp*	*sqr*
sinh		

The bailout value is the variable that determines when Fractint should call it quits on the iterations and assign the pixel a color. The default value is 4.

EXPLORER

For feathery, nested spirals of the LambdaSine and the frost-on-glass patterns of the LambdaCosine, make the real part of c equal to 1 and the imaginary part anywhere ranging from 0.1 to 0.4. The best patterns are closer to 0.4. For the tongue and blobs of LambdaExponent, try a real part of 0.379 for c and an imaginary part of 0.479.

WARNINGS

In the older versions of Fractint, drawing these fractals virtually required your machine to use an 80387 coprocessor. But, thanks to Stone Souper Mark Peterson, the newer versions (including the one with this book) calculate the transcendentals using his high-speed integer mathematics. There is a trade-off, though, of speed for accuracy. After a couple of maximum zooms you will exceed the accuracy range of the integer math. In this case Fractint will automatically switch to floating-point math. If you don't have an 80387 or an 80486, take a long vacation. The drawing may be finished by the time you come back.

HISTORY AND CREDITS

Mark Peterson wrote the code for the trigonometric fractals, and Tim Wegner coded the exponential and logarithmic fractals.

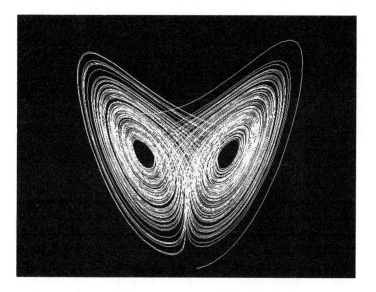

LORENZ FRACTAL

FRACTAL CATEGORY	Orbital fractal
FORMAL NAME	Lorenz
FRACTAL TYPE	lorenz and lorenz3d
FORMULA	$x' = x - (ax + ay)dt$
	$y' = y + (bx - y - zx)dt$
	$z' = z - (cz + xy)dt$

COMMAND LINE

```
fractint map=altern type=lorenz
```

DESCRIPTION

A single-point loop draws out a path of two double spirals, cocked at an angle of a butterfly's wings in flight. The point spirals for a time in one loop, then unexpectedly jumps to the other loop. If you let it spiral for an eternity, it will never return to any spot it has already been as it travels on its journey through its private infinity.

This fractal originally came from three simultaneous equations to describe the motion of a water wheel. The three variables, x, y, and z, completely describe the motion of the dynamic system from one point in time to the next. Water flows directly into the buckets on top of the water wheel. The buckets themselves have holes in them that drain the water. This creates a chaotic, dynamic system where the water wheel continually changes speed and sporadically changes direction.

If you're tired of strictly visual effects, turn on the sound with the ⓧ key and you can listen to the Lorenz fractal as it's formed! Set the sound variable to "x," "y," or "z." Fractint will change the sound frequency proportional to the orbital position along one of those three axes.

PARAMETERS

Time step	*0.02*
a	*5*
b	*15*
c	*1*

The time step variable is used to set the value of *dt* in the formula. The smaller this value is, the slower the plotting, but you will get more detail. Higher values will plot more quickly, but the image can look rather chunky.

The variables *a*, *b*, and *c* change the corresponding variables in the formula. Higher values of *a* and *c* tend to collapse the spirals into circles. Higher values of *b* make the fractal larger.

EXPLORER

Another good set of variables to try is twice the default values:

Time step	*0.02*
a	*10*
b	*30*
c	*2*

SPECIAL EFFECTS

There are actually two versions of the Lorenz fractal. The fractal type lorenz produces the two-dimensional garden variety Lorenz. The fractal type lorenz3d is the same set of equations, but with the added twist of showing the orbits using Fractint's perspective 3-D routines. These routines expect you to be wearing the red/blue funny glasses. They plot a red and blue point for each orbital position so as to fool the brain into thinking the point is positioned in three-dimensional space.

The default perspectives values ($x = 60$, $y = 30$, $z = 0$) are not the best ones to use for fun viewing. Try other angles, such as 20/0/0 and 40/0/0. While you're at it, try a nonzero perspective point and view the fractal from *inside* the orbits.

HISTORY AND CREDITS

Edward Lorenz originally described this fractal (though it wasn't *called* a fractal at the time) in an article entitled "Deterministic Non-Periodic Flow," which was published in the *Journal of the Atmospheric Sciences* in 1963. Unfortunately, there were not too many mathematicians or physicists who read that particular journal, so it was quite a while before Lorenz's work became widely known.

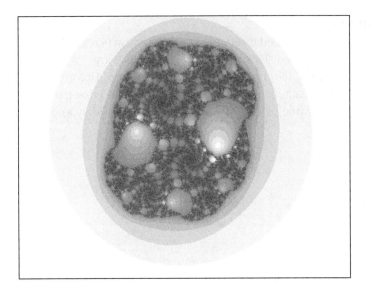

MAGNETISM FRACTAL TYPES

FRACTAL CATEGORY   Escape-time fractals

FORMAL NAME   Magnetism Model Type I & II

FRACTAL TYPES   magnet1j, magnet2j, magnet1m, and magnet2m

FORMULA

$$\frac{[z^2 + c - 1]^2}{[2z + c - 2]^2} \qquad \text{Type I}$$

$$\frac{[z^3 + 3(c\text{-}1)z + (c\text{-}1)(c\text{-}2)]^2}{[3z^2 + 3(c\text{-}2)z + c^2 - 3c + 3)]^2} \qquad \text{Type II}$$

COMMAND LINE

```
fractint params=0.35/1.3 maxiter=20000 map=altern logmap=-
1 inside=255 type=magnet1j
```

DESCRIPTION

These fractals are a descriptive model of the phase transition of a ferromagnetic material from a magnetic state to a nonmagnetic state as its temperature is raised. The derivation of the formulas is well beyond the scope of this book, but an in-depth discussion of the topic can be found in *The Beauty of Fractals*, pp. 129–46.

These magnet1j and magnet2j fractal types form the family of Julia sets associated with the formulas. The magnetm1 and magnetm2 fractal types are the associated Mandelbrot sets.

PARAMETERS

Real part of parameter	*0.3*
Imaginary part of parameter	*0.6*
Bailout value (0 means use default)	*0*

The real part of parameter and imaginary part of parameter are used to set the real and imaginary portion of the variable c in the formula for the Julia fractal types, magnet1j and magnet2j. The bailout value is the variable that determines when Fractint should stop iterating and assign the pixel a color. The default value is 4.

Real perturbation of z(0)	*0*
Imaginary perturbation of z(0)	*0*

The real perturbation of $z(0)$ and imaginary perturbation of $z(0)$ have a warping effect on the magnet1m and magnet2m fractal types when they are nonzero.

EXPLORER

Miniature copies of the classical Mandelbrot sets are located at these settings:

```
fractint type=magnet1m corners=1.81/2.27/1.46/1.81
fractint type=magnet2m corners=1.9176/1.9713/.8829/.9276
```

Generate a spiral using these command-line parameters:

```
fractint type=magnet1m corners=1.2793/1.3023/.9639/.9811
maxiter=20000 map=firestrm logmap=-1
```

Since the magnet1m and magnet2m fractal types are the Mandelbrot sets for the formulas, they are actually a map of all the various Julia sets. These are your best guides to the most interesting Julia sets associated with the magnet1j and magnet2j fractal types.

ALTERNATE COLOR MAPS

Smooth color maps, such as altern.map and firestrm.map, work best with this fractal type.

HISTORY AND CREDITS

This fractal was adapted from the description in *The Beauty of Fractals*, by H. O. Peitgen and P. H. Richter, pp. 129–46.

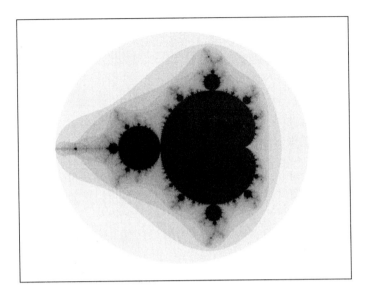

THE MANDELBROT SET

FRACTAL CATEGORY	Escape-time fractal
FORMAL NAME	Mandelbrot Set
FRACTAL TYPE	mandel
FORMULA	$z^2 + c$

COMMAND LINE
```
fractint maxiter=20000 inside=255 map=altern logmap=-1
type=mandel
```

DESCRIPTION	See Chapter 1.

PARAMETERS

Real perturbation of $z(0)$	*0*
Imaginary perturbation of $z(0)$	*0*
Bailout value (0 means use default)	*0*

The real perturbation of $z(0)$ and imaginary perturbation of $z(0)$ have a warping effect on the Mandelbrot set when they are nonzero. The bailout value is the variable that determines when Fractint should call it quits on the iterations and assign the pixel a color. The default value is 4. Pressing the space bar toggles the fractal type to the Julia set. Fractint uses the point in the center of the screen as the c value when it makes the switch. Pressing the space bar again toggles back to the Mandelbrot set. This feature is disabled if you are using perturbation parameters.

If you are in a hurry and want to bypass the zoom boxes, set the center-mag= parameter in the command line and go directly to the spot you want at correct magnification.

EXPLORER

The most interesting places in the Mandelbrot set are in the nooks and crannies of the spheroids.

Delicate flowers bloom within the crease of the heart:
```
fractint type=mandel center-mag=.28261/-.01077/465
```

Spiral whirlpools:
```
fractint type=mandel center-mag=-.16894/-.65747/500.
```

Mandelbrot buds:
```
fractint type=mandel center-mag=-.745277/.124755/300
```

Extending from the tips of the spheres are more straight-line images. Sword blades lash out of the negative tail:
```
fractint type=mandel center-mag=-1.5/0/80.
```

Jagged lightning strokes spawning more Mandelbrot sets in their path:
```
fractint type=mandel center-mag=-0.614/.9784/130
```

For speed, use the default setting of 150 to draw the image. Much of the image at the higher magnification levels will appear blue, meaning either the area is part of the Mandelbrot lake or the iteration limit was exceeded before Fractint could determine the color. Call up the options menu using the ⓧ key and raise the value of maximum iterations to around 1000 or so. This will also sharpen the image. Some people frequently use settings around 30,000. Fractint can easily handle iteration levels in the tens of thousands with only a marginal increase in calculation time through the use of its periodicity-checking algorithm. Thanks to periodicity and solid checking, Fractint can handle those high iteration levels and still draw the image in short order.

Whenever the iteration level exceeds the available number of colors in a video mode, an "overflow" occurs creating a jumbled mish-mash of disjointed colors. When this happens, try setting the log palette to 1 if you are using the default palette, or -1 if you are using a continuous palette such as firestrm.map.

SPECIAL EFFECTS

Try the distest parameter from the command line. Continuous potential provides the best, but slowest, viewing of this fractal.

WARNINGS

Mandelbrot exploration is highly addictive! People have been known to lock themselves behind closed doors for days on end feverishly searching for that perfect fractal. Have a friend check on you occasionally just to remind you what time it is. But don't let your friend look at the screen—he or she might get caught up in it also!

HISTORY AND CREDITS

Benoit B. Mandelbrot (b.1924) is credited with the discovery of this fractal. In 1979 he created a catalogue of Julia sets which he planned on using as a guide in exploration of Julia sets. The Mandelbrot set is that catalogue. Bert Tyler, the original author of Fractint, wrote the high-speed generation algorithm. Mark Peterson added the algorithm for periodicity checking. Tim Wegner added symmetry and solid-guessing. Many others added inversion, boundary tracing, faster calculation methods, and more.

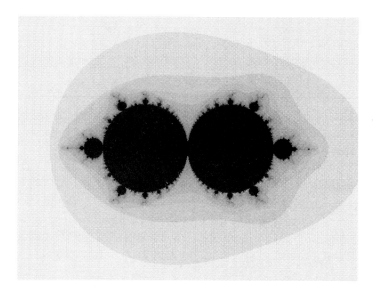

MANDELBROT LAMBDA

FRACTAL CATEGORY	Escape-time fractal
FORMAL NAME	None
FRACTAL TYPE	mandellambda
FORMULA	$cz(1 - z)$

COMMAND LINE

```
fractint maxiter=20000 inside=255 map=altern logmap=-1
type=mandellambda
```

DESCRIPTION

This is the Mandelbrot map of the lambda fractal type. You should note that this fractal type uses the same formula as lambda, however the fractal is generated so as to produce a Mandelbrot set rather than a Julia set. In the lambda fractal, which produces a family of Julia sets, the value of the variable c is kept constant and the initial value of z is changed from pixel to pixel to correspond with the associated Cartesian coordinates. Since the Mandelbrot lambda is a Mandelbrot set, the initial value of z is kept constant at 0.5, a *critical point* for the formula, and the value of c is changed from pixel to pixel to correspond with the Cartesian coordinates. For information on determining a formula's critical point, refer to *The Science of Fractal Images,* 1988, p 156.

PARAMETERS

Real perturbation of z(0)	*0*
Imaginary perturbation of z(0)	*0*
Bailout value (0 means use default)	*0*

The real perturbation of $z(0)$ and imaginary perturbation of $z(0)$ have a warping effect on the set when they are nonzero. During normal generation of the fractal, a new value of c is used for each pixel. The value of the variable p (*perturbation*), however, is kept constant throughout the drawing.

The bailout value is the variable that determines when Fractint should stop iterating and assign the pixel a color. The default value is 4.

Pressing the space bar toggles the fractal type to the Julia set. Fractint uses the point in the center of the screen as the c value when it makes the switch. Pressing the space bar again toggles back to the Mandelbrot set. This feature is disabled if you are using a nonzero value for the Perturbation parameters.

EXPLORER

These settings will show you one of the local spirals:

```
fractint type=mandellambda center-mag=1.9255/1.0429/120
maxiter=20000 map=firestrm logmap=-1
```

And these will show you the source of the commotion nearby—a tiny Mandelbrot set:

```
fractint type=mandellambda maxiter=30000 logmap=-1
map=firestrm inside=0 corners=1.93233/1.93422/1.03954/
1.04096
```

HISTORY AND CREDITS

See the Lambda fractal type.

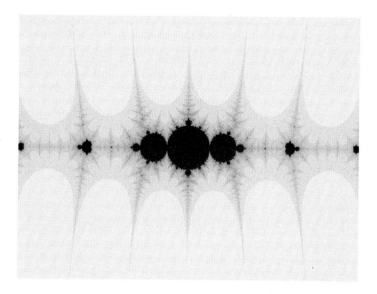

MANDELBROT LAMBDA FUNCTION

FRACTAL CATEGORY	Escape-time fractal
FORMAL NAME	None
FRACTAL TYPE	mandelfn
FORMULA	$c\,(\mathrm{fn}(z))$,
	$\mathrm{fn}(z) = \sin(z),\ \cos(z),\ \sinh(z),\ \cosh(z),\ e^z,\ \ln(z),\ z^2$

COMMAND LINE

```
fractint maxiter=20000 inside=255 map=altern logmap=-1
type=mandelfn
```

DESCRIPTION

These are variants of the classic Mandelbrot set. Instead of the traditional z^2, we've substituted a transcendental function multiplied by c. As with all Mandelbrot sets, associated with any of the function fractals is an entire family of Julia sets.

The trigonometric functions appear rather spiky. This is because Fractint watches only the real portion of z rather than checking the modulus of z. The Formula Compiler (see type formula) can be used to view these fractals with a modulus bailout check. A formula for the Mandelbrot fractal based on the sine function would look like this:

```
MandelSine = {
   z = pixel:
      z = pixel * sin(z),
   |z| < 32
}
```

```
fractint corners=8/-8/6/-6 type=formula
formulaname=mandelsine
```

The lambdafn fractal types are the Julia sets associated with each of the functions.

Not all the default fractals are really Mandelbrot sets, however, because the initial value of z is always set to zero. To obtain a real Mandelbrot fractal the initorbit= parameter must be set in the Fractint command line to the fractal's critical point. The *critical point* is defined as the point where the derivative of the function is equal to zero.

PARAMETERS

Real perturbation of z(0)	*0*
Imaginary perturbation of z(0)	*0*
First function	*sin*
Bailout value (0 means use default)	*0*

Using a nonzero value for the real perturbation of $z(0)$ and the imaginary perturbation of $z(0)$ will warp the original fractal. The first function parameter accepts any one of these seven parameters to generate a fractal:

sin	*cosh*	*log*
cos	*exp*	*sqr*
sinh		

The bailout value is the variable that determines when Fractint should stop the iterations and assign the pixel a color. The default value is 4.

EXPLORER

Even though the initial value of the cosine fractal is off, there is still a tiny copy of the Mandelbrot set located at these coordinates:

```
fractint type=mandelfn function=cos corners=4.68/4.76/-
.03/.03
```

SPECIAL EFFECTS

Like almost all the fractals in Fractint, these can be redrawn in 3-D, transformed onto a sphere, or made into a starfield.

WARNINGS

See the warning for lambdafn.

HISTORY AND CREDITS

Mark Peterson wrote the code for the trigonometric fractals, and Tim Wegner coded the exponential and logarithmic fractals.

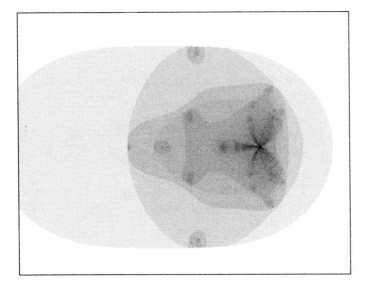

MANOWAR

FRACTAL CATEGORY	Escape-time fractal
FORMAL NAME	None
FRACTAL TYPE	manowar, manowarj
FORMULA	$z' = z^2 + m + c$; $m' = z$;

COMMAND LINE

```
fractint maxiter=20000 inside=255 map=altern logmap=-1
type=manowar
```

DESCRIPTION

This fractal looks like an oblong tube with several fractal spots, including one main chaotic area on the right-hand side. Pressing the space bar will toggle from the Mandelbrot mapping of the formula to the Julia sets.

PARAMETERS

These are the parameters for the manowar fractal type

Real perturbation of z0)	*0*
Imaginary perturbation of z(0)	*0*
Bailout value (0 means use default)	*0*

As with other Mandelbrot types, the real and imaginary perturbation parameters warp the image by perturbing the initial orbit value.

For the manowarj fractal type the parameters are as follows:

Real part of parameter   *0.0*
Imaginary part of parameter   *0.0*
Bailout value (0 means use default)   *0*

The values for the real and imaginary part of parameter are used to set the value of the variable c in the formula.

EXPLORER

Negative values of the real parameter result in the manowarj fractal breaking up into two globules when the imaginary parameter is 0. Try these values:

Real part of parameter   *-1.9*
Imaginary part of parameter   *0.0*

As you slowly make the real parameter less negative, the two globules will merge. The value when they just touch is -1.75.

HISTORY AND CREDITS

The original formula is from Art Matrix. Tim Wegner added the Julia version.

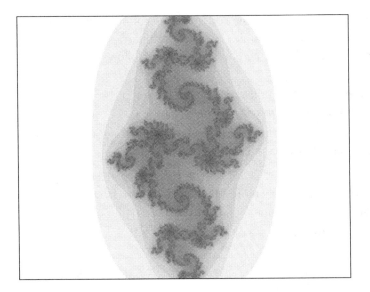

MARK'S JULIA

FRACTAL CATEGORY	Escape-time fractal
FORMAL NAME	Mark's Julia
FRACTAL TYPE	marksjulia
FORMULA	$z^2 c^{(p-1)} + c$

COMMAND LINE

```
fractint maxiter=20000 inside=255 map=altern logmap=-1
type=marksjulia
```

DESCRIPTION

These fractals are the Julia sets associated with the different points from Mark's Mandelbrot. Pressing the space bar toggles back to Complex Mark's Mandelbrot.

PARAMETERS

Real part of parameter	*0.1*
Imaginary part of parameter	*0.9*
Parameter exponent (>0)	*0*
Bailout value (0 means use default)	*0*

The real and imaginary parameters define the value of c in the formula. The value of z is initialized to the coordinates of the pixel color being calculated. The parameter exponent is used to set the complex value of p in the formula.

EXPLORER

With an infinite number of sets to choose from, exploration of this fractal type could take awhile. Fortunately, the marksmand fractal is a catalog of all the different Julia sets associated with this formula. Find an interesting spot in marksmand and press the space bar to toggle to the Julia set associated with the point in the center of the screen.

HISTORY AND CREDITS

See Complex Mark's Mandelbrot.

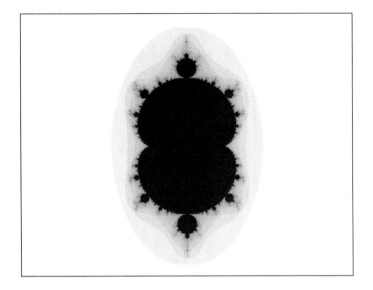

MARK'S MANDELBROT

FRACTAL CATEGORY	Escape-time fractal
FORMAL NAME	Mark's Mandelbrot
FRACTAL TYPE	marksmandel
FORMULA	$z^2 c^{(p-1)} + c$

COMMAND LINE
```
fractint maxiter=20000 inside=255 map=altern logmap=-1
type=marksmandel
```

DESCRIPTION

Mark's Mandelbrot is the faster version of Complex Mark's Mandelbrot originally written for Fractint. By restricting the variable p to real integers greater than 1, the fractal algorithm can be calculated much more quickly.

The marksjulia fractal draws the Julia sets associated with each point on this fractal. Cmplxmarksmand is a slower version of this fractal that allows the value of the variable p to be complex.

PARAMETERS

Real perturbation of z(0)	*0*
Imaginary perturbation of z(0)	*0*
Parameter exponent (>0)	*1*
Bailout value (0 means use default)	*0*

The real and imaginary perturbations warp the drawings. For exploration we'd recommend using zeros for these parameters. The parameter exponent is used to set the complex value of p in the fractal formula. These default settings draw a traditional Mandelbrot set. Using a value of 2 for the exponent draws a double Mandelbrot set. A value of 3 draws a triangular Mandelbrot set. A setting of 4 draws a square Mandelbrot.

HISTORY AND CREDITS

See Complex Mark's Mandelbrot.

NEWTON

FRACTAL CATEGORY   Escape-time fractal

FORMAL NAME   Newton

FRACTAL TYPE   newton

FORMULA

$$\frac{(n-1)z^n+1}{nz^{(n-1)}}$$

COMMAND LINE

```
fractint type=newton center-mag=0/0/1.5 params=4 logmap=-1
maxiter=750 map=firestrm.map
```

DESCRIPTION

Strings of fiery pearls flung from the core of a hot dwarf sun. This fractal is a faster version of complexnewton. The iteration formula above is a generalization of Newton's method for finding solutions to $z = \sqrt[n]{1}$, where z is a complex number and n is a positive integer greater than or equal to 3. The fractal description for complexbasin has a detailed explanation of Newton's method.

The newtbasin is the same fractal, except the color displayed represents the solution obtained by Newton's method rather than the number of iterations required. The complexnewton and complexbasin are slower, but they allow any complex value to be used for n.

PARAMETERS

Polynomial degree (>2)   *3*

The default parameters tell Fractint to look for the solutions to the equation $x = \sqrt[3]{1}$. The polynomial degree parameter sets the value of n in the formula. An odd integer value for the degree produces one fractal arm along the negative x-axis and n-1 evenly spaced arms extending outward from the origin. The actual solutions to $x = \sqrt[3]{1}$ are $(1+i0)$, and $(-\frac{1}{2} + i\frac{\sqrt{3}}{2})$, and $(-\frac{1}{2} - i\frac{\sqrt{3}}{2})$.

The fractal arms are always found between the actual solutions to the equation.

Polynomial degree (> 2)   *4*

The polynomial degree determines how many fractal arms will appear in the image. In this case, four evenly spaced fractal arms extend outward from the origin. If the polynomial degree is odd, one of the arms will be along the negative x-axis.

EXPLORER

The Newton fractals are similar to Julia sets in that the images on the smaller scales are copies of the overall image. Large zooms out from the origin create a tunnel effect with the fractal arms shrinking in size as they approach the origin.

ALTERNATE COLOR MAPS

As with other escape-time fractals, a smooth color palette is a good variation. These palettes are best used with a logarithmic color option.

HISTORY AND CREDITS

The actual fractal characteristics of Newton's method for roots was first discovered by John Hubbard in Orsay, France. The first fractal types newton and newtbasin were coded into Fractint by Tim Wegner. Lee Crocker wrote a more efficient algorithm using FPU-specific assembly language.

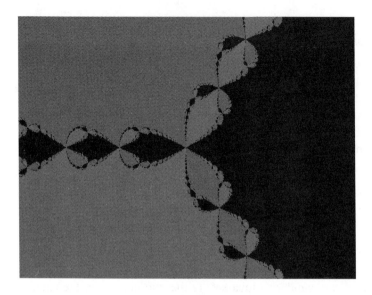

NEWTON'S BASIN

FRACTAL CATEGORY	Escape-time fractal
FORMAL NAME	Newton's Basin
FRACTAL TYPE	newtbasin

COMMAND LINE
```
fractint type=newtbasin params=3
```

DESCRIPTION

This fractal is identical to the fractal type newton except the colors represent the solution itself rather than the number of iterations Fractint required to find the solution. See the description of the newton fractal type for more information.

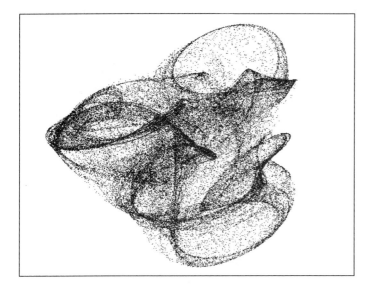

PICKOVER ATTRACTORS

FRACTAL CATEGORY	Orbital fractal
FORMAL NAME	None
FRACTAL TYPE	pickover
FORMULA	$x' = \sin(ax) - z\cos(bx)$
	$y' = z\sin(cx) - \cos(dy)$
	$z' = \sin(x)$

COMMAND LINE

```
fractint map=altern maxiter=20000 type=pickover
```

DESCRIPTION

This fractal forms a three-dimensional wispy cloud of points as they orbit through the iterations. A majority of the points collect along the fractal's strange attractors.

Setting the sound frequency to one of the axes will make your computer *sound* like a computer. Try it and you'll see what we mean!

PARAMETERS

a	*2.24*
b	*0.43*
c	*-0.65*
d	*-2.43*

The parameters *a*, *b*, *c*, and *d* correspond to the applicable variables in the formula. Changing these will produce an entirely different fractal.

SPECIAL EFFECTS

Since this fractal is three-dimensional, we've included an option in Fractint for viewing with the red/blue 3-D glasses. Select the 3D Transforms menu by pressing the Ⓣ key and selecting the 3D Transform Parameters option. Set the stereo parameter to either 1 or 2. Selecting 2 will give you the best viewing.

HISTORY AND CREDITS

This fractal type was developed by Clifford A. Pickover of IBM's Thomas J. Watson Research Center.

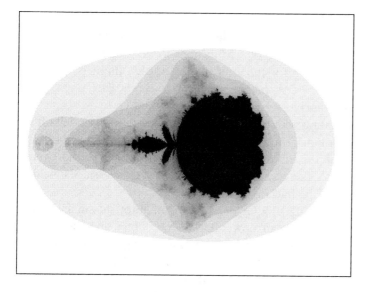

PICKOVER M/J FRACTALS

FRACTAL CATEGORY	Escape-time fractal
FORMAL NAME	Mandelbrot and Julia sets
FRACTAL TYPES	manzpower, julzpower manzzpwr, julzzpwr mandel4, julia4
	manfn+zsqrd, julfn+zsqrd manfn+exp, julfn+exp
FORMULAS	$zm + c$ $z^z + z^m + c$ $z^4 + c$
	$\text{fn}(z) + z^2 + c$ $\text{fn}(z) + e^z + c$ $\text{fn}(z) = \sin(z), \cos(z), \sinh(z), \cosh(z), e^z, z^2$

COMMAND LINE

```
fractint maxiter=20000 inside=255 map=altern logmap=-1
type=manfn+zsqrd
```

DESCRIPTION

This is another collection of variations of the classical Mandelbrot and Julia sets. The last two types allow any one of six functions to be used to generate the fractal. As with all Mandelbrot/Julia set combinations, there is only one Mandelbrot set associated with a complete family of Julia sets. Each point on the Mandelbrot set corresponds to a unique Julia set.

The fractal types starting with the "man" prefix generate the Mandelbrot set associated with the formula. The fractal types with the "jul" prefix are used to generate the Julia sets for the formula. No matter how bizarre the overall Mandelbrot set may look, there are always tiny copies of the classic Mandelbrot set scattered throughout the fractal.

The manzpower fractal is another periodic Mandelbrot set similar to the marksmandel fractal. With the manzpower fractal type, subtracting one from the value of m is the period. For example, the default settings use a value of 2, which is z^2+c, or the classic Mandelbrot set with a period of 1. A value for m of 3 produces a double Mandelbrot set, or a period of 3 -1 = 2. Currently, Fractint only allows positive integer values to be used for m. The mandel4 fractal type is a faster version of manzpower using a parameter of 4 for m.

Pressing the space bar will toggle from the Mandelbrot set to the Julia set corresponding to the point in the center of the screen.

EXPLORER

Turn on the biomorph option from the command line to create organic-looking fractals. Try the following:

```
fractint type=manfn+sqrd biomorph=0 corners=-8/8/-6/6
function=sin
```

to see a big biomorph digesting little biomorphs!

ALTERNATE COLOR MAPS

All the color maps work well with these fractals.

HISTORY AND CREDITS

These types have been explored by Clifford A. Pickover of IBM's Thomas J. Watson Research Center.

PLASMA CLOUDS

FRACTAL CATEGORY   Random fractal

FORMAL NAME   Midpoint Displacement

FRACTAL TYPE   plasma

FORMULA   N/A

COMMAND LINE

`fractint type=plasma map=altern`

DESCRIPTION

Plasma clouds are generated using a recursive algorithm that randomly picks the four corner colors, picks a color for the center, and then recursively quarters the four new rectangles. Random colors are averaged with those of the outer rectangles so the small adjacent points differ only slightly, creating a smoothed-out, cloudlike effect. The more colors your video mode is capable of, the better. The images can be saved and viewed in a 3-D mode as a fractal landscape. Your clouds are transformed into mountains!

Using the Ⓐ key, Plasma Clouds can be used as a template for generating realistic starfields, if your video mode supports at least 256 colors. The starfield default settings work best in an 800 × 600 video mode. See the Starfields section for details on the different parameters.

Color cycling for this fractal is required for all users of Fractint! The result is an eye-catching cauldron of writhing colors!

PARAMETERS

Graininess factor (.1 to 50, default is 2)

The graininess factor determines how abruptly the colors change from one pixel to the next. A value of .5 yields the smoothest clouds, while 50 yields the grainiest.

SPECIAL EFFECTS

These fractals make excellent landscapes using the landscap.map. They also make excellent planets with spherical projection!

EXPLORER

Zooming does not work with this fractal because the image is randomly created each time. See the guided tour at the beginning of Chapter 2 for an example of how to create a landscape from a plasma image.

HISTORY AND CREDITS

The midpoint displacement algorithm was first used by Archimedes as a method for constructing parabolas. Later, around 1900, the number theorist Teiji Takagi used a variation on the method to create a fractal curve between two points that had an infinite length. The algorithm in Fractint was adapted from Pascal code written by Bret Mulvey.

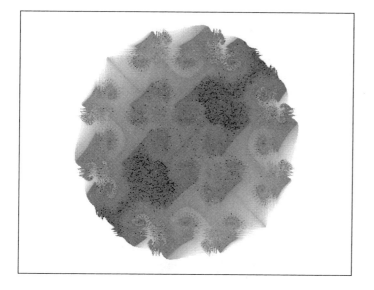

POPCORN JULIA SET

FRACTAL CATEGORY	Escape-time fractal
FORMAL NAME	None
FRACTAL TYPE	popcornjul
FORMULA	$x' = x - 0.05 \sin(y) + \tan(3y)$
	$y' = y - 0.05 \sin(x) + \tan(3x)$

COMMAND LINE

```
fractint maxiter=20000 inside=255 map=altern logmap=-1
type=popcornjul
```

DESCRIPTION

This fractal is the Julia set associated with the popcorn fractal type. Recall that the Julia set uses the screen coordinates for the corresponding pixel as the initial values for the variables x and y. The iterations continue until the value of $x^2 + y^2$ becomes higher than the bailout value, the orbits become periodic, or the maximum allowable number of iterations is reached. The pixel's color is assigned according to the number of iterations Fractint performed.

Pressing the ⊚ key will toggle on the orbits plotted in the popcorn fractal type. Color cycling works well with this fractal.

PARAMETERS

Bailout value (0 means use default)   0

Fractint uses the bailout value as one of the criteria to stop the iterations. Fractint will stop the iterations when the value of $x^2 + y^2$ is greater than or equal to the bailout value.

EXPLORER

Unlike most of the Julia fractal types in Fractint that have an entire family of sets, this fractal type has only one Julia set associated with the formula. Zooming in on any section of the fractal will show the same overall pattern only at higher iteration levels.

ALTERNATE COLOR MAPS

Smooth color maps at high iteration levels work best with this fractal type. If the iteration level exceeds the number of colors available on your screen, turn on the logarithmic color mapping from the Ⓧ key options menu or set the command-line parameter logmap= to 1 or -1.

HISTORY AND CREDITS

Clifford A. Pickover of IBM's Thomas J. Watson Research Center originated the popcorn fractal type.

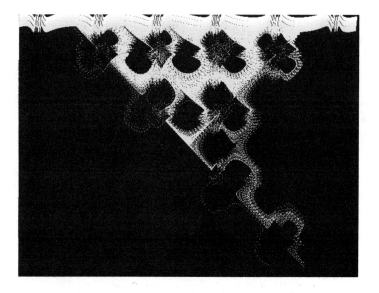

POPCORN FRACTALS

FRACTAL CATEGORY	Orbital fractal
FORMAL NAME	None
FRACTAL TYPE	popcorn
FORMULA	$x' = x - 0.05 \sin(y) + \tan(3y)$ $y' = y - 0.05 \sin(x) + \tan(3x)$

COMMAND LINE

```
fractint maxiter=20000 inside=255 map=altern type=popcorn
```

DESCRIPTION

This fractal is called "popcorn" because it looks like a bowl of popped popcorn on the screen. The screen coordinates are used as the initial values for the variables x and y. With each iteration the new x and y positions are plotted to the screen. Each new iteration cycle is plotted in the next sequential color from the current color palette.

The orbits frequently occur outside of the screen boundaries. To view the fractal in its entirety, set the preview option from the Ⓥ key options menu.

PARAMETERS

Bailout value (0 means use default)   0

Fractint uses the bailout value as one of the criteria to stop the iterations. Fractint will stop the iterations when the value of $x^2 + y^2$ is greater than or equal to the bailout value. The default value is 4. To increase the number of iterations, raise the value of maximum iterations in the $\textcircled{x}$ key options menu or use the command-line parameter maxiter=.

SPECIAL EFFECTS

Try pressing (RETURN) during color cycling to see teaser changes in the colors. This fractal looks best in a low-resolution mode such as $320 \times 200 \times 256$ (video mode F3).

ALTERNATE COLOR MAPS

Smooth color maps are not recommended for this fractal type.

HISTORY AND CREDITS

Clifford A. Pickover of IBM's Thomas J. Watson Research Center originated this fractal type.

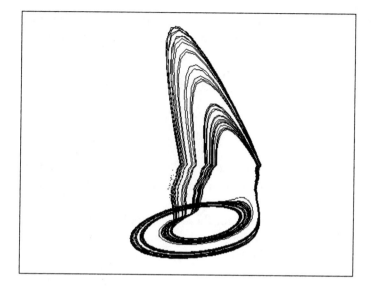

ROSSLER THREE D

FRACTAL CATEGORY	Orbital fractal
FORMAL NAME	Rossler
FRACTAL TYPE	rossler3d
FORMULA	$x' = x - (y - x)dt$
	$y' = y + (x + ay)dt$
	$z' = z + (b + xz - cz)dt$

COMMAND LINE

```
fractint maxiter=20000 inside=255 map=altern
type=rossler3d
```

DESCRIPTION

Named after its originator, Dr. Otto Rossler, this fractal is very similar to the Lorenz fractal. The three variables, x, y, and z, plot a position in three-dimensional space. The dt term is the time increment.

The way Dr. Rossler describes the fractal is, "a sausage in a sausage in a sausage in a sausage. Take it out, fold it, squeeze it, put it back." Dr. Rossler takes a very philosophical view of this fractal, which he imagines as a wind sock in an airfield: "an open hose with a hole in the end, and the wind forces its way in. Then the wind is trapped. Against its will, energy is doing something productive, like the devil in medieval history. The principle is that nature does something against its own will and, by self-entanglement, produces beauty." (James Gleick, *Chaos—Making a New Science*, pp 141–2.)

PARAMETERS

Time step	*0.04*
a	*0.2*
b	*0.2*
c	*5.7*

The time step parameter is used as the *dt* term in the formula. Higher values generate the fractal more quickly but produce many sharp corners. Lower values take longer and smooth out the curves.

The parameters *a*, *b*, and *c* are used for the corresponding variables in the formula. Changing the values of *a* and *b* will generally destroy the fractal. Changing the value of *c* will alter the fractal's size.

SPECIAL EFFECTS

Since this fractal is inherently three-dimensional it is possible to generate it as an anaglyph for viewing with the red/blue glasses. The perspective, rotation, and other parameters need to be altered for proper viewing.

HISTORY AND CREDITS

This fractal was discovered by Otto Rossler, a nonpracticing medical doctor in Germany. Dr. Rossler became interested in chaos through his studies of chemistry and theoretical biology.

SCOTT TAYLOR FRACTALS

FRACTAL CATEGORY	Escape-time fractal
FORMAL NAME	None
FRACTAL TYPES	fn($z*z$), fn*fn, fn*z+z, fn+fn, sqr(1/fn), sqr(fn)
FORMULAS	fn(z^2)
	fn(z)fn(z)
	fn+fn
	$p_1$fn(z) + $p_2 z$
	$p_1$fn(z) + $p_2$fn(z)
	1/fn(z)^2
	fn(z)^2
	fn(z) = sin(z), cos(z), sinh(z), cosh(z), e^z, ln(z), z^2

COMMAND LINE

```
fractint maxiter=20000 inside=255 map=altern logmap=-1
type=fn(z*z)
```

DESCRIPTION

When Fractint was first released with the Formula Compiler, one person in particular went on a wild rampage generating new fractal types. Stone Soup was getting so many different fractals from this person that names could not be created quickly enough! So we lumped them all together here.

The short list of six different types is deceptive. Considering that the fn*fn fractal type allows you to select the same or different functions for each of the functions to be multiplied, that one fractal type alone is actually 28 different types in disguise! Toss in changes in the two parameters and the number of variations is mind-boggling.

PARAMETERS

Real coefficient first function	*1*
Imag coefficient first function	*0*
Real coefficient second function	*1*
Imag coefficient second function	*0*
First function	*sin*
Second function	*sqr*
Bailout value (0 means use default)	*0*

The real coefficient and imag coefficient of the first four parameters refer to the complex variables p_1 and p_2 of the formulas. The first function and second function accept one of the following function types:

sin	*cosh*	*log*
cos	*exp*	*sqr*
sinh		

The bailout value is the variable that determines when Fractint should stop the iterations and assign the pixel a color. The default value is 4.

EXPLORER

These fractals will get you well on your way in exploring this immense fractal type:

```
fractint inside=255 function=cosh potential=255/128/0
type=fn(z*z) corners=-3.28023/3.27637/-2.45584/2.46025

fractint inside=255 function=cosh potential=255/255/0
type=fn(z*z) corners=-2.3798/-1.4890/+1.6200/+2.2881

fractint inside=255 function=cosh/sin potential=255/255/0
type=fn+fn corners=-4.48415/4.47702/-3.35977/3.36304
params=1/0/1/0

fractint inside=255 function=cosh/sin potential=255/300/0
type=fn+fn corners=+1.2202/+2.7584/+1.6218/+2.7756
params=1/0/1/0

fractint inside=255 function=sinh potential=255/128/0
type=sqr(1/fn) corners=-2.1286/+2.1256/-1.5916/+1.5966
```

```
fractint inside=255 function=cosh potential=255/128/0
type=sqr(fn) corners=-4/3.99739/-2.99709/3

fractint inside=255 function=cosh potential=255/128/0
type=sqr(fn) corners=+0.7835/+1.8690/+0.4091/+1.2229

fractint inside=255 function=sqr potential=255/200/0
type=sqr(1/fn) corners=-2.7044/+2.6985/-2.0207/+2.0284
maxiter=5192
```

HISTORY AND CREDITS

These fractal types were contributed to Fractint by Scott Taylor. Tim Wegner programmed the types into Fractint.

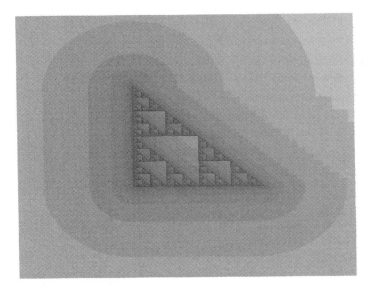

SIERPINSKI

FRACTAL CATEGORY	Escape-time fractal
FORMAL NAME	Sierpinski's Gasket
FRACTAL TYPE	sierpinski
FORMULA	$x' = 2x - 1, x > .5$
	$x' = 2x, x <= .5$
	$y' = 2y - 1, y > .5$
	$y' = 2y, y <= .5$

COMMAND LINE
```
fractint maxiter=20000 inside=255 map=altern logmap=-1
type=sierpinski
```

DESCRIPTION

This fractal, named after its mathematician originator, is full of so many holes that there is nothing left of it. The overall shape is that of a triangle. Cut out of the triangle are successively smaller triangles carried on into infinity. Imagine a Swiss cheese where there are only holes remaining and no cheese. That's the way Sierpinski acts, except the holes are triangles.

The reason there is "no cheese" is because the fractal exists between the first and second dimensions. One-dimensional objects are lines which have a length.

Two-dimensional objects are planes which have a length and width that can be used to calculate the object's circumference and surface area. The sierpinski fractal has a circumference but no surface area. It is more than a line and yet less than a plane. It exists in a fractional dimension between the two.

PARAMETERS

Bailout value (0 means use default)   0

The bailout value determines at what level the iterations should cease. The default value is 4. Lower values are ignored. Changing this parameter to higher values alters the overall color of the fractal but otherwise has no appreciable effect.

EXPLORER

Zoom in and you will find smaller and smaller triangles.

HISTORY AND CREDITS

The original mathematical concept of the fractal came from a mathematician named Sierpinski in the early twentieth century. The fractal code was obtained from a basic program in *Fractals Everywhere* by Michael Barnsley (p. 251).

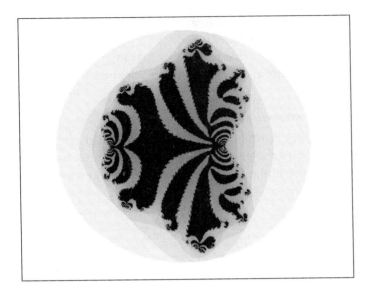

SPIDER

FRACTAL CATEGORY	Escape-time fractal
FORMAL NAME	None
FRACTAL TYPE	spider

FORMULA

$$z' = z^2 + c$$
$$c' = \frac{c}{2} + z'$$

COMMAND LINE

```
fractint maxiter=20000 inside=255 map=altern logmap=-1
type=spider
```

DESCRIPTION

The name tells it all—this type looks like a spider!

PARAMETERS

As with other Mandelbrot types, the parameters warp the image by perturbing
the initial orbit value.

EXPLORER

Try zooming in on the area where the legs appear to be converging.

HISTORY AND CREDITS

This fractal type came from the program *Fractal Magic 5* by way of Lee Skinner.

TETRATION FRACTAL

FRACTAL CATEGORY	Escape-time fractal
FORMAL NAME	None
FRACTAL TYPE	tetrate
FORMULA	c^z

COMMAND LINE

```
fractint type=tetrate maxiter=1023 potential=255/511 in-
side=255 corners=1.58675/2.77/3.22225/4.10550
```

DESCRIPTION

This fractal type orginated from an investigation into the properties of the generalized Ackerman exponential. Fractint initializes the variables z and c to the complex value corresponding to the screen pixel color being evaluated. By successively raising the variable c in the fractal formula to the z power with each iteration, Fractint is performing a *tetration* of z, hence the name.

The examples below show the wide range of images that the tetration type can produce. The fractal named "The Tunnel" has smoothly varying colors that seem to form the sides of a cavern. The smooth colors come from the use of the continuous potential option, which turns bright stripes into blending hues. The other examples have more of a crazy-quilt appearance with solid colored patches.

PARAMETERS

Real part of parameter	*0*
Imaginary part of parameter	*0*
Bailout value (0 means use default)	*0*

The real part of parameter and imaginary part of parameter are added to the initial value of z for each pixel calculation. Fractint compares the bailout value parameter to the modulus of z with each iteration. When the modulus is greater than or equal to the bailout value, Fractint stops iterating and assigns a color to the pixel.

EXPLORER

Here are a few places to visit to start you on your explorations. Try the following commands from the DOS command line:

The Land

```
fractint type=tetrate maxiter=1023 inside=0 corners=-6/6
-4.5/4.5
```

The Tunnel

```
fractint type=tetrate maxiter=1023 potential=255/511
inside=255 corners=1.58675/2.77/3.22225/4.10550
```

Circles

```
fractint type=tetrate maxiter=1023 inside=0 corners=-.32/
.15/-.18/.18
```

The Star Spiral

```
fractint type=tetrate maxiter=1023 inside=0 corners=
-1.59911/-1.58942/.584366/.591539
```

WARNINGS

Every iteration of this fractal requires a complex power calculation. If you do not have a floating-point coprocessor this fractal type will take a very long time to generate.

HISTORY AND CREDITS

This fractal type was created by Lee Skinner from Albuquerque, New Mexico.

UNITY

FRACTAL CATEGORY	Escape-time fractal
FORMAL NAME	Unity
FORMULA:	$One = x^2 + y^2$
	$y' = (2 - One) * x;$
	$x' = (2 - One) * y';$

COMMAND LINE

```
fractint type=unity logmap=-1 maxiter=20000
```

DESCRIPTION

> *Circles in circles and lines within lines.*
> *Zoom in closer and see what you find.*
> *Patterns pertaining to a search, you'll see,*
> *Of x chasing y to Unity.*

The Unity fractal is abased on a round-about approximation of the number 1. The first line of the formula is the equation for a unit circle. From there, the next *y* is calculated based on how far it deviated from the correct answer. The next *x* is based on how far the *y'* variable deviates from the correct answer. As soon as the variable *One* approximates the real number 1 to with one pixel width, the iterations top and the number of iterations required to that point are displayed to the screen as a color.

This is the only fractal where the bailout criterion is based on the width of a pixel on the screen. This creates some interesting effects. As you zoom in to the fractal, some lines expand while others become smaller. Also, if you change to a higher-resolution drawing, more lines develop. In all the drawings the line of the unit circle is always one pixel wide.

EXPLORER

The most interesting section is where both the x- and y-coordinates are close to the square root of two.

HISTORY AND CREDITS

Mark Peterson originated this fractal and adapted it to Fractint. At the time he was intrigued by Newton's fractal, which approximates complex roots, and wondered if other approximations algorithms would also produce fractals. In this case, one did.

USER-DEFINED FRACTALS

Fractint has a feature unique among fractal programs. It lets you enter your own fractal formulas and then it will generate the corresponding image on the screen. You can thus explore your own ideas and create previously unknown fractals. You use the formula and lsystem fractal types to explore these new fractal formulas. Zoom into unexplored depths—translate to dazzling 3-D—the only limits are your own imagination!

THE FORMULA COMPILER

The Formula Compiler interprets algebraic expressions into a series of program instructions. These instructions are then turned over to the powerful Fractint engine, which quickly generates the corresponding fractal. All the resources available to other fractal types in Fractint can also be used with your own formulas.

To compile a formula, set type=formula in either sstools.ini or from the command line. Fractint will later ask you which text file you would like it to use. Just press (RETURN) to use the default fractint.frm file, or enter a different file name. Fractint will scan the text file and create a list of the available formulas for you to choose from. Use the arrow keys to highlight the formula you'd like to use. As you will see, you can add your own formulas to this file.

If you are running in the batch mode, you can bypass the queries from Fractint by setting formulafile= to the text file containing the list of formulas and also setting formulaname= to the name of the formula you want to run. Fractint will then skip the queries and go straight to work.

Formula Files

The Formula Compiler reads and compiles formulas from a DOS text file. Operationally, the formula compiler is divided into three major sections. The first section separates the formula names from the actual formula to create the list of names. Once you tell Fractint which formula will be used, it passes the formula information to an internal interpreter section called the *Parser*. The Parser compiles the formula into a set of instructions that are then executed by Fractint.

Formula Names and Comments

The Formula Compiler distinguishes names from formulas by looking for a set of curly brackets. It treats any text enclosed in curly brackets as a formula and the text immediately before the brackets as the name, as follows:

FormulaName = { … Formula … }

The "=" symbol is optional. Comments can also be placed in the file if they are named explicitly as "comments" and if the text is enclosed in the curly brackets:

```
comment = {
          Comments can be placed right before your fractal
          formulas. This is where you would describe all
          the wonderful properties of your formula, its
          history, or whatever. The comment section can
          take up as many lines as you like, provided they are
          enclosed within curly brackets.

}
```

Any number of comment sections can be placed in the formula file. The use of the "comment" name informs the compiler that the text in the enclosing brackets is not a formula and should be disregarded.

The Parser

The Parser looks for three distinct sections in every formula. The first section it looks for is the initial conditions. Generally, this section defines the values for your variables. The second section details the math operations performed on each iteration. The third section specifies the conditions under which the iterations should continue. There can be any number of math operations in each of the sections, provided the total number of characters between the curly brackets is fewer than 200. The Parser looks for each of the sections to be separated by a different punctuation marking:

MyFractal { Initial Condition: Iteration, Condition }

The full colon separates the initial conditions from the iterations. The comma separates the iterations from the conditionals. Multiple math statements should be separated by semicolons.

These three sections can be placed on separate lines for clarity, but the required punctuation must be used:

MyFractal { $c = z = 1/pixel$: $z = $ sqr $(z) + c$, $|z| <= 4$ }

or

```
MyFractal {
c = z = 1/pixel:
        z = sqr (z) + c,
|z| <= 4
}
```

Let's walk through this example and say what each part of this formula does. "MyFractal" is the name that will appear in the list of formula types loaded from your *.FRM file. The variable *pixel* always refers to the complex number mapped to the screen pixel color being calculated. The calculation is repeated for all the values of the variable *pixel* needed to cover the screen. The line "$c = z = 1/pixel$" defines two variables c and z and initializes them to $1/pixel$. This initialization is done once for each pixel calculation. The formula "$z - sqr(z) + c$" is the calculation that is iterated over and over. In this case, in each iteration, z is changed to be the sum of the square root of the previous z and c. The last formula, "$|z| <= 4$," is true. When this condition fails to be true, the iteration is halted. If periodicity checking is enabled, the default condition and then the iterations are halted when the successive values of z fall into a periodic loop.

Note that either upper- or lowercase may be used. The entry

$$z = a + sin(z * pixel \wedge z)$$

is the same as:

$$Z = A + SIN(Z * PIXEL \wedge Z)$$

The chart below shows the precedence rules that are in effect when your formula is parsed and interpreted. These rules govern the order in which operations are performed if not explicitly determined with parentheses. The lower-numbered precedence level operations are done before the higher-numbered ones.

PRECEDENCE LEVEL 1

2.34543	*Convert from a real constant to a complex real constant*
(1.32, -7.64)	*Convert from a Cartesian constant to a complex constant*
MyVariable	*Creation of automatic complex variable*
Abs ( )	*Converts both real and imaginary components to positive numbers*
Cos ( )	*Complex Cosine*
Cosh ( )	*Complex Hyperbolic Cosine*
Conj ( )	*Complex Conjugate*
Exp ( )	*Complex Exponential*
Imag ( )	*Replaces the real component with the imaginary component, then sets the imaginary portion to zero, creating a pure real number*
Log ( )	*Complex Logarithm*
Real ( )	*Zeros the imaginary component, creating a pure real number*

Sin ( )	*Complex Sine*
Sinh ( )	*Complex Hyperbolic Sine*
Sqr ( )	*Complex Square*

PRECEDENCE LEVEL 2

| - | *Complex Negation* |
| ∧ | *Complex Power* |

PRECEDENCE LEVEL 3

| * | *Complex Multiplication* |
| / | *Complex Division* |

PRECEDENCE LEVEL 4

| + | *Complex Addition* |
| - | *Complex Subtraction* |

PRECEDENCE LEVEL 5

| = | *Assignment* |

PRECEDENCE LEVEL 6

| < | *Real Component Comparison (Less than)* |
| <= | *Real Component Comparison (Less than or equal to)* |

These are the operations and functions supported by the formula compiler. The formula compiler also supports nested parentheses of an unlimited depth (well, in reality it's limited by the size of the computer's stack space) and a modulus squared operator " | ... | ".

Precedence

If you've never written computer programs you may be unfamiliar with the term *precedence*, although you are probably familiar with the concept. If you were to calculate the expression $a + 4bc^3$, where $a = 7$, $b = 2$ and $c = 3$, you know you need to cube the value of c before multiplying by $4b$, and you need to perform the multiplication before the addition to a. This way the expression evaluates to 223. Powers are performed before multiplication because they have a higher *precedence*. Likewise, multiplication and division are performed before addition or subtraction. An expression suitable for the Formula Compiler equivalent to $a + 4bc^3$ would be:

$$a + 4 * b * c\wedge3$$

If, on the other hand, you wanted 4 added to a before multiplying and then you wanted to cube the entire expression, you would write the expression as

$((a + 4)bc)^3$. Here you are overriding the normal precedence of the expression by enclosing the portion you'd like calculated first within parentheses. The Parser equivalent in this case would be:

$$((a + 4) * b * c) \wedge 3$$

Predefined Variables

Variable	Function
z	*Used in periodicity checking*
p1	*Command-line parameters 1 and 2*
p2	*Command-line parameters 3 and 4*
pixel	*Screen coordinates being calculated*

Table 3-1 Predefined variables used by the Formula Compiler

The Formula Compiler uses several predefined variables (see Table 3-1) as an aid in interfacing with the rest of Fractint. The most important among these is the predefined variable z. The Fractint fractal engine performs an occasional check on the value of z to determine whether iterations of the equation have fallen into a periodic loop. By maintaining the value of z current with the results of the iteration, Fractint will use this periodicity check to speed the drawing of your fractal (see Appendix C for more details on periodicity).

Another important predefined variable is *pixel*. This variable is updated by Fractint as it calculates the color of each pixel on the screen. It sets the value of *pixel* to the complex number equivalent to the current position on the screen relative to the values of the screen corners. For example, if you started Fractint with corners=4/-4/3/-3, then for the first calculation Fractint would set the value of *pixel* to the complex number equivalent to the upper left-hand corner of the screen, or $-4 + i3$. If the resolution you are working in is 320 × 200 pixels, then when Fractint calculates the color of the next adjacent pixel it will set the value of *pixel* to $(-4 + i3) + ((4 - (-4))/320)$ or $4.025 + i3$. If you chose to zoom into a portion of your fractal, Fractint will automatically keep track of the screen corner values.

Two other useful variables are $p1$ and $p2$. These variables are set by the Formula Compiler as each color is calculated with the params= parameter passed from either the command line or SSTOOLS.INI. The variable $p1$ is composed of the first two parameters in params=, and $p2$ is composed of the second two. If you set params=1/2/3/4, then Fractint will set $p1$ equal to $1 + i2$ and $p2$ equal to $3 + i4$. This is very useful in the batch mode, where you can generate a number of similar fractals based on the same formula but differing only by one or two complex constants.

Parser Errors

As the Parser compiles a formula it looks for syntax errors. These are errors in the formula that make no mathematical sense. If you were to try compiling:

$$\text{Bogus1 } \{ z = 0 \colon z = z + * 2, \ |z| <= 4 \}$$

the Parser would tell you

TABLE OF PARSER ERRORS

Number	Error	Explanation
Error(0)	*Should be an Argument*	*An operator was found when the Parser was expecting an variable, constant, or the value returned by a function.*
Error(1)	*Should be an Operator*	*An argument was found when the Parser was expecting an operator.*
Error(2)	*')' needs a matching '('*	*There are more close parentheses than open parentheses.*
Error(3)	*Need more ')'*	*There were more open parentheses than close parentheses.*
Error(4)	*Undefined Operator*	*An operator was used, such as '!' or '%', that is not supported by the Parser. The "Precedence Level" charts, above, list all supported operators.*
Error(5)	*Undefined Function*	*A function was used, such as tan(...), that is not supported by the Parser. The "Precedence Level" charts, above, list all supported operators.*
Error(6)	*More than one ','*	*There can be only one comma in a formula. This separates the iteration portion from the conditional. If more than one statement is required, use a semicolon.*

```
Error(0):   Should be an Argument
```
$$z = 0:\ z = z + * 2;\ |z| <= 4$$
$$\wedge$$
```
...Press any key to continue...
```

meaning the Parser was expecting you to try adding something to z before multiplying by 2. After you press a key, Fractint will return to the Fractal Types list. The preceeding table is a complete list of Parser errors.

After the Parser has completed compiling a formula without encountering any errors, it passes the set of instructions to Fractint's fractal engine for immediate execution.

Formula Examples

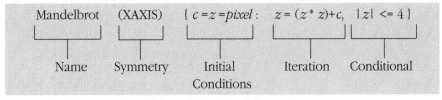

Figure 3-3 Different sections of the traditional Mandelbrot set

The above diagram breaks down the different sections of the traditional Mandelbrot set. After compiling the formula, the Parser will give Fractint a set of instructions which read, "When drawing the screen assume the fractal is symmetrical about the x-axis. For each pixel on the screen set z equivalent to the Cartesian coordinate on the screen and set the automatic variable c equal to z. Then successively perform the iterations until the conditional is false (z is not less than 4), the maximum limit to the number of iterations is reached, or the value of z falls into a periodic loop."

Fractint will execute the instructions using the currently set math mode (see Appendix C for a description of various math types), and each pixel on the screen will be colored according to the number of iterations performed. If the maximum allowable number of iterations was performed or z went into a periodic loop, the color is set to the value of the variable *inside*.

Formula Compiler Hints

There are a few things to consider when using the Formula Compiler. Specify a symmetry only after you are sure the fractal is symmetrical, otherwise Fractint will draw a false picture. Second, remember that integer mathematics, which is

the default math mode, has a limited range. The range is fine for additions, sub-
tractions, and multiplications, but when the formulas involve powers or trigonometric functions, the range of this math mode is easily exceeded. When this
happens, the iterations stop and Fractint draws however many iterations it took
before the overflow occurred. This also creates false pictures that are not real
fractals. They are not *real* fractals because the drawing is based on the limitations of the integer mathematics rather than the mathematics described in the
formula. You should always try drawing the fractal using floating-point math at
one time or another to see if it matches the integer drawing. This way you can
be sure you are looking at the real McCoy.

Many functions that are not supported can be calculated using the available
functions. For example, a Mandelbrot set based on a tangent function can be
written using a sine and a cosine, as follows:

> MandelTangent {
>> z = *pixel* :
>>> z = *pixel* * $(\sin(z) / \cos(z))$,
>> | real(z) | <= 32
> }

With your text editor you can modify or create any formula that comes to mind.

> Mandel3 = {
>> z = *pixel*; c = $\sin(z)$:
>>> z = $(z * z) + c$;
>>> z = $z * 1/c$,
>> | z | <= 4
> }

Don't be bashful. There is a fractal out there with your name on it.

L-Systems

L-systems were developed in 1968 by A. Lindenmayer as a method for modeling
the growth of living organisms. A. R. Smith and P. Prusinkiewicz both applied
the system to computer graphics. This drawing system enables drawing not only
lifelike trees and plants, but also abstract fractals such as the Koch curve and the
classic Sierpinski gasket. More important, Fractint will run the L-system definitions you create using your text editor! The L-system definitions are listed in
Table 3-3.

You write L-system definitions in a text file in a format similar to the one used
by the fractal type formula. If you are within the Fractint program and select the
lsystem fractal type, Fractint will prompt you for the file you want to use con-

Command	Function
nn	*Specifies a number. The number* nn *can be prefixed by "I" to mean 1/*nn*, by "Q" to mean* $\sqrt{nn}$, *or by a combination of the two.*
Angle nn	*Specifies the primary turning angle in fractions of a circle (360/*nn *degrees).*
Axiom string	*Character string containing the initial turtle drawing instructions.*
c = string	*Instructs Fractint to recursively replace each occurrence of* c *in this and all other strings with string.*
F	*Move forward, and draw a line.*
G	*Move forward, but don't draw a line.*
+	*Instructs the turtle to turn left (counterclockwise) using the primary angle.*
-	*Instructs the turtle to turn right (clockwise) using the primary angle.*
\nn	*Creates a secondary angle which is* nn *degrees higher than the primary angle.*
/nn	*Creates a secondary angle which is* nn *degrees lower than the primary angle.*
D	*Turn using the secondary angle, move forward, and draw a line.*
M	*Turn using the secondary angle, move forward, but do not draw a line.*
C nn	*Set the drawing color to color number* nn.
< nn	*Add* nn *to the drawing color number.*
> nn	*Subtract* nn *from the drawing color number.*
!	*Toggles the use of negative angles for instructions "+", "-", "\", and "/", but not "D" or "M".*
@ nn	*Multiply the line segment by* nn.
[	*Save the current state of the turtle (position, primary and secondary angles) and continue drawing.*
]	*Restore the previously saved state of the turtle.*
;;	*Designates a comment line.*

Table 3-3 Commands within an L-system definition

taining the L-systems definitions. It will then scan the file and create a list of names for you to choose from. This selection process can also be done from the Fractint command line using lfile= to specify the definition text file and lname for the name of the L-system definition Fractint is to run.

The L-system definition consists of a name followed by the definition enclosed in curly brackets, as follows:

MyLSystemName { . . . L-system Definition . . . }

The use of curly brackets helps Fractint separate the definition names from the actual definitions. Using a definition name of "Comment" tells Fractint to ignore whatever text is enclosed within the curly brackets. Text lines within an L-system definition beginning with ";;" also designate comments.

Comment {

This text, and the name "Comment," is completely ignored by Fractint.

}

BogusDefinition {

;; This is a comment line within an L-system definition since it begins with ";;".

}

Fractint interprets the instructions within the definition via a Logo-like turtle graphics interpreter. Fractint uses a "turtle," which follows simple instructions, such as "Draw a line" and "Turn left," to draw the L-system fractal. These instructions are contained within the string declared by the keyword *Axiom.*

Initially, the turtle is pointed directly towards the right side of the screen. The F and G characters instruct the turtle to move in the direction it is pointing. For the F command, the turtle moves forward in the direction it is pointing and draws a line between the new point and where it was before it moved. The G command instructs the turtle to move forward in the direction it is pointing and not draw a line.

The + and - characters are turning instructions. Somewhere in the definition the turning angle is specified by the keyword *Angle* followed by a number. Note that all numbers can be prefixed by I, Q, or both to mean the inverse of the number or the square root of the number, respectively. Declaring "Angle 6" tells the turtle to turn one-sixth of a full circle (360/6 degrees) whenever a turning instruction is used. The + character turns the turtle to the left and - turns the turtle to the right.

Creating a Koch curve using these instructions is a snap:

```
KochCurve {
        Angle 6
        Axiom F
        F=F+F -- F+F
}
```

The "Angle 6" instruction declares a turning angle of one-sixth of a circle, or 60 degrees. The axiom is to simply draw a line. The definition of a straight line, however, is modified to have a triangular hump in the middle. This is done by declaring "F = F+F -- F+F", which reads as "draw a line forward, turn left, draw a line forward, turn right twice, draw a line forward, turn left, draw a line forward."

Notice that the definition of a line, "F =", uses line statement F. If Fractint is instructed to go only one level deep, it will go down one level and use the original definition of a straight line, When it returns to the previous level, the definition of a line has been modified to have the triangular hump. Instructing Fractint to go two levels deep creates a line with a triangular hump on the first level. On the second level a straight line is defined as a triangular hump drawn using lines with triangular humps. With each level the length of the lines used is increasingly smaller.

Other characters can be used as needed to define subaxioms. Here is an example:

```
DragonCurve {
        Angle 4
        Axiom X
        X=X-YF-
        Y=+FX+Y
}
```

Here the characters X and Y are used to define subaxioms.

```
Bush {
        Angle 16
        Axiom ++++F
        F=FF-[-F+F+F]+[+F-F-F]
}
```

Bushes and trees utilize the "[" and "]" symbols, which save and restore the turtle's position and angle. This enables the turtle to draw branches and sub-branches and still be able to return to the previous branch or trunk to continue the drawing. The Bush example consists of two "[]" pairs which create forked branche. This particular example creates a plant that looks like wind-blown sagebrush.

PARAMETERS

OPTIONS FOR FRACTAL TYPE LSYSTEM

Order   2

The order parameter determines how deeply Fractint will apply the character string substitutions. The deeper the level, the more detailed the image. With each level of depth the time required to generate the image is squared. If an image takes 10 minutes to draw at level 6 it will take 100 minutes to draw at level 7 and 10,000 minutes at level 8.

The L-system code is new to Fractint, so you're swimming in uncharted territory. Other L-systems to try are the following:

```
ColorTriangleGasket {
  Angle 6
  Axiom -- X
  X=++FXF++FXF++FXF>1
  F=FF
}


SierpinskiSquare {
  Angle 4
  Axiom F+F+F+F
  F=FF+F+F+F+FF
}
```

APPENDIX A

FRACTINT, VIDEO, ADAPTERS, AND MONITORS

In order to see fractals on your PC, you need a graphics adapter. Support of a variety of graphics hardware is a strong point of Fractint, and fortunately so, because a large variety of graphics adapters are available on the market. Fractint supports four different IBM graphics standards, the CGA, EGA, VGA, and 8514a. In addition to these, many manufacturers have offered VGA boards with enhanced features, called super-VGA boards. These enhanced features usually include some higher resolution modes that fractal creators love. Unfortunately, these boards use a variety of methods of accessing their super-VGA modes, although some of the newer ones are beginning to use the emerging VESA standard. Fractint attempts to detect which board you have and adjust its pixel-writing procedures accordingly. Most of the super-VGA adapters on the market are supported. Then there are the Hercules-compatible monochrome graphics boards, and, finally, the Truevision Targa boards, which are popular among multimedia professionals. Since each of these boards has multiple graphics modes, you can see why the Fractint mode list is so long!

THE VIDEO ROUTINES

Fractint supports a wide variety of video adapters—from Hercules monochrome graphics to the third-party VESA adapter capable of displaying 1280 × 1024 × 256 colors. By pressing (RETURN) twice when starting Fractint you can select from a list of various video modes and select one to fit whatever video hardware is used by your computer. These modes are divided up into several different categories: standard modes, super-EGA/VGA modes, tweaked modes, and disk video modes.

In most cases, Fractint uses your machine's built-in BIOS routines to set the video mode. This ensures that when we select a mode, the computer will know how to do it regardless of the particular video display installed. For reading and writing individual pixel colors, however, Fractint bypasses the machine's BIOS and uses direct video access as a faster and more versatile drawing method. This approach requires Fractint to use many different read/write routines depending on the video mode you select. This is handled internally by using several different C language function pointers for reading and writing pixels. (See Appendix C, "For Programmers Only.")

The use of function pointers allows the actual video mode you select to be transparent to the rest of the Fractint program. That is, the fractal generation algorithms are concerned only with the screen resolution and the number of available colors. In the C source code, this information is available through the global variables *xdots*, *ydots*, and *colors*. These variables and the function pointers are set right after Fractint calls the BIOS to place the video adapter into the mode you select.

ALL VIDEO ADAPTERS ARE DIFFERENT

Fractint has dedicated routines for writing in CGA, EGA, VGA/MCGA and Hercules Graphics modes. Separate routines are required because each of the adapters uses a different method for utilizing the video memory to display the color information. For example, the CGA adapter uses a memory address of b800h for the beginning of its video RAM while the Hercules Graphics adapter uses b000h. Different video modes also use different color mapping techniques. EGA uses a color map system where the video processor has to be instructed directly with each read/write operation how the color information should be handled. VGA and MCGA use a 1 for 1 color map where a color index byte is written directly to the video memory.

In Fractint, the video modes marked as "Super VGA/VESA Autodetect" support most of the high-resolution adapters available for MS-DOS machines. Fractint uses a slightly modified version of John Bridges' Super-VGA and Autodetect logic. John Bridges' SVGA adapter code is free for use in all commercial, shareware, freeware, or public domain programs. John's code automatically detects the presence of Cirrus, Video7, Tseng, Genoa, Orchid, Willow, Paradise, Chips & Technology, Trident, ATI, Everex, Ahead, and Oak Tech video boards and chip sets. Other video adapters supported by Fractint include: Video 7 EGA, ATI EGAWonder, Everex EGA, Genoa EGA, Paradise EGA, Tandy 1000, AT&T 6300, Targa, and the NEC GB-1. You can contact the Stone Soup Group forum on Compuserve to determine if your new adapter is covered in a later version.

Super-VGA boards, which are VGA adapters supporting 256 colors at greater than the IBM VGA 320 × 200 resolution (such as 640 × 400 or 640 × 480), utilize memory areas in excess of the 64K of memory located at the normal VGA memory address of A000h. To get around this limitation the boards incorporate a concept known as *bank switching*. This involves calling a routine to switch a different area of video memory to the A000h address. The 800 × 600 × 256 color modes divide their video memory into seven banks of 64K each. For each pixel read/write operation Fractint determines which bank the pixel is located in and switches that bank to the A000h address. After the bank is switched Fractint can then perform the operation. The latest version of the code is always available in the PICS forum on CompuServe, library 14, in the file called VGAKIT.ZIP. This code is mostly assembly language.

TWEAKED VGA MODES

Fractint contains code that sets up the IBM (or any truly register-compatible) VGA adapter for several special-purpose, high-resolution extended modes such as 704 × 528, 736 × 552, 768 × 576, and 800 × 600 at 16 colors, and 320 × 400, 360 × 480, and all the way up to 400 × 600 at 256 colors. Even though most super-VGA adapters have built-in modes higher than the tweaked modes, these tweaked modes have an advantage: they are universal. Suppose you are going to show off your fractals at a computer user group, and you know they have a VGA. It is really too bad to be limited to the plain VGA 320 × 200 256-color mode. You can use the 320 × 400 or 360 × 480 256-color modes instead, which look much better, and still have reasonable confidence that those modes are supported on the user group's VGA.

The tweaked modes work by programming the VGA controller to use the fastest dot-clock on the IBM adapter (28.322 MHz), displaying more pixels per scan line, and reducing the refresh rate to make up the difference. These modes push many monitors beyond their rated specs, in terms of both resolution and refresh rate. Signs that your monitor is having problems with a particular tweaked mode include the following:

- vertical or horizontal overscan (displaying dots beyond the edges of your visible CRT area)

- bad flickering (caused by a too-slow refresh rate, although some flickering is normal for the higher-resolution tweaked modes)
- vertical roll or total garbage on the screen (your monitor simply can't keep up or is attempting to "force" the image into a preset mode that doesn't fit)

If your monitor exhibits any of these symptoms DO NOT continue using that video mode. Continued use could damage your monitor. The 320 × 400 and 360 × 480 256-color modes are both very useful and very conservative, and they should not create any problems, which show up mostly for the highest-resolution tweaked modes.

We have successfully tested the modes up to 768 × 576 on an IBM PS/2 Model 80 connected to IBM 8513, IBM 8514, NEC Multisync II, Sony CPD-1302, and Zenith 1490 monitors (all of which exhibit some overscan and flicker at the highest rates), and we have tested 800 × 600 mode on the NEC Multisync II and Sony CPD-1302 (although it takes some twiddling of the vertical-size control).

DISK VIDEO

Often you would like to generate high-resolution fractals using a lower-resolution adapter. You might want to make a transparency for artwork or projection. Fractint offers disk video modes to handle this need. The disk video modes do not involve a video adapter at all. They use your expanded memory, extended memory, or disk storage to hold the color information during fractal generation. These modes are very useful for creating images beyond the capacity of your video adapter, up to the current internal limit of 2048 × 2048 × 256.

Disk video mode is ideally suited for Windows 3.0, where you can generate fractals in the "background" mode. This means you can make big fractals while simultaneously working on a word processor, calculating a spreadsheet, or downloading a file. The nondisk video modes attempt to write directly to the screen, which is not allowed in multitasking environments, such as Windows 3.0. The disk video mode gives Fractint someplace to put the Fractal image without wreaking havoc with your word processing screen.

While you are in a disk video mode, your screen will display text information indicating whether memory or your disk drive is being used, and what portion of the "screen" is being read from or written to. A "Cache size" figure is also displayed. This is the amount of memory reserved by Fractint to use as a storage buffer before sending the data to the disk. 24K is the maximum cache size. If you see a number less than this, it means that you don't have a large amount of memory free, so performance will be less than optimum. With a very low cache size such as 4K or 6K, performance will become considerably worse in cases using solid-guessing, boundary tracing, plasma, or anything else that paints the screen nonlinearly. If you have such a problem, we suggest removing most of your TSR utilities, any non-essential drivers (*.sys files) in your CONFIG.SYS file, and reducing a high BUFFERS value down to BUFFERS=20. Changing the value of FILES will have no effect, since Fractint only opens one file at a time.

Both the orbit feature and the zoom box are disabled during disk video mode since you couldn't see where the fractal is anyway. If you decide to use a magnetic disk for your disk video, Fractint will not generate some "attractor" types (e.g., Lorenz fractals) or IFS images, because excessive disk accesses would wear out the disk drive in short order. Boundary tracing is allowed with disk video, but it may give your drive a bit of a workout; it is, however, generally tolerable.

In order to use extended memory to store your disk video images (which will be fast), you must have Microsoft's HIMEM.SYS driver or an equivalent that supports the XMS 2.0 extended-memory standard or higher. HIMEM.SYS is distributed with Microsoft Windows 286/386 and 3.0.

To use expanded memory, you must have either a hardware expanded memory board or a software driver that causes extended memory to emulate expanded memory. Just make sure that the expanded memory is properly set up on your machine; Fractint will then be able to detect its presence.

WHEN YOUR VIDEO CARD ISN'T SUPPORTED BY FRACTINT—FRACTINT.CFG

If you have a favorite adapter/video mode that you would like to *add* to Fractint, or you just want to *remove* the table entries that do not apply to your particular system, or if you're unhappy with the key combinations, or if you are using a nonenhanced keyboard so that you can't *use* a particular combination, you'll want to modify the CFG (configure) file. Fractint can be made to create an external, editable video configuration file called FRACTINT.CFG. Once this has been made Fractint will use the file FRACTINT.CFG instead of its internal table as long as it can locate it somewhere along the DOS path. To create this file, enter

```
fractint batch=config
```

You will get a default file with an entry for every one of the internal video table entries. You can now go to work on it with a text editor.

Any line in the file that begins with a tab or a space (or is empty) is treated as a comment. The rest of the lines must consist of ten fields separated by commas. Thus a typical line in FRACTINT.CFG would look like this:

```
adapter/mode        AX BX CX   DX  mode   x    y   clrs  comments
IBM 16-Color EGA    10  0  0    0    2   640  350   16   EGA hi-res
```

The ten fields are defined as follows:

1. The name of the adapter/video mode (25 chars max, no leading blanks). This is the name Fractint will display on the Select Video Mode menu. The next four lines tell Fractint what values should be placed in the AX, BX, CX, and DX registers before calling the video BIOS via INT 10h. The users manual for your video adapter should describe the proper settings. These should be in hexadecimal format. The other fields use standard decimal notation.

2. AX register value

3. BX register value

4. CX register value

5. DX register value

6. An encoded value describing the type of video memory Fractint should assume is present. This is used for reading and writing colors to and from the screen.

Currently available codes are as follows:

CODE MEANING

1. Use the BIOS (INT 10H, AH=12/13, AL=color) (last resort—this option is SLOW!)
2. Pretend it's a (perhaps super-res) EGA/VGA
3. Pretend it's an MCGA
4. SuperVGA 256-color mode using the Tseng Labs chipset
5. SuperVGA 256-color mode using the Paradise chipset
6. SuperVGA 256-color mode using the Video-7 chipset
7. Nonstandard IBM VGA 360 × 480 × 256-color mode
8. SuperVGA 1024 × 768 × 16 mode for the Everex chipset
9. Targa video modes
10. Hercules video mode
11. Nonvideo, i.e., disk video
12. 8514/A video modes
13. CGA 320 × 200 × 4-color and 640 × 200 × 2-color modes
14. Reserved for Tandy 1000 video modes
15. SuperVGA 256-color mode using the Trident chipset

16. SuperVGA 256-color mode using the Chips & Tech chipset
17. SuperVGA 256-color mode using the ATI VGA Wonder chipset
18. SuperVGA 256-color mode using the Everex chipset
19. Roll-your-own video mode (as you've defined it in yourvid.c)
20. SuperVGA 1024 × 768 × 16 mode for the ATI VGA Wonder chipset
21. SuperVGA 1024 × 768 × 16 mode for the Tseng Labs chipset
22. SuperVGA 1024 × 768 × 16 mode for the Trident chipset
23. SuperVGA 1024 × 768 × 16 mode for the Video 7 chipset
24. SuperVGA 1024 × 768 × 16 mode for the Paradise chipset
25. SuperVGA 1024 × 768 × 16 mode for the Chips & Tech chipset
26. SuperVGA 1024 × 768 × 16 mode for the Everex chipset
27. SuperVGA Auto-Detect mode (we poke around looking for your adapter)
28. VESA modes (Add 100, 200, 300, or 400 to this code to specify an override "textsafe" option to be used with the mode. The textsafe option is explained in Chapter 2. Adding 100 to the code sets textsafe=yes, adding 200 sets textsafe=no, adding 300 sets textsafe=bios, and adding 400 sets textsafe=save. For example, if you wish to set textsafe=save with a VESA mode, use 28 + 400 or 428.)
7. The number of pixels across the screen (160 to 2048)
8. The number of pixels down the screen (160 to 2048)
9. The number of available colors (2, 4, 16, or 256)
10. A comment describing this mode (25 chars max, leading blanks are OK)

If you look closely at the default entries, you will notice that the IBM VGA entries labeled "tweaked" and "nonstandard" have entries in the table with AX = BX = CX = 0, and DX = some other number. Those are special flags that Fractint uses to custom-program the VGA adapter and are NOT undocumented BIOS calls.

If you have a fancy adapter with a new video mode that is not currently supported, please get the information to the Fractint authors! If you are a programmer, send us a version of the file video.asm modified to support your video board. Otherwise, send whatever information you have about your board, including how modes are set and how bank switching is accomplished. We will add the video mode to the list on our next release and give you credit for it. Which brings up another point: If you can confirm that a particular video adapter/mode works (or that it doesn't), and the program says it is untested, please get that information to us also. To contact the Stone Soup Group, please see p.306.

PALETTE MAPS

If you have a VGA, Super-VGA, 8514/a, or Targa video adapter, you can save and restore the color palette for these adaptors using special color-map files. While these adapters can display only 256 colors at one time, those 256 colors can be from any combination of colors from a palette of over 262,144 different colors. Fractint uses *palette maps* that allow you to decide which 256 colors from this enormous palette are actually used to draw the fractal. These maps are loaded into the digital-to-analog converter (DAC) registers when Fractint starts. Maps consist of a text file defining the amount of red, green, and blue to use for each of the 256 pixel color index entries and are made when Fractint is started. In other words, we can specify for each of the 256 colors exactly what percentage of red, blue, and green to add to produce it. These files can be used in Fractint by specifying "map=" from the command line, as in:

```
fractint map=altern . . . .
```

or in the SSTOOLS.INI file:

```
[fractint]

   . . .

   map=altern

   . . .
```

You can also load a color map interactively. From the Main menu, or while an image is displaying, press Ⓒ to enter color cycling mode. Then press Ⓛ to load a color map. You will be presented with the usual Fractint file selection screen. If there are no color maps listed, type in the path where they are found, and the list should appear. Move the highlight to the desired map, press (ENTER) to select it, and press (ESC) to leave color cycling mode. Fractint reads the file and assigns the color values specified on a given line to the corresponding color index.

```
0    0    0          This is a comment. . .
0    0    168        . . . any text out here is ignored.
0    168  0
```

Here are the first three lines of the 256 color definitions in the map called DEFAULT.MAP. The first line defines the RGB (red, green, blue) "gun" values for the color index 0. The "gun" is the beam of electrons sent to the screen inside the CRT. Since all three guns are set to zero, the color must be black. The next line defines the gun values for color index 1. Since the only gun with a nonzero value is the blue gun, the color will appear a medium bright blue. The next line defines color index 2 to be green at the same intensity as color index 1.

Fractint automatically loads this DEFAULT.MAP file when it is first started and stores the color information somewhere in memory. Immediately before Fractint starts to generate the image, Fractint performs a high-speed dump of the color information map into the DAC registers of the video adapter, which sets the display adapter colors to the values stored in memory.

Color cycling of fractals is performed by loading the DEFAULT.MAP to the video adapter's, but instead of starting with the first color index, Fractint loads the DAC register with the *second* color and places the first color at the end of the palette. After those colors are displayed to the screen, Fractint reloads the DAC register starting with the *third* color index and places the first two at the end. Fractint continues this process with the fourth, fifth, sixth, and so on through to the end of the palette and then starts over again. This results in a rotation of the colors as the index values are bumped up one at a time.

APPENDIX B

GIF: THE GRAPHICS INTERCHANGE FORMAT

Fractint uses a standard format for saving and loading its images that is very popular. It is called the Graphics Interchange Format, or GIF (pronounced "jif"). CompuServe created and maintains this machine-independent standard format for distributing graphics images. All files saved in this format end with the .GIF extension. This graphics standard is supported by a wide range of software. You can display a GIF image on any computer with graphics hardware using GIF decoder software written for that machine. Many different GIF programs have been written for the PC. Decoders are available for the Mac II, Atari, Amiga, C-64, TI Professional, DEC Rainbow, Sun Workstations, and X-Windows. Various GIF decoders can be downloaded from CompuServe's PICS forum, library 3.

An image stored as a GIF file is composed of two different tables. One short table contains a list of gun colors for each of the color index values similar to the .MAP files described in Appendix A, "Fractint, Video, Adapters, and Monitors". The other table contains the image data. The image data table is comprised of color index numbers. This table is compressed using an LZW compression algorithm to keep the size of the file as small as possible. Therefore, compression utilities such as PKZIP will usually store a GIF file without compression—it's already compressed! At the most these utilities will provide 2 percent compression by squeezing down the header and color table.

Older versions of Fractint saved the fractal images in files ending with a .FRA extension. These files used a modified version of an earlier GIF specification called GIF87a. The GIF87a standard was fine for saving graphics images, but it did not provide space to store other information required by Fractint, such as information on the fractal type and the coordinates for the corners, which is needed so it can reload a drawing and continue working where it left off.

To get around the limitations of the GIF87a standard, older versions of Fractint stored the images in the GIF87a format and then tacked the extra information needed onto the end of the file. Since this extra information deviated from the CompuServe standard, Fractint appended a .FRA extension to the file to avoid confusing other GIF decoders and infringing on the license granted by CompuServe. Fractint would also save the images without the extra information in a file conforming to the GIF87a standard and readable by other decoders, paint programs, and the like. Such files were appended with the traditional .GIF extension. This was important, since CompuServe will only accept graphics files for posting if they adhere to the GIF standard.

All this changed when the GIF89a standard was released for general use. The GIF89a standard set aside space in multiple extension blocks for the extra information needed by Fractint and other applications. Fractint now uses several of these extension blocks to its fullest advantage. For example, when a fractal is saved while it is still generating the image, Fractint saves all the information it needs to pick up right where it left off. This is perfect for generating detailed fractals requiring intense calculations that can't be completed in one session.

The complete GIF89a standard is available on CompuServe in a file called GIF89A.DOC or GIF89A.ARC in the PICS forum, library 14. This library also contains examples and explanations of the LZW encoding and decoding methods used for GIFs.

APPENDIX C

FOR PROGAMMERS ONLY

This appendix is for programmers who would like to know a little more about how Fractint achieves its phenomenal performance. We assume the reader has a working knowledge of C and of the 80x86 processor family. The full source code for Fractint is available on CompuServe in the COMART (Computer Art) forum, section 15 (Fractals) in the file FRASRC.EXE. The source code is self-extracting. The source code requires Microsoft C 5.1 and up to compile.

There are many techniques unique to fractals that can be used to shorten the generation time and other techniques to reduce the amount of programming code. Calculation techniques between many fractal type variations are similar. Fractint uses generalized sections of code wherever it does not hinder generation speed. Some fractals are symmetrical, so Fractint capitalizes on this by calculating only one section of the image and then duplicating it in the redundant areas of the screen.

Most fractals have sections that decay into periodic orbits that go on forever. Fractint keeps a watch on the iterations and looks for these decayed orbits. When it discovers an orbit has decayed into a periodic loop, Fractint knows the orbits will continue indefinitely and quits early.

Often, large areas of the screen have the same color. Fractint will find these areas and "box in" regions with the same color. The Fractint program will then save time by skipping the calculations for that section and simply filling in the boxed section with the appropriate color.

THE FRACTAL ENGINE—
MULTIPLYING TYPES AND OPTIONS

As noted earlier in the book, fractal types can be broken down into several different categories. Indeed, virtually all fractal categories can be generalized into a single fractal computational "engine." The differences between the fractal types within a category are grouped into sets of type-specific subroutines. These type-specific routines are often shared between closely related fractal types, with only one subroutine different between them.

Single-Pass Engine

Implementing a single-pass fractal engine is the simplest, most straightforward, accurate, and *slowest* method for generating fractals. The Mandelbrot and Julia set fractal types are the most common types in the escape-time fractal category. These are all calculated in a similar manner, as follows:

```
void (*SetupConstants)();
void (*PerPixelSubroutine)();
int (*IterationLoop)();
void (*Plot)()

SetupConstants();
for(y = 0; y < ydots; y++) {
   for(x = 0; x < xdots; x++) {
        PerPixelSubroutine(x, y);
        for(color = 0; color < maxiter; color++)
             if(IterationLoop())
                    break;
        Plot(x, y, color);
   }
}
```

The above code is part of a greatly simplified version of a fractal engine for escape-time fractal types without any speed enhancements, such as solid-guessing or periodicity checking, or checks on the status of the system mouse or keyboard. The *SetupConstants* routine extracts any information needed from the params=statement from the Fractint command line or as set from the interactive fractal type list. It is also responsible for setting the values of any constants required by the fractal formula. The *PerPixelSubroutine* is responsible for updating the variables that change from one pixel to the next. The *IterationLoop* routine actually performs the iterations of the fractal formula to determine the appropriate pixel color. After the color of the pixel is determined, the function *Plot* updates the color on the screen.

When you select a specific fractal type such as julia from the fractal type list (accessed with Ⓣ), Fractint scans a type table and sets the function pointers to the appropriate routines. In this case, Fractint would set the function pointers as follows:

```
SetupConstants = JuliaSetup;
PerPixelSubroutine = julia_per_pixel;
IterationLoop = JuliaFractal;
```

The *JuliaSetup* routine sets the value of the variable c in the formula $z^2 + c$ equal to the values passed to Fractint from the command-line statement params= or to the values set during the interactive session following selection of a fractal type. The *julia_per_pixel* function updates the initial value of z in the formula as the color of each pixel is calculated. The function *JuliaFractal* actually performs the formula calculation and determines whether the modulus of the variable z has exceeded the bailout value.

The function pointer *Plot* in escape-time fractals is usually set to a function that plots the points to the screen according to the fractal's symmetry. For example, the top half of the Mandelbrot set is a mirror image of the bottom half. By only calculating the top half of the image and then plotting the mirrored pixels on the bottom half, the image is generated in half the time! This is why you see the Mandelbrot fractal grow from the top and bottom of the screen towards the center.

To prepare the fractal engine to calculate a Mandelbrot, the function pointers are set this way:

```
SetupConstants      = MandelSetup;
PerPixelSubroutine  = mandel_per_pixel;
IterationLoop       = JuliaFractal;
```

The *MandelSetup* is similar to the *JuliaSetup* except that this function places the two parameters from "params=" or the interactive session into a variable designed to warp the Mandelbrot set. The *mandel_per_pixel* routine updates the value of c from pixel to pixel and reinitializes the variable z to zero (Fractint actually sets the value of z equal to the variable c, thereby skipping the first iteration calculation). The formula used for the Mandelbrot set is identical to the Julia fractals, so the same subroutine is used.

From within the *color* loop, in which the orbit formula is repeatedly iterated, other features can be added. Function calls are made from within the loop that check the mouse and keyboard. Checks are also made on the value of z to see if it has fallen into a periodic loop (see the section on "Periodicity Checking"). Solid-guessing and boundary tracing, on the other hand, require different types of engines.

SOLID-GUESSING AND BOUNDARY TRACING

Solid-guessing is a technique that calculates every fourth pixel on every fourth line of the fractal image looking for sections that appear to have only one color. If a box is formed with four corner pixels of the same color, Fractint assumes the remaining pixels within the box are also the same color and skips the calculations within the box by simply filling in the appropriate color.

On subsequent passes, Fractint calculates the color of the pixels on either side of the box boundaries, working its way towards the center of the box on either side. If it finds consecutive colors, Fractint assumes the rest of the box is the same color and moves on to more profitable areas.

The *boundary tracing method* is a more sophisticated implementation of the solid-guessing algorithm. This method scans along a single line. When this algorithm finds a boundary between two different colors, it follows along the color boundary and encloses the entire region. Once the region is enclosed, it fills it with the appropriate color and moves on to the next pixel.

PERIODICITY CHECKING

Periodicity checking is the algorithm that keeps a watch on the iteration loop and waits to see if the iterations will cause the value of z to decay into a periodic orbit. For example, consider the Mandelbrot calculation for the point (.1429, 0.7575). Eventually the calculations start to look like this:

Iteration	Points
#60	(-0.1408, 0.7574)
#61	(-0.6968, 0.5442)
#63	(0.0464, -0.0009)
#64	(-0.1408, 0.7574)
#65	(-0.6968, 0.5442)
#66	(0.0464, -0.0009)
#67	(-0.1408, 0.7574)

The iterations keep coming up with the same three numbers. The iterations are caught in a periodic loop. Since we know the iterations are caught in a loop, why bother to continue calculating? Fractint is smart enough to recognize this and stop calculating as soon as it spots the situation.

The code to look for this situation is rather simple:

```
void InitializeChecking(void) {
   Savedx = Savedy = 0;
   Periodicity = LastPeriod = 1;
   CheckEvery = 3;
}


int PeriodicityCheck(void) {
   if((x == Savedx) && (y == Savedy)) {
      if(LastPeriod == Periodicity)
         return(Periodicity);
      else {
         LastPeriod = Periodicity;
         Periodicity = 1;
      }
   }
   else {
      if(Periodicity++ >= CheckEvery) {
         CheckEvery *= 2;
         Periodicity = 1;
            Savedx = x;
            Savedy = y;
      }
   }
   return(0);
}
```

The first statement checks to see if the values of x and y are equal to *Savedx* and *Savedy*, which were initialized to zero at the start of the iterations. If they weren't, then a check is made against the variable *CheckEvery* to see if it is time to update the values of *Savedx* and *Savedy* to a number from the current iteration. If it is time, then the *Periodicity* variable is reset to 1 and the values of *Savedx* and *Savedy* are updated with the current x and y. If the next x and y are equal to the *Savedx* and *Savedy* then the iterations are run through again to determine the periodicity level. To speed the calculations, Fractint normally skips this step.

The value of *CheckEvery* is continually increased. This is because if it remained at a level of 3, larger periodic loops, such as 4 or 20, would be missed. If the *CheckEvery* variable were initially set to too high a number, many times quite a few iterations would have to go by before the algorithm would spot that the orbit had become periodic.

HOW FRACTINT HANDLES MATH

Fractint is *fast*. The key to its phenomenal speed is Fractint's ability to adapt to individual hardware configurations. In this way it can take advantage of the capabilities of a particular machine and at the same time minimize the aspects which could bog down the program. This is accomplished by using three different number formats. Each format has advantages and disadvantages depending on the machine running Fractint.

Fractint uses separate sets of math routines depending on the type of CPU and also whether a math coprocessor is installed. The 80386, 80386SX, and 80486 machines are all capable of 32-bit mathematics, and using 32-bit mathematics can quadruple the speed of integer and MP math routines, which both use arithmetic that does not require a coprocessor (see "The MP Math Format" section below). Fractint checks for the presence of a 32-bit processor and uses special 32-bit routines to optimize their use.

Fractint treats machines with an 80486 processor as if they were an 80386 with an 80387 math coprocessor installed, which is exactly what an 80486 is from a programming standpoint. Also, Fractint considers the 80387SX as functionally equivalent to the 80387. The 80387 and its cousins can perform a simultaneous calculation of a number's sine and cosine. The 80387 coprocessor is also more tolerant of the acceptable range of numbers for some calculations. Fractint bypasses the additional code overhead required by the 8087 and 80287 if it detects the presence of an 80387.

None of the coprocessors will calculate a number's hyperbolic sine and cosine in one operation. This ability would enhance the speed of calculating trigonometric values for complex numbers. Fractint goes the extra mile and uses dedicated routines for this purpose and gets the most calculating power in the least amount of processor time.

Where significantly less accuracy is required than 15 decimal places, Fractint automatically switches to the faster integer trigonometry. This format performs the calculations 20 to 60 times faster than emulated floating-point, almost twice as fast as an 8087 or 80287, and 50 percent faster than an 80387 (if the sine and cosine are calculated separately).

FIXED-POINT MATHEMATICS AND THE FRACTINT FUDGE FACTOR

The first release of Fractint was written to run only on an 80386 using 32-bit integer math instructions. The name "Fractint" came from Bert Tyler's contraction of the words "fractal" and "integer." While Fractint has expanded to other math formats, neither the name nor the program's commitment to speed has changed. Because of its superior speed on virtually all machine configurations, integer mathematics is still the default math type for almost all fractal types.

Floating-point mathematics always return a result in the form of a mantissa (without leading zeros) and a binary exponent. Removing the leading zeros and recalculating the binary exponent takes a considerable amount of time. Integer mathematics, on the other hand, is a form of fixed-point mathematics where the result is returned with the binary decimal point fixed in one location. The location of this binary decimal point is referred to as a *fudge factor*. Fractint uses a fudge factor of 29 for calculating Mandelbrot and Julia fractals. This means 29 of the least significant bits are used to represent the fractional portion of the number, two bits represent the integer portion, and the most significant bit represents the sign.

The speed of the integer format is due largely to the time required to perform addition and subtraction operations. Calculation time for normal multiplication and division is roughly equal between integer and coprocessor floating-point, but with addition and subtraction there is a significant difference. Even the fastest coprocessor requires at least 40 clock cycles to perform an addition or subtraction of two floating-point numbers. Using 32-bit integer mathematics, Fractint performs these operations in just 2 clock cycles.

Multiplication and division by powers of 2, a very common operation in most fractal calculations, typically takes 200 clock cycles using a coprocessor and eons in emulated floating-point. But with 32-bit mathematics multiplication and division by powers of 2 is accomplished using logical bit shifts, which typically require only 5 clock cycles. Fractint performs logical bit shifts in lieu of multiplication or division whenever possible.

The MP Math Format

Integer mathematics is very limited in its dynamic range. Small numbers lose significant digits and some math operations, like exponentials, rapidly exceed the range of the format. Fractals such as Newton or Newton's Basin need a large dynamic range and cannot be generated using integer mathematics. Fractint uses MP math ("MP" stands for Mark Peterson) to fill the gap between integer mathematics and floating-point. This format is similar to the normal IEEE floating-point format in that it uses an unsigned mantissa and a binary exponent. However, the format is designed specifically for high-speed execution on 32-bit processors. Consequently, it uses a 32-bit mantissa and a 14-bit exponent with 1 bit to represent the sign of the number and another for the sign of the exponent.

The 32-bit mantissa provides an accuracy of greater than 1 part in 2^{30}, or 1 part in 1,073,741,824. The size of the mantissa is small enough that the math operations can be handled internally by the processor. The 14-bit exponent allows numbers to be as large as 1×10^{4932} or as small as 1×10^{-4932}. Fractint's use of this format allows it to generate fractals, such as Newton, five times faster than emulated floating-point!

APPENDIX D

COMPLEX MATHEMATICS

This appendix is for the readers who are curious about the mechanics of manipulating complex numbers mathematically and who desire a limited dialog on the geometric interpretations. The first section on basic algebraic manipulations (addition, subtraction, multiplication, and division) assumes the reader has a working knowledge of basic algebra. The last section concerns complex transcendentals and assumes a working knowledge of trigonometry.

For programmers, examples of C code are listed in strategically placed boxes. Be forewarned that these examples are not the most efficient methods of implementation. They are written only to help explain the topic. More efficient methods can be found in the Fractint source code.

For the mathematically pure at heart, the term *number* is used to mean *real number* (double or float to you programmers out there) as opposed to an integer. If you have never done any programming and are only interested in the math content, just skip over the code.

THE CARTESIAN PLANE

Fractint maps the pixels on the screen to a corresponding mathematical map called the Cartesian plane. The meaning of "Cartesian" is "of or relating to René Descartes (1596–1650) or his philosophy." (Webster's Ninth New Collegiate Dictionary, 1985, p. 210) At the very center of the Cartesian plane is a point

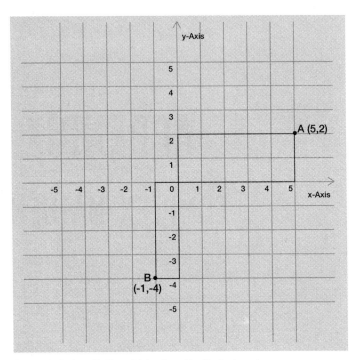

Figure 1 Points (5, 2) and (-1, -4) on the Cartesian plane

called the *origin*. Extending out to the left and right of the origin is a number line called the *x-axis*. Extending vertically out of the origin is a number line called the *y-axis*. At the origin is the number zero for both the *x*- and *y*-axes. The positive numbers of the *x*-axis are to the right of the origin and the negative numbers are to the left. The positive numbers of the *y*-axis extend upwards from the origin and the negative numbers are below.

Every spot on a Cartesian plane is referenced first by its horizontal distance from the origin followed by its vertical distance, as shown in Figure 1. Point A is five units to the right of the origin along the *x*-axis and two units up, so it is located at point (5, 2). This is shorthand for saying point A has an *x*-coordinate of 5 and a *y*-coordinate of 2.

Since point B is one unit to the left of the origin and three units down, it is located at (-1, -4). Or, written out long-hand, point B has an *x*-coordinate of -1 and a *y*-coordinate of -4.

As shown in Figure 2, Fractint uses the default settings of -2.5/1.5/1.5/-1.5 for the screen corners of the Mandelbrot set. The first and third parameters designate the upper left-hand corner of the screen as point (-2.5, 1.5), the second and

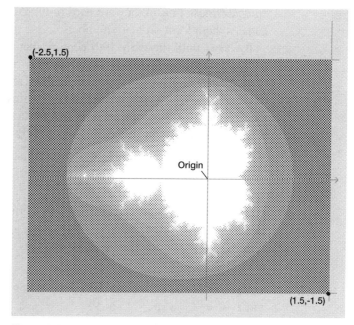

Figure 2 Fractint's default settings for screen corners of the Mandelbrot set

third designate the upper right-hand corner as (1.5, 1.5), the first and last mark the lower left-hand corner as (-2.5, -1.5), and the second and last designate the lower right-hand corner as (1.5, -1.5). These settings place the origin of the Cartesian plane at the vertical center of the screen and off to the right of the horizontal center. These coordinates were chosen as the default settings because they provide the best viewing of the entire Mandelbrot set by placing it in the middle of the screen. Overriding the default settings for the corners and changing them to -2.0/2.0/-1.5/1.5 will place the origin of the Cartesian plane in the center of the screen. This is done by typing in from the DOS command line:

```
fractint corners=-2.0/2.0/-1.5/1.5
```

ADDITION AND SUBTRACTION

Points on the Cartesian plane are added or subtracted from one another in exactly the same manner as regular numbers. Every mathematical operation that is performed on regular numbers can be done with points on the Cartesian plane. First, though, they have to be written out as *complex numbers*. The term *complex* doesn't mean they are hard or difficult to understand. The term differentiates them from ordinary numbers.

It wasn't until the early 19th century that Fredrich Gauss (1777–1855) formally proved the modern system of complex numbers. Gauss labeled the y-axis of the Cartesian plane as i, which he defined as equal to the points on the x-axis times $\sqrt{-1}$. To write a coordinate from the Cartesian plane as a complex number, the x portion of the coordinate is first written as is. The y-coordinate is then written as multiplied by the coefficient i and added to the x-coordinate, as follows:

$$\text{complex number} = (x\text{-coordinate}) + i\,(y\text{-coordinate})$$
$$A = 5 + i2$$
$$B = -1 - i4$$

These statements are literally read as "*A* equals 5 plus *i* times 2 and *B* equals -1 minus *i* times 4."

In C, complex numbers are represented as a structure containing two float or double variables:

```
typedef struct { double x, y; } CPLX;
CPLX A = {  5.0,  2.0 };
CPLX B = { -1.0, -4.0 };
```

With the two points, *A* and *B*, represented as complex numbers, addition is a matter of adding together the like terms (see Figure 2):

$$
\begin{aligned}
C &= A + B \\
&= (5 + i2) + (-1 + -i4) \\
&= 5 + i2 - 1 - i4 \\
&= (5 - 1) + i(2 - 4) \\
&= 4 - i2
\end{aligned}
$$

To plot the point represented by the complex number $4 - i2$, the number that is the coefficient of i, which in this case is -2, is the y-coordinate, and the number without the i coefficient is the x-coordinate. Point C is plotted at (4,-2) or four units to the right of the origin and two units down.

Subtraction is performed in the same way:

$$
\begin{aligned}
D &= A - B \\
&= (5 + i2) - (-1 + -i4) \\
&= 5 + i2 + 1 + i4 \\
&= (5 + 1) + i(2 + 4) \\
&= 6 + i6
\end{aligned}
$$

The complex number *D* corresponds to point (6, 6) on the Cartesian plane. Here are the addition and subtraction functions in C:

```
/* AddCplx returns _a + b  */
CPLX AddCplx(CPLX a, CPLX b) {
  CPLX Ans;

  Ans.x = a.x + b.x;
  Ans.y = a.y + b.y;
  return(Ans);
}


/* SubCplx returns _a - b  */
CPLX SubCplx(CPLX a, CPLX b) {
  CPLX Ans;

  Ans.x = a.x - b.x;
  Ans.y = a.y - b.y;
  return(Ans);
}
```

The process of adding and subtracting points has an application in the real world in addition to generating beautiful fractals. Adding the points A and B together is the same as combining two *force vectors,* that is, two forces pushing on an object from different directions.

IMAGINARY NUMBERS

Many people start to get confused at this point—the i coefficient and $\sqrt{-1}$ are each called an *imaginary number*. The portion of a complex number without the i coefficient is referred to as the *real* part, and the term with the i coefficient is called the *imaginary* portion. Likewise, the x-axis of the Cartesian plane is called the *real axis*, and the y-axis can also be called the *imaginary axis*.

Many people place an almost mystical aura on the location and meaning of imaginary numbers. The term *imaginary* is an unfortunate holdover from the days before mathematicians defined and started working with complex numbers from a geometric point of view. In the words of James Newman, "The word *imaginary* is the great algebraical calamity, but it is too well established for mathematicians to eradicate. It should never have been used." (James R. Newman, *The World of Mathematics*, New York: Simon and Shuster, 1956, p. 309.)

"Imaginary numbers" do not exist in some "imaginary world" any more than "negative numbers" exist in a "negative world." In fact, the best way to think of the coefficient i is in the same way you treat the negation operator, "-".We take for granted the existence of negative numbers. To us the concept is quite obvious. An everyday example of a negative number is a check written against a bank account. Positive numbers are deposits. We add them all together and determine the current balance. Geometrically, negative numbers exist on a number line to the left of zero. Algebraically, a negative number is a positive number multiplied by -1. The negation operator in the term -A is actually shorthand for (-1)(A). Multiplication is a special case where -1 times -1 equals a positive 1.

Geometrically, imaginary numbers are located on the y-axis, both above and below the x-axis. Algebraically, imaginary numbers are either positive or negative numbers multiplied by $\sqrt{-1}$. The use of the i coefficient in the term $i2$ is mathematical shorthand for ($\sqrt{-1}$)(2). Multiplication of i times i can be rewritten as $\sqrt{-1}$ times $\sqrt{-1}$, which intuitively is equal to -1.

Imaginary numbers should also be taken for granted. You see them every day even though you probably don't realize it. Let's switch our number example from checkbooks to moving boxes around. You and a friend are trying to move a box across a room. You push the box forward four feet and your friend pushes it back at you two feet. The work you did was positive and your friend negated some of your work by pushing in the opposite direction—he performed negative work. Added, the net distance is two feet.

You explain to your friend that he isn't helping matters any and he should be pushing from a different direction. This time you push the box forward another four feet and your friend pushes the box at a 90 degree angle for two feet (like a scene from "The Three Stooges"). Again, the work you accomplished was positive because you pushed the box in the positive direction. Your friend, on the other hand, pushed the box in what is geometrically called the *imaginary* direction. Your friend's work was *imaginary* in the sense that it didn't help or hinder you from moving the box in the desired direction, but it did move the box. This time we say the net distance is a complex number. The distance moved is 4+i2 feet. Since the value is complex, that is, it has a direction off the real number line, it's called a *vector* so as to distinguish it from a linear distance.

CHECKING THE LINEAR DISTANCE

Perhaps you and your friend are curious exactly how far the box was moved on your last pushing effort. You could take out a ruler and measure the distance from the start of the last push on an angle to the resulting destination. Or, knowing the vector distance each of you pushed the box, you could determine the linear distance by taking the *modulus* of the complex number 4 + i2. This is

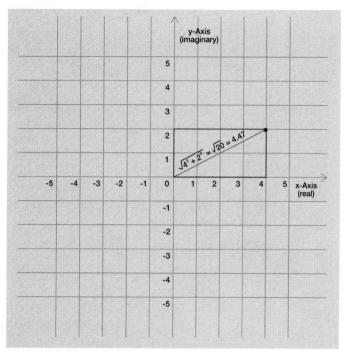

Figure 3 Determining the linear distance by taking the modulus of a complex number.

done by using the Pythagorean theorem: $a^2 + b^2 = c^2$. In this example (Figure 3) the linear distance moved was

$$c = \sqrt{a^2 + b^2}$$

$$c = \sqrt{4^2 + 2^2}$$

$$c = \sqrt{20} = 4.47 \text{ feet}$$

Determining the modulus of a complex number is a fundamental part of almost all the fractal calculations performed by Fractint. With the Mandelbrot fractal we know that if z falls outside a 2-unit circle around the origin, successive iterations will always take it to infinity. This is analogous to determining that the net distance the box was pushed resulted in its being outside a certain circle about the starting point. So the modulus of z (our linear distance to z) is checked after each iteration to determine its distance from the origin.

MULTIPLICATION: SPINNING AROUND THE ORIGIN

Multiplication of complex numbers involves the Distributive law. In this rule, both terms of one complex number are multiplied by each of the terms in the other complex number and totaled:

$$(a + ib)(c + id) = a(c + id) + ib(c + id)$$
$$= ac + iad + ibc + (i*i)(bd)$$

Remember, the coefficient i is shorthand for $\sqrt{-1}$ and that multiplication of i times itself is equal to -1:

$$= ac + iad + ibc + (-1)(bd)$$
$$= (ac - bd) + i(ad + bc)$$

The equations are even simpler when a complex number is multiplied times itself, or *squared*:

$$(a + ib)(a + ib)= a(a + ib) + ib(a + ib)$$
$$= a^2 + iab + iab + (i*i)b^2$$
$$= (a^2 - b^2) + i(2ab)$$

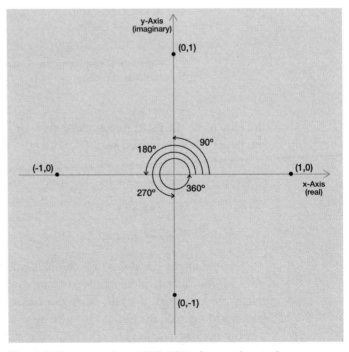

Figure 4 The successive multiplication of a complex number

In terms of our box analogy, multiplication of complex numbers has the effect of rotating a vector around the origin in a counterclockwise direction. A vector can be thought of as a hand of a clock. The process multiplies the modulus of each number and adds the angle (in our box example, 90 degrees). A simple example, as shown in Figure 4, is the successive multiplication of the complex number $1 + i0$ by $0 + i1$, each of which has a modulus of 1. The first multiplication by $0 + i1$ rotates the initial vector, $1+i0$, 90 degrees off the x-axis. A second multiplication results in $-1 + i0$ for a total of 180 degrees of rotation. Two more multiplications by $0 + i1$ will rotate the vector back to $1 + i0$.

As long as you perform successive multiplication of a complex number with a modulus of one it will eventually return to its original value. However, successive multiplications by a complex number with a modulus less than one will continually spiral the vector closer and closer to the origin. Successive multiplication by a complex number with a modulus greater than one will continually spiral the vector away from the origin. An example using Fractint's Formula Compiler follows:

SuccessiveMult = { $z = c = pixel$: $z = z * c$, $|z| < 4$ }

This formula, when used in Fractint's Formula Compiler (see type formula in Chapter 3), sets the initial values of the complex numbers z and c to the complex number corresponding to a pixel on the screen. The value of z is then successively multiplied until the modulus squared is less than 4. Note that the Fractint Formula Compiler interprets the notation $|z|$ as the modulus squared, rather than the traditional modulus in mathematics. This avoids performing a time-consuming square root calculation which, for most fractals, is not required in the calculation. If you try running this formula under Fractint and then press the ⊙ key, you can watch the orbits formed by this successive multiplication—the series of white dots being a spiral plot of the location of z after each iteration.

The orbital decay accelerates when, instead of successive multiplication, the values are successively squared. Try running this formula and watching the orbits:

SuccessiveSqr = { $z = pixel$: $z = z * z$, $|z| < 4$ }

This formula starts with a given screen point and successively squares the value until the modulus squared is less than 4. Mixing successive squaring with addition changes the orbital decay from an accelerated process to one of chaos. If you run this formula with the orbits turned on, you can look right into the heart of the chaos. The batch file uses the Formula Compiler for the following:

Mandelbrot = { $z = pixel$: $(z * z) + pixel$, $|z| < 4$ }

Division of Complex Numbers

Geometrically, division of complex numbers is the same as multiplication except the rotation is clockwise instead of counterclockwise. The modulus of the numerator is also multiplied by the inverse of the denominator's modulus. Algebraically, the process can be derived by writing the two numbers as a complex fraction and simplifying:

$$\frac{a + ib}{c + id} = \frac{(a + ib)(c - id)}{(c + id)(c - id)} = \frac{(ac + bd) + i(bc - ad)}{c^2 + d^2}$$

Here are examples of complex multiplication, squaring, and division in C:

```
/* MultiplyCplx return _a * b  */
CPLX MultiplyCplx(CPLX a, CPLX b) {
   CPLX Ans;

   Ans.x = (a.x * b.x) - (a.y * b.y);
   Ans.y = (a.x * b.y) + (a.y * b.x);
   return(Ans);
}


/* SquareCplx returns _a * a  */
CPLX SquareCplx(CPLX a) {
   CPLX Ans;

   Ans.x = (a.x * a.x) - (a.y * a.y);
   Ans.y = a.x * a.y * 2.0;
   return(Ans);
}


/* DivideCplx returns _a / b  */
CPLX DivideCplx(CPLX a, CPLX b) {
   CPLX Ans;
   double Modulus_of_b;

   Modulus_of_b = (b.x * b.x) + (b.y * b.y);
   Ans.x = ((a.x * b.x) + (a.y * b.y)) / Modulus_of_b;
   Ans.y = ((a.x * b.y) - (a.y * b.x)) / Modulus_of_b;
   return(Ans);
}
```

MORE EXOTIC FRACTINT OPERATIONS: COMPLEX TRANSCENDENTALS

The transcendental functions, combined with addition, subtraction, multiplication, division, powers, and roots, generate the most interesting kinds of fractal images. The reason they are documented here is because the beauty of these fractals can only be fully appreciated with an understanding of the mathematics behind them. In addition, it is very difficult to *find* any text on the subject. This section assumes the reader has an understanding of the principles of logarithms and trigonometry. As in the previous section, programming examples in C will be used for each math function.

The real beauty of complex mathematics can be more fully appreciated when applied to the transcendental functions. Algebraic numbers are actually a subset of real numbers, corresponding to the roots of algebraic equations with integer coefficients. Transcendental numbers are real numbers for which this is not true; that is, they are not roots of any equations with integer constants. Transcendental numbers solve an important class of equations involving what are called, naturally, transcendental functions. The elementary transcendental functions are the exponential, logarithm, trignometric fuctions (sin, cos, and tan), and hyperboloid functions (sinh, cosh, and tanh). These transcendental numbers can be generalized to the domain of complex numbers. They are very convenient building blocks for creating fractal formulas. A large number of fractal types in Fractint use them.

One beautiful aspect of complex transcendental numbers is that all functions, except for division by zero, have valid solutions. Pick up any calculator and try taking a square root or a logarithm of a negative number. Try an inverse sine on a number greater than one. In each case the calculator will complain of an error because it can only handle real numbers. In the complex domain, those same calculations give valid results.

EXPONENTIALS, LOGARITHMS, POWERS, AND ROOTS

Exponentials of complex numbers are closely related to the polar coordinates system, where the vector modulas and the angle are used to position a point on a plane. Geometrically, the exponential of a complex number is performed by interpreting the imaginary component of the complex number as the angle of a vector in radians. See Figure 5(a). The modulus of the vector is *e* raised to the power of the real component. Expressed algebraically this is:

$$e^{(x + iy)} = e^x e^{iy}$$
$$e^{iy} = \cos(y) + i\sin(y)$$
$$e^x e^{iy} = e^x(\cos(y) + i\sin(y))$$
$$= e^x\cos(y) + ie^x\sin(y)$$

Here is the exponential of a complex number in C:

```
/* ExpCplx return e**a */
CPLX ExpCplx(CPLX a) {
  CPLX Ans;
  double ExpX;

  ExpX = exp(a.x);
  Ans.x = ExpX * cos(a.y);
  Ans.y = ExpX * sin(a.y);
  return(Ans);
}
```

The real-number transcendental functions described here are familiar to students of trigonometry and calculus. Furthermore, most computer languages or

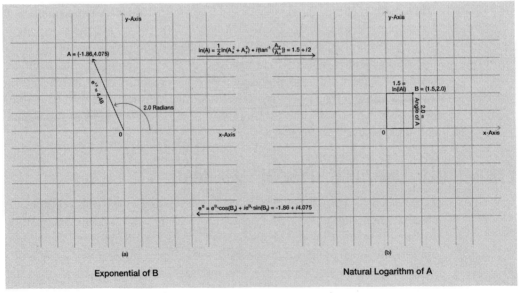

(a) Exponential of B   (b) Natural Logarithm of A

Figure 5

programming libraries provide the real-valued versions of these functions. But for fractals, we need the complex versions of these functions. In order to do fractal programming, formulas are needed that show how to calculate the complex versions of these functions from the real versions. In the above example, to take the exponential of a complex number $x + iy$, the formula

$$e^{x+iy} = e^x[\cos(y)] + i[e^x\sin(y)]$$

is used. The functions on the right side of the equation are the ordinary and familiar exponential, cosine, and sine applied to real numbers (the "x" and "y" parts of the complex number $x + iy$ are real numbers). The formula reduces the calculation of the unfamiliar complex exponential to the more familiar real versions of the exponential, sine, and cosine. The C program listing for the same exponential calculation shows the point of this formula. The exp, sin, and cos real-valued functions are all a part of the standard C library.

Logarithms are the opposite of exponentials in that the real component of the solution is the natural logarithm of the complex number. The imaginary portion of the solution is the partial inverse tangent of the vector angle. The real portion is the natural logarithm of the modulus. See Figure 5(b).

A partial inverse tangent differs from the regular inverse tangent. The regular variant produces angles in the range of $\frac{-\pi}{2}$ to $\frac{\pi}{2}$, which is only quadrants I and IV of the Cartesian plane. The partial inverse tangent, on the other hand, provides a full circle of angles ranging from $-\pi$ to π, hitting all four quadrants.

The algebraic formula for a complex logarithm is:

$$\ln(x \pm iy) = 1/2 \ln(x^2 + y^2) \pm i(\tan^{-1}(y, x) \pm k2\pi),$$
$$k = 0, 1, 2, 3, 4, \ldots$$

Here is a complex logarithm and power in C:

```
/* LogCplx returns _ln(a)   */
CPLX LogCplx(CPLX a) {
   CPLX Ans;

   Ans.x = log((a.x * a.x) + (a.y * a.y)) / 2.0;
   Ans.y = atan2(a.y, a.x);
   return(Ans);
}


/* PwrCplx returns _a^b   */
CPLX PwrCplx(CPLX a, CPLX b) {
   CPLX Ans;
```

```
    a = LogCplx(a);
    b = LogCplx(b);
    Ans = MultiplyCplx(a, b);
    Ans = ExpCplx(Ans);
    return(Ans);
}
```

The term $k2\pi$ complicates matters in that there are an infinite number of logarithms for any given complex number. This is more easily seen if the logarithms are viewed in terms of reverse exponentials. Consider the solution for $\ln(1 + i0)$. The most obvious answer is zero, since $e^0 = 1$. However, two equally valid solutions are $0 + i2\pi$ and $0 - i2\pi$, since $e^{(x+i2\pi)} = e^x$. Generally, only the *prime* logarithm, where k is equal to zero, is used.

The multiplicity of solutions is readily apparent in any of the complex fractals. A glance at a complex Newton fractal sometimes shows an apparent split along the negative x-axis and within the subsequent smaller copies. This is because a logarithm is used in the computation and only the prime solution is used. Fractint performs logarithmic calculations in the complex plane based on angles between $-\pi$ and $+\pi$. If the inverse partial tangent were calculated in only units of positive 2π then the split would be along the positive x-axis where an angle of 2π is equal to an angle of zero.

With addition of complex logarithms it is possible to conceptualize the rotation effect of complex multiplication. Computing the logarithm of two complex numbers results in the log of the modulus of each as the real components and the angles as the imaginaries. Addition of the two logarithms followed by an exponential is equivalent to multiplying the two original numbers.

As promised, it is possible to perform a logarithm of a negative number. An example would be the logarithm of -1, which in the complex domain is $-1 + i0$:

$$\ln(-1 + i0) = 1/2 \ln((-1)^2) + aptan(-1, 0)$$
$$= 1/2 \ln(1) + i\pi$$
$$= 0 + i\pi$$

A quick check using the complex exponential verifies the above as correct:

$$e^{(0 + i\pi)} \quad = e^0(\cos(\pi) + i\sin(\pi))$$
$$= 1(-1 + i0)$$
$$= -1$$

Complex logarithms, multiplication, and exponentials are all the ingredients needed to raise any number to a complex power. Raising a complex number a to a complex b power requires taking the complex logarithm of a, multiplying it by b, and calculating the exponential. To find a complex root, perform a division instead of multiplication.

COMPLEX TRIGONOMETRIC AND HYPERBOLIC FUNCTIONS

Fractint generates many fractals, such as lambdafn and mandelfn, based on complex trigonometric and hyperbolic functions. Computing the sine of a complex number may seem rather strange at first. You are, after all, dealing with an angle that has both a real and imaginary component. Since each number has two dimensions, the diagramming of these functions requires four dimensions. As such, it is extremely difficult to diagram trigonometric and hyperboloid functions in a two-dimensional illustration.

Sines and cosines of imaginary angles are the same as the hyperbolic functions of their real counterparts:

$$\sin(iy) = i \sinh(y)$$
$$\cos(iy) = \cosh(y)$$

Armed with the above information, the calculation of a complex sine is a trivial application of the identity:

$$\sin(a + b) = \sin(a) \cos(b) + \cos(a) \sin(b)$$

A straightforward substitution yields:

$$\sin(x + iy) = \sin(x) \cos(iy) + \cos(x) \sin(iy)$$
$$= \sin(x) \cosh(y) + i(\cos(x) \sinh(y))$$

The same procedure can be used to derive a complex cosine:

$$\cos(a + b) = \cos(a) \cos(b) - \sin(a) \sin(b)$$
$$\cos(x + iy) = \cos(x) \cos(iy) - \sin(x) \sin(iy)$$
$$= \cos(x) \cosh(y) - i(\sin(x) \sinh(y))$$

Here are the complex sine and cosine in C:

```
/* SinCplx returns _sin(a)  */
CPLX SinCplx(CPLX a) {
  CPLX Ans;

  Ans.x = sin(a.x) * cosh(a.y);
  Ans.y = cos(a.x) * sinh(a.y);
  return(Ans);
}

/* CosCplx returns _cos(a)  */
CPLX CosCplx(CPLX a) {
  CPLX Ans;

  Ans.x = cos(a.x) * cosh(a.y);
  Ans.y = -sin(a.x) * sinh(a.y);
  return(Ans);
}
```

Although inverse trigonometric functions are not currently supported by Fractint, it is worth noting that in the complex domain there are valid solutions to inverse sines and cosines greater than one. Consider the inverse sine of 2. As a complex number this would be represented as $2 + i0$. The inverse sine of $2 + i0$ is $\frac{\pi}{2} + i1.4436$. This is verified using the complex sine formula:

$$\sin(\tfrac{\pi}{2} + i1.4436) = \sin(\tfrac{\pi}{2}) \cosh(1.4436) + i\cos(\tfrac{\pi}{2})\sinh(1.4436)$$
$$= 2$$

The formulas to solve complex hyperbolic equations are derived from a similar set of identities as the complex sine and cosine, namely:

$$\sinh(iy) \qquad = i \sin(y)$$
$$\cosh(iy) \qquad = \cos(y)$$
$$\sinh(a + b) \quad = \sinh(a) \cosh(b) + \cosh(a) \sinh(b)$$
$$\cosh(a + b) \quad = \cosh(a) \cosh(b) + \sinh(a) \sinh(b)$$

Solving for complex numbers yields:

$$\sinh(x + iy) \quad = \sinh(x) \cos(y) + i\cosh(x) \sin(y)$$
$$\cosh(x + iy) \quad = \cosh(x) \cos(y) + i\cosh(x) \sin(y)$$

Here are the complex hyperbolic sine and cosine in C:

```
/* SinhCplx returns _sinh(a)   */
CPLX SinhCplx(CPLX a) {
  CPLX Ans;

  Ans.x = sinh(a.x) * cos(a.y);
  Ans.y = cosh(a.x) * sin(a.y);
  return(Ans);
}


/* CoshCplx return _cosh(a) */
CPLX CoshCplx(CPLX a) {
  CPLX Ans;

  Ans.x = cosh(a.x) * cos(a.y);
  Ans.x = sinh(a.x) * sin(a.y);
  return(Ans);
}
```

Fractint generates many Mandelbrot and Julia set fractals based on complex trigonometric formulas. There are a surprising number of similarities between the different variants. For instance, all the Mandelbrot sets, even those based on the trig formulas, have the complete Mandelbrot set buried somewhere in the fractal. Another similarity can be noted between the Mandelsine fractal and the Mandelbrot fractal based on a hyperbolic cosine. The hyperbolic cosine appears to be a vertical variant of the horizontal sine fractal. See Chapter 3 for more details.

Fractal images give the viewer a much better intuition of what transcendental functions are really all about in the first place. And, an understanding of transcendental functions opens an entirely new insight into the beautiful mathematical world of fractals.

SUGGESTED READING

Books

Barnsley, Michael, *Fractals Everywhere*, San Diego: Academic Press, 1988.

Fractals as limits of iterated function systems; rigorous, yet witty; numerous examples and exercises.

Devaney, Robert L, *An Introduction to Chaotic Dynamical Systems*, 2nd ed., Menlo Park, CA: Addison-Wesley, 1989.

A mathematically rigorous treatment of maps presupposing a solid background in real and complex analysis; a solid mathematics textbook with many exercises.

Devaney, Robert, *Chaos, Fractals, and Dynamics: Computer Experiments in Mathematics*, Menlo Park, CA: Addison-Wesley, 1990.

The most elementary (requires only a strong algebra background), yet comprehensive introduction to discrete dynamical systems available; replete with exercises, experiments and programming projects, including nine simple BASIC programs.

Devaney, R.L. and L. Keen, eds., *Chaos and Fractals: The Mathematics Behind the Computer Graphics*, Proceedings of Symposia in Applied Mathematics, V. 39, Providence, RI: The American Mathematical Society, 1989.

Proceedings of a very successful short course given at the AMS Centennial Celebration in Providence, Rhode Island, in August 1988; contributions by Devaney, Holmes, Alligood & Yorke, Keen, Branner, Harrison, and Barnsley.

Gleick, James, *Chaos: Making a New Science*, New York: Viking, 1987.

A popular, historical account of recent developments in nonlinear dynamics.

Mandelbrot, Benoît, *The Fractal Geometry of Nature*, New York: W.H. Freeman & Co., 1983.

A classic work by the "father of fractals."

Peitgen, H.-O. and P.H. Richter, *The Beauty of Fractals: Images of Complex Dynamical Systems*, New York: Springer-Verlag, 1986.

Many strikingly beautiful color images of Julia and Mandelbrot sets.

Peitgen, H.-O. and P.H. Ritcher, eds, *The Science of Fractal Images*, New York: Spring-Verlag, 1988.

Includes contributions by Barnsley, Devaney, Mandelbrot, Voss, and others, with numerous algorithms.

Pickover, Clifford A., *Computers, Patterns, Chaos and Beauty*, New York: St. Martin's Press, 1990.

A wide variety of images and topics by one of the virtuosi of fractals.

Prunsinkiewicz, Przémyslaw, Aristid Lindenmayer, with James S. Hanan, et.al. *The Algorithmic Beauty of Plants*, New York: Spring-Verlag, 1990.

Beautiful pictures of plant simulations and L-Systems theory.

Articles

Dewdney, A.K., "A computer microscope zooms in for a look at the most complex object in mathematics," *Scientific American* 253(2), 16-24 (August 1985).

The Mandelbrot set; iterations over finite sets; Pollard's rho-method.

Dewdney, A.K., "Of fractal mountain's, grafted plants, and computer graphics at Pixar," *Scientific American* 255(6), 14-20 (December 1986).

Three-dimensional fractal mountains, L-systems, ray-tracing, and computer animation.

Dewdney, A.K., "Beauty and profundity: the Mandelbrot set and a flock of its cousins called Julia," *Scientific American* 257(5), 140-145 (November 1987).

More on the Mandelbrot set and its associated Julia sets.

Hofstadter, Douglas R., "Strange attractors: mathematical patterns delicately poised between order and chaos," *Scientific American* 245(5), 22-43 (November 1981).

The logistic map; Duffing's equation; the Hénon map.

Jürgens, Hartmut, Heinz-Otto Peitgen, and Dietmar Saupe, "The language of fractals," *Scientific American* 263(2), 60-67 (August 1990).

Topics in three-dimensional fractals, fractal landscapes, iterated function systems, and complex maps.

Kenner, Hugh, "In darkest self-similarity," *Byte* 15(6), 382-3 (June 1990).

A review of books and software devoted to fractals.

Prunsinkiewicz, Przemyslaw and James Hanan, "Lindenmayer systems, fractals and plants," Department of Computer Science, University of Regina, Regina, Saskatchewan, Canada, S4S 0A2, April 15, 1988 (published under the same title as a volume in: Lecture Notes in Biomathematics, Vol. 79, Springer-Verlag, New York, 1989.

Relationships between fractals and formal languages; includes an interpreter (written in C) that converts a grammar into a fractal; applications to biology, especially developmental botany.

Goldberger, Ary L., David R. Rigney, and Bruce J. West, "Chaos and Fractals in Human Physiology," *Scientific American* 262(2), (February 1990).

A fascinating study of fractal structures found in the human body.

Master C Order Form

Okay, I'm ready to take the plunge and learn C. I understand that Master C will teach me C—the most powerul computer programming language in use today. Master C is a disk-based self-training system that turns my IBM PC into a C instructor. It keeps score. It uses modern computer based training techniques to teach me C, including quizzes, accumulating blackboards, and answer judgment. It presents a complete course in C from fundamentals through advanced concepts. The book New C Primer Plus runs parallel with this course but I don't need the book to use this software. This product is NOT a compiler.

To order by phone, call 415-331-0575 or 331-1075 (FAX)

Name

Company

Address
Street Address Only, No P.O. Box

City State ZIP

Daytime Phone

Quantity and Type

Master C training system	CBT-1	Quantity	x $44.95 =

Sales Tax—California addresses add 6% sales tax.

Shipping—Add $5 USA, $10 Canada, or $30 Foreign for shipping and handling. Standard shipping is UPS Gound. Allow 3 to 4 weeks. Prices subject to change.Purchase orders subject to credit approval, and verbal purchase orders will not be accepted.

Sales Tax

Shipping

Total Due

Disk Type: ☐ 5.25-inch ☐ 3.5-inch

Method of Payment

Checks or money orders, payable to The Waite Group. To pay by credit card, complete the following:

☐ Visa ☐ MasterCard Card Number

Cardholder's Name _____ Exp. Date

Cardholder's Signature _____

Waite Group Satisfaction Report Card

Please fill out this card if you wish to know of future updates to *The Waite Group's Fractal Creations*, or to receive our catalog.

Company Name: _____

Division: _____ **Mail Stop:** _____

Last Name: _____ **First Name:** _____ **Middle Initial:** _____

Street Address: _____

City: _____ **State:** _____ **Zip:** _____

Daytime telephone: (　　　) _____

Date product was acquired: Month _____ **Day** _____ **Year** _____ **Your Occupation:** _____

Overall, how would you rate *The Waite Group's Fractal Creations*?
☐ Excellent ☐ Very Good ☐ Good
☐ Fair ☐ Below Average ☐ Poor

What did you like MOST about this book/disk? _____
_____
_____

What did you like LEAST about this book/disk? _____
_____
_____

How do you like the Fractint program? _____
_____

How do you use this book (education, diversion, relaxation...) ____
_____

Are you interested in similar products? Any particular subject? (Imaging, graphics, etc.) _____
_____

Did you have any problems with running or installing Fractint? ____
_____
_____

What is your level of computer expertise?
☐ Reluctant user ☐ Informed user
☐ Power user ☐ Programmer ☐ Wizard

If you are a computer programmer, what language(s) do you know?
_____

What type of computer, graphics card, and monitor are you running Fractint on? _____
_____

Where did you buy this book?
☐ Bookstore (name) _____
☐ Discount store (name) _____
☐ Computer store (name) _____
☐ Catalog (name) _____
☐ Direct from WGP ☐ Other _____

What price did you pay for this book? _____

What influenced your purchase of this book?
☐ Recommendation ☐ Store display
☐ Subject matter ☐ Mailing
☐ Advertisement ☐ Book's format
☐ Magazine review ☐ Reputation of The Waite Group
☐ Other _____

How many computer books do you buy each year? _____

How many other Waite Group books do you own? _____

What is your favorite Waite Group book? _____
_____

Any other comments? _____
_____

☐ Check here for free Waite Group catalog

BUSINESS REPLY MAIL

FIRST CLASS MAIL   PERMIT NO. 33   MILL VALLEY, CA

POSTAGE WILL BE PAID BY ADDRESSEE

ATTENTION: FRACTAL CREATIONS
WAITE GROUP PRESS, INC.
100 SHORELINE HIGHWAY, SUITE A-285
MILL VALLEY, CA 94941-9840

FOLD HERE

THE STONE SOUP GROUP

AND THE FRACTINT AUTHORS

Fractint is the product of an informal association of programmers and fractal enthusiasts known as the Stone Soup Group. Here is the explanation of the origin of that name and an introduction to the Fractint authors.

THE FABLE OF STONE SOUP

Once upon a time, somewhere in Eastern Europe, there was a great famine. People jealously hoarded whatever food they could find, hiding it even from their friends and neighbors. One day a peddler drove his wagon into a village, sold a few of his wares, and began asking questions as if he planned to stay for the night.

"There's not a bite to eat in the whole province," he was told. "Better keep moving on."

"Oh, I have everything I need," he said. "In fact, I was thinking of making some stone soup to share with all of you." He pulled an iron cauldron from his wagon, filled it with water, and built a fire under it. Then, with great ceremony, he drew an ordinary-looking stone from a velvet bag and dropped it into the water.

By now, hearing the rumor of food, most of the villagers had come to the square or watched from their windows. As the peddler sniffed the "broth" and licked his lips in anticipation, hunger began to overcome the villagers' skepticism.

"Ahh," the peddler said to himself rather loudly, "I do like a tasty stone soup. Of course, stone soup with *cabbage*—that's hard to beat."

Soon a villager approached hesitantly, holding a cabbage he'd retrieved from its hiding place, and added it to the pot. "Capital!" cried the peddler. "You know, I once had stone soup with cabbage and a bit of salt beef as well, and it was fit for a king."

The villager butcher managed to find some salt beef...and so it went, through potatoes, onions, carrots, mushrooms, and so on, until there was indeed a delicious meal for all. The villagers offered the peddler a great deal of money for the magic stone, but he refused to sell and traveled on the next day. And from that time on, long after the famine had ended, they reminisced about the finest soup they'd ever had.

THE ORIGIN OF FRACTINT

Fractint has grown and developed just like the soup in the fable, with quite a bit of magic, although without the element of deception. You don't have to deceive programmers to make them think that hours of painstaking, often frustrating work is fun—they think that already! The developers who have banded together to develop Fractint and its sister programs have decided to call themselves the "Stone Soup Group" to reflect the spirit of cooperation and openness that has characterized Fractint's evolution.

The original "stone" was the program FRA386.exe, written by Bert Tyler, which is still available on some computer bulletin boards. It is a little unfair to compare Bert's original program to a humble stone, since FRA386 is a highly polished and capable fractal generator. Its claim to fame was that it is "blindingly fast." But a comparison between the original program and the copy of Fractint packaged with this book shows why the "stone" metaphor is apt. If FRA386 is a tasty morsel, then Fractint is a gourmet feast! The reason is that for several years now fractal enthusiasts from around the world have been sending Bert programming onions, potatoes, and spices to add to the soup! You are a beneficiary of this enthusiastic outpouring of creativity, because Fractint is the state of the art of PC fractal programming. It would take a large software development effort to duplicate Fractint's features in a commercial program, and by then Fractint would have added still more features. And the software with this book has this unique advantage: it comes with free updates forever!

A WORD ABOUT FRACTINT'S AUTHORS

Fractint is the result of a synergy between the main authors, many contributors, and published sources. All four of the main authors have had a hand in many aspects of the code. At the time of writing, none of the four had ever met; the intense collaboration resulting in Fractint has been conducted entirely by electronic conferencing in the COMART (short for "Computer Art") forum of the CompuServe Information Service. You are welcome to join in the discussions of Fractint and fractals; just type in GO COMART when you log onto CompuServe.

Here is some background on each of the four main authors. Their pictures are not only for your benefit. By now, each of the authors has a copy of this book, so for the first time, they all know what each other look like!

TIM WEGNER

Tim Wegner considers himself more of a "math type" than a programmer, although some of the programming skills of the rest of the team may have rubbed off a little on him. He first discovered Bert's FRA386 program in late 1988, and he remembers pestering Bert to alter the program so it would run on low-end PCs. Tim's reasons were entirely selfish: he wanted to modify Bert's code to add features, and FRA386 wouldn't run on his PC. Bert rewrote the program so that it would run on any PC and renamed it Fractint. As soon as Fractint was released in January of 1989, Tim began to barrage Bert with ideas and code. These included support for super-VGA graphics boards, the now-famous color cycling feature, new fractal types, and 3-D transformation capabilities. Together, Tim and Bert hammered out the main outlines of Fractint's "StandardFractal" architecture and data structures. Tim has been labeled by his cohorts as being "obsessed with options," but he has now paid the price: as a coauthor of this book, Tim had to document all the options he so enthusiastically added!

Tim has BA and MA degrees in mathematics from Carleton College and the University of California Berkeley. He worked for seven years overseas as a volunteer, doing things like working with Egyptian villagers building water systems. Since returning to the United States in 1982, he has written shuttle navigation software and a software support environment prototype and supported strategic information planning, all at NASA's Johnson Space Center. He currently is a Member of the Technical Staff of MITRE Houston.

MARK PETERSON

The Fractint team first heard from Mark in early 1989 when Mark sent an electronic mail message about an "artificial intelligence" algorithm for greatly speeding up fractal calculations. Bert and Tim didn't take him very seriously at first, but Mark's persistence paid off, and what is now called the periodicity checking speedup became a feature of Fractint. In short order Mark began coming up with significant and unique Fractint enhancements. Mark didn't just look in fractal texts for new fractal types, he invented brand new ones! Among his new fractal types are the unity fractal type and the four-dimensional Julibrot. Mark wrote the formula parser and greatly speeded up the Fractint code with a library of hand-coded assembler routines for calculating transcendental functions such as sine and cosine.

Mark's interest in fractals started with the book *Chaos* by James Gleick. Mark currently works for Northeast Utilities and also as a freelance programming consultant in the Hartford, Connecticut area.

BERT TYLER

Bert Tyler is Fractint's original author. He wrote the "blindingly fast" Intel 80386-specific integer math code and the original video mode logic. At one point, Bert understood every line in Fractint's source code, but these days there are so many goodies in there from so many developers that now Bert claims he has no idea what some of the routines are doing. His fortes are writing fast 80x86 assembler, his knowledge of a variety of video hardware, and his skill at hacking up the code everybody sends him. Bert's involvement with Fractint began when he downloaded a "Mandelbrot Generator" program, fired it up on his brand-new, Intel 80386-based PC with no math coprocessor, and then broke out of the program two hours later when it had drawn only half of its first image. Bert had heard of a way of programming fixed-point mathematics that does not require a math coprocessor in the PC, so he thought he would try it. (You can find out more about Fractint's fixed-point math in Appendix C.) The result was FRA386.EXE version 1.00.

When asked what his best contributions to Fractint have been, Bert answered that they were his decisions to distribute the program with full source code and to give full credit to anyone who sent him improvements. To this day, the authors receive major improvements from people they've never heard of before on an almost daily basis.

Bert has a BA in mathematics from Cornell University. He has been in programming since he got a job at the computer center in his sophomore year at college—in other words, he says, he hasn't done an honest day's work in his life. Bert has been known to pass himself off as a PC expert, a UNIX expert, a statistician, and even a financial modeling expert. He is currently an independent PC consultant, supporting PC-to-mainframe communications. Fractint is Bert's first effort at building a graphics program. His latest Stone Soup Group project has been porting Fractint to the Microsoft Windows 3.0 environment.

PIETER BRANDERHORST

Pieter was the last of the four authors to join the team, but his impact has been extensive. Pieter first tried a couple of fractal programs in 1989, but he didn't explore them much because they were too slow. Then a friend sent him a copy of Fractint, and he was impressed with the speed. But Pieter has never seen a program he didn't think he could make a little faster, so he obtained the source code and dived in. As a result, Fractint will never be the same! Pieter sees himself as one of the no-holds-barred programming types in the group. He has already touched so many parts of the Fractint code that is would be impossible to list all his contributions, but they include major code speedups, rotating zoom box support, the save-and-resume logic, and the colorful point-and-shoot user interface. At this time Pieter has personally massaged the entire source code more than any of the authors.

Pieter was been programming computers for twenty years, since he left high school. He has worked on more types of computers and in more languages than he can remember. He currently works as an independent computer consultant. When asked to describe his work in one sentence he says "I've never designed any hardware."

How the Stone Soup Team Works

Whenever anyone comes up with ideas for Fractint, those ideas are shared and passed around in the COMART forum. A feature makes it into the program if someone cares enough to incorporate the feature by writing the code. Since the source code is available, many of the new capabilities were coded by the contributors and sent to the authors as fully integrated code. Other features started life as suggestions that eventually were implemented by one of the authors.

One of the Fractint authors wrote this statement, which sums up the experience of being a Stone Souper: "There is something unique about the way this group works. We get along well without a formal structure or responsibilities, without clashes, and somehow everyone's efforts come together. Don't ask me how—I think some kind of magic is involved, and certainly some good humor."

Accessing the Authors

Communication among the authors for development of the next version of Fractint takes place in COMART (Computer Art) Section 15 (Fractals) of CompuServe (CIS). Access to this area is open to any and all interested in computer-generated images. Stop on by if you have any questions or just want to take a peek at what's getting tossed into the soup! This is a good way to get your Fractint questions answered. The authors are always happy to help Fractint users and to hear suggestions for improving the program. They can all be reached on CompuServe Information Services.

Bert Tyler [73477,433] on CIS, btyler on BIX

Timothy Wegner [71320,675] on CIS

Mark Peterson [70441,3353] on CIS

Pieter Branderhorst [72611,2257] on CIS

INDEX

All the production for this book was done using desktop publishing techniques and every phase of the book involved the use of computer technology. Never did production have to use traditional typesetting, stats, or photos, and everything for this book, from the fractal images to the formatted text, was saved on disk.

The authors wrote the text of this book on a IBM PC AT clone computer using the Windows 3 operating system and Microsoft Word for Windows word processing software. The fractals appearing throughout the book were generated on the same computer using Fractint Version 15.1. The text was saved in Microsoft Word for DOS, compressed with PKZIP, and uploaded to a CompuServe Information Service account from the AT using Procomm communications software.

The zipped text files were downloaded at the Waite Group offices to a Macintosh IIcx computer, using the Microphone II Version 3.0 communications software. The MacBinary option had to be turned off. The files were unzipped, then opened by Microsoft Word for the Macintosh, and saved in Macintosh format.

All the fractal images were saved in GIF format, then packaged with PKZIP, and uploaded to CompuServe. The fractals were downloaded to the Macintosh, unzipped, and opened in Adobe Photoshop. Photoshop was used to turn the GIFs to gray scale and then they where saved as TIFF files for the PageMaker desktop publishing software. All page formatting and book design was done in PageMaker Version 4.0. Illustrations were done from the authors' sketches using Freehand and saved as EPS files for placement in PageMaker. Backmatter figures was done on a Macintosh IIfx using Freehand.

Corrected files were sent on three SyQuest 44 Mb removable disk cartridges to the printer, R. R. Donnelley, where they were directly imposed to film through a Macintosh IIfx and Linotronic 530 phototypesetting machine, utilizing Adobe and Monotype fonts. Plates were then made from the film.

●

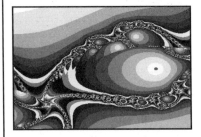

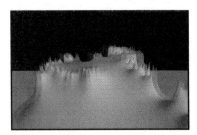

Fractal Creations Fractal Disk Order Form

You've explored Fractint and you want more! You can't go another day without seeing what the masters of Fractal hunting have discovered, to focus on the best of what Fractint can do. So fill out this post-paid card today and get ready to stare at the most beautiful images you have ever seen.

To order by phone call 415-331-0575 or 331-1075 (FAX)

Name

Company

Address
Street Address Only, No P.O. Box

City   State   ZIP

Daytime Phone

Quantity and Type

EGA and VGA Fractals	FC-1-VEGA	Quantity	☐	x $15 =	
SuperVGA Fractals	FC-2-SVGA	Quantity	☐	x $15 =	
Landscape Fractals	FC-3-LAND	Quantity	☐	x $15 =	
3-D Fractals	FC-4-3DRB	Quantity	☐	x $15 =	
ALL FOUR SETS	FC-5-ALL4	Quantity	☐	x $50 =	

Sales Tax—California addresses add 6% sales tax.

Shipping—Add $5 USA, $10 Canada, or $30 Foreign for shipping and handling. Standard shipping is UPS Gound. Allow 3 to 4 weeks. Prices subject to change.Purchase orders subject to credit approval, and verbal purchase orders will not be accepted.

Sub Total

Sales Tax

Shipping

Total Due

Disk Type: ☐ 5.25-inch ☐ 3.5-inch

Method of Payment

Checks or money orders, payable to The Waite Group. To pay by credit card, complete the following:

☐ Visa   ☐ Mastercard   Card Number

Cardholder's Name _____   Exp. Date

Cardholder's Signature _____

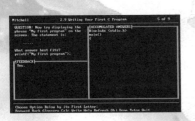

Master C Order Form

Okay, I'm ready to take the plunge and learn C. I understand that Master C will teach me C—the most powerul computer programming language in use today. Master C is a disk-based self-training system that turns my IBM PC into a C instructor. It keeps score. It uses modern computer based training techniques to teach me C, including quizzes, accumulating blackboards, and answer judgment. It presents a complete course in C from fundamentals through advanced concepts. The book New C Primer Plus runs parallel with this course but I don't need the book to use this software. This product is NOT a compiler.

To order by phone, call 415-331-0575 or 331-1075 (FAX)

Name

Company

Address
Street Address Only, No P.O. Box

City   State   ZIP   —

Daytime Phone

Quantity and Type

Master C training system   CBT-1   Quantity   x $44.95 =

Sales Tax—California addresses add 6% sales tax.

Shipping—Add $5 USA, $10 Canada, or $30 Foreign for shipping and handling. Standard shipping is UPS Gound. Allow 3 to 4 weeks. Prices subject to change.Purchase orders subject to credit approval, and verbal purchase orders will not be accepted.

Sales Tax

Shipping

Total Due

Disk Type: ☐ 5.25-inch ☐ 3.5-inch

Method of Payment

Checks or money orders, payable to The Waite Group. To pay by credit card, complete the following:

☐ Visa ☐ MasterCard   Card Number

Cardholder's Name _____   Exp. Date

Cardholder's Signature _____

RELATED TITLES FROM WAITE GROUP® PRESS

The Waite Group's C++ Primer Plus
Stephen Prata

Computer mavens expect the new programming language C++ to eventually displace C from its position of near-universal preference. An extension of C, C++ treats data and functions as objects (hence the term object-oriented programming or OOP), making it possible to clone, modify, and build upon them. Unlike existing books on the subject, *C++ Primer Plus* is addressed to those without an extensive programming background. It provides a simple introduction to C++ while also covering the essential concepts of C. It teaches the basics of OOP and shows how to build programs that are flexible and readily modified.

In the friendly, easy-to-follow style of *C Primer Plus* (the author's best-selling work), *C++ Primer Plus* illustrates the language's fundamentals with short sample programs that are easy to key in and experiment with. A companion disk (available through the order card included with the book) contains all the sample programs and projects. The book is compatible with any AT&T Version 2.0 compliant compiler.

500 Pages, 7 × 9, Softbound　　　　　　　　　　**ISBN: 1-878739-02-6, $26.95**

The Waite Group's Turbo Pascal How-To
Gary Syck

Turbo Pascal How-To is a working programmer's dream: hundreds of typical programming problems, with creative ways to solve them, in an easy-to-use reference format. The solutions provided are designed to work with the latest, "object-oriented" Version 6.0 of Turbo Pascal, as well as earlier versions. Experienced programmers will appreciate the ease of incorporating these solutions, which will allow them to concentrate on their program's unique characteristics and not waste time solving problems. At the same time, novice programmers will find they can quickly begin creating functional programs just by building on the modular examples provided here. Borland's new Turbo Vision interface system as well as the new Windows 3.0 extensions are presented for the first time.

The Waite Group's *Turbo Pascal How-To* answers the most practical questions any programmer has, such as: "How do I put information in a window? How do I build a fancy pull-down menu system? How do I scroll the screen? Create a directory? Save memory?" And more. In short, this book has everything readers need to know to write professional Turbo Pascal programs.

500 Pages, 7 × 9, Softbound　　　　　　　　　　**ISBN: 1-878739-04-2, $24.95**

The Waite Group's Master C: *Let the PC Teach You C*
Mitchell Waite, Stephen Prata, Rex Woollard

The programming language known as C has become one of the languages of choice among programmers, due to its enormous range and flexibility which allows it to be used in simple applications as well as advanced operating systems. *Master C: Let the PC Teach You C* is a revolutionary new book/disk package designed to use the power and speed of the IBM PC to provide the fastest, most effective way to learn C. Master C has features not found in books. It automatically guides the user through C topics, notices problems, and recommends action. Sophisticated answer judgment accepts rough responses (even misspellings). "Remediation paths" send the user to review material not understood. All in all, there is no better or faster way to learn C today than with Master C.

256 Pages, 7 × 9, 3 5.25" disks, Softbound　　　　　　　**ISBN: 1-878739-00-X, $44.95**

LICENSE AND WARRANTY

THIS IS A LEGAL AGREEMENT BETWEEN YOU, THE END USER, AND THE WAITE GROUP, INC. ("TWG"). BY OPENING THIS PACKAGE, YOU AGREE TO BE BOUND BY THIS AGREEMENT. IF YOU DO NOT AGREE WITH THE TERMS OF THIS AGREEMENT, PROMPTLY RETURN THE UNOPENED DISK PACKAGE AND THE ACCOMPANYING USER MANUAL FOR A REFUND.

SOFTWARE LICENSE

1. TWG grants you a nonexclusive license to use one copy of the enclosed program on a single computer system (whether a single CPU, part of a licensed network, or a terminal connected to a single CPU). Each user of the program must obtain his or her own copy of the program user manual and book from TWG.

2. TWG or its licensor owns all rights in the program, including all U.S. and foreign copyrights in the program. You may make one copy of the program for backup purposes, or you may transfer a copy of the program to one hard disk drive, using the original for backup. You may make no other copies of the program or its user manual and book. You may not decompile, disassemble or reverse engineer the program.

3. You may not rent the program or the right to use the program to others, but you may transfer all of your rights in the program and its user manual if you retain no copies of either and if the recipient agrees to the terms of this agreement.

LIMITED WARRANTY

TWG warrants that the program will perform substantially as described in the accompanying user manual and book for a period of ninety days from your receipt of it. This limited warranty does not apply if the program is the object of misuse, accident or abuse.

TWG's entire liability and your exclusive remedy for breach of this limited warranty will be, at TWG's option, either replacement of the program or a refund of the price paid. You must return a copy of your original receipt along with the program to obtain a refund.

DISCLAIMER OF WARRANTIES, LIMITATION OF LIABILITY

TWG makes no other warranty, express or implied, regarding the program, its user manual, or their merchantability or fitness for a particular purpose. TWG shall not be liable for any indirect, special, incidental or consequential damages (including lost profits, loss of information or other economic loss) resulting from the use of or inability to use the program, even if you have advised TWG of the possibility of such damages.

Some states do not allow the exclusion or limitation of implied warranties or liability for incidental or consequential damages, so these exclusions may not apply to you. This limited warranty gives you specific legal rights; you may have others, which vary from state to state.